Introduction to

LAW AND LEGAL OBLIGATIONS

Introduction to

LAW AND LEGAL OBLIGATIONS

General Editor

Dale McFadzean

Lecturer in Law, University of Paisley

DUNDEE UNIVERSITY PRESS
2006

First published in Great Britain in 2006 by
Dundee University Press
University of Dundee
Dundee DD1 4HN

www.dundee.ac.uk/dup

ISBN 1–84586–014–4
EAN 978–1–84586–014–1

No natural forests were destroyed to make this product;
only farmed timber was used and replanted.

British Library Cataloguing-in-Publication Data
A catalogue record for this book is available on request from the British Library

Typeset by Hewer Text UK Ltd, Edinburgh
Printed and bound by Bell & Bain Ltd, Glasgow

FOREWORD

This book facilitates the teaching and learning of law at an introductory level for the considerable number of students who now undertake legal studies outwith the traditional LL.B. stream in a range of institutions across Scotland.

From my experience as class leader for a number of years on the first-year Introduction to Law and Legal Obligations class for B.A. Arts and Business students at Strathclyde University, this is an excellent, readable and very user-friendly book for a range of students in further and higher education who are studying law at a fairly basic level. It covers all the key topics which are taught in most of the introductory classes in law for University B.A. students and for college students undertaking Cert.H.E. law or H.N.C. law, notably the key legal process/system topics: Sources of Law (Chapter 1), Scottish Legal System (Chapter 2) and the increasingly important areas of Dispute Resolution (Chapter 6) and Constitutional Law (Chapter 3), together with the core private law areas of Delict and Contract (Chapters 4 and 5 respectively).

For accounting students, this book's coverage satisfies the requirements for professional accreditation purposes by the treatment of Company Law (Chapter 8) and the increasingly significant area of Intellectual Property Law (Chapter 9), in addition to the basic Chapters 1–5.

The addition of a chapter on Employment Law (Chapter 7) will be helpful in particular for HRM professional accreditation purposes and should in any event be relevant as a matter of personal and professional interest for all students.

Accordingly, the book provides a comprehensive yet focused introduction to law, a "one-stop shop" in particular for satisfaction of the professional requirements of Accounting and HRM students, and avoids the failings of some textbooks which seek to cover too many topics and are consequently too broad in scope and do not consider the particular learning needs of the students.

It should not be underestimated how difficult law can appear for a student being introduced to it as part of a wider educational curriculum. Students will certainly find that this book makes the study of law accessible. The text is clear, presented well and easy to follow, with the use of paragraph numbering, bold headings and bullet points. Footnotes have been used to avoid the text becoming too cluttered but these are kept to a minimum. The vivid discussion of case law in various chapters such as those on contract and delict, where it is used to elucidate legal principles, should enable students to understand better how to apply the law. A number of additional features will facilitate student learning, such as the addition, in Chapter 1 on Sources of Scots Law, of a key to reading a statute, which can otherwise be a formidable exercise for a student new to law. Furthermore, the insertion of emboldened sections with essential facts and essential cases at the end of all chapters is a useful educational tool to allow students to review their learning on a topic, and these will also act as an *aide-mémoire* on key issues and case law. Finally, academics can often mistakenly assume that students are familiar with legal jargon, and the addition of a Glossary of terms will be welcomed by students struggling to come to terms with key legal terminology.

Barry J Rodger
July 2006

CONTENTS

TABLE OF CASES

TABLE OF STATUTES

TABLE OF STATUTORY INSTRUMENTS

TABLE OF EUROPEAN LEGISLATION

1 SOURCES OF SCOTS LAW

WHAT IS LAW?

The definitions of law are wide and varied. It has been described by White and Willock as   **1.1**
". . . the words of someone in authority who has the power to intervene in other people's
affairs . . . and if they do not comply something unpleasant is liable to befall them",[1] while
the *Oxford English Dictionary* describes law as a ". . . body of rules, whether proceeding
from formal enactment or custom, which a particular state or community recognises as
binding on its members or subjects".[2] Law may have many descriptions but it has only one
main practical purpose – to restrict and regulate certain kinds of behaviour. The fact that
there are laws which most people obey means that you can generally go about your
business secure in the knowledge that someone is not going to assault you, or steal your
belongings, or generally put your life in danger by failing to take proper care. If someone
does carry out this kind of behaviour then the law creates legal consequences. If you
commit a crime then you could be fined or sent to prison. If you have injured someone
through negligence then you may be forced to pay compensation or damages.

CATEGORISING THE LAW

PUBLIC AND PRIVATE LAW

Scots law deals with many specific subject areas, such as criminal law, the law of contract,   **1.2**
and the law of delict, among others. Each of these areas is known as a "branch" of law. For
simplicity, each of these branches is further categorised into two distinct groupings: public
law and private law. There is no real technical reason for these groupings. It is simply a
useful way of categorising the various branches of law under separate headings.

With "public law", the involvement of the state is paramount. Public law relates to   **1.3**
the operation of government and the regulation of the relationship between government
and citizens. It also regulates other public bodies such as the courts, the Scottish
Parliament, local government, and even the police. Key branches of public law include
constitutional law, administrative law and criminal law.

On the other hand, with "private law" the involvement of the State is minimal.   **1.4**
Instead, private law is more concerned with the regulation of relationships between
individual citizens and/or companies and organisations. For example, when a legal
relationship between individuals breaks down, such as a contract, this concerns private
law. Key branches of private law include contract law, delict and family law.

---

[1] White and Willock, *The Scottish Legal System* (2nd edn, 1999).
[2] *Oxford English Dictionary*, vol VI.

CIVIL AND CRIMINAL LAW

1.5   As well as categorising the various branches of law into both public and private, the law can also be described in terms of civil or criminal. The main difference between civil and criminal law is that a different court structure is used to regulate each.[3] Under criminal law, a special set of criminal courts exists which aims to punish criminal behaviour and impose sanctions on individual liberty. Cases brought before the criminal courts are known as prosecutions and are brought by officials representing the state. In Scotland these are the Procurator Fiscal, the Lord Advocate, or one of their deputies (known as Depute Procurators Fiscal and Advocates Depute). The person against whom the prosecution is brought is called the *accused*. The standard of proof in a criminal prosecution is "beyond all reasonable doubt". This means that if a jury has a reasonably held doubt, based upon the evidence, as to the accused's guilt, then they must acquit. The standard of proof is set at a high level in order to safeguard the liberty of the accused who may ultimately face imprisonment.

1.6   Under civil law, a special set of civil courts exists which deals with disputes arising between two or more parties, where the conduct of one party has caused unjustified loss to another. Such disputes are known as civil cases and when brought before the civil courts they are referred to as "litigation". The person bringing the case to court is known as the *pursuer* and the person against whom the action is taken is called the *defender*. Examples of civil cases include a DIY company damaging your home while fitting a new bathroom suite, or a driver running into your vehicle and causing you to suffer from whiplash. In each of these examples, the aggrieved party may attempt to sue the other party before the civil courts if they have failed to fulfil their obligations or pay compensation for any damage caused by their actions. Under the civil law, courts have no power to interfere with individual liberty. Instead of punishment through imprisonment or fine, the civil courts focus upon reparation whereby aggrieved parties are financially recompensed for any loss suffered. As such, the standard of proof is lower than that of the criminal courts and is based upon the "balance of probabilities".

Overlap between civil and criminal law

1.7   Often there can be an overlap between the civil and criminal law. This can happen when a type of behaviour occurs which is both criminal and civil in nature. For example, if an individual assaults another person in the street, that individual has committed a crime which can then result in a prosecution taking place before the criminal courts. However, that assault can also be dealt with under the civil law,[4] in that the victim could attempt to sue his assailant for compensation, using the civil courts.

SOURCES OF LAW

INTRODUCTION

1.8   All legal systems must have sources of law. It is these sources which give authority to the rules and principles within any given system. However, the approach to

---

[3] See further Chapter 2.
[4] Specifically under the branch of delict.

creating and defining these sources will differ according to the type of legal system. Civil law systems, on the whole, are codified. They have been heavily influenced throughout the ages by Roman law and are based upon codified rules and principles logically set out in often encyclopaedic documents. These "codes" are the main source of law.

Common law systems, on the other hand, have developed quite independently of the **1.9** influence of Roman law. Instead of reliance upon codes as a source of law, they rely upon judicial precedent. As a source of law, precedent consists of the decisions of judges made in cases which are heard before them. From these decisions, legal principles can be drawn from the judges' written decisions which together form a major source of law. Common law systems have been greatly influenced by English law which was little affected by the spread of Roman law.

There is a third type of legal system which is known as the *hybrid* system. This is the **1.10** system to which Scots law adheres and it has developed in such a way that it does not conform exclusively to either civil or common law. Instead, it is a mixed system in which one can discern elements of civil or Roman law but also the influence of common law and precedent. This is certainly true of Scotland where, for example, the branch of criminal law is almost wholly derived from common law whereas other branches, such as company law, rely almost entirely on Acts of Parliament which codify them.

FORMAL SOURCES OF SCOTS LAW

Within the Scottish legal system, there are a number of formal sources of law. Each of **1.11** these sources has varying importance and can effectively be "ranked" in terms of their authority. In order of importance the sources are:

(1)   legislation;
(2)   judicial precedent;
(3)   institutional writings;
(4)   custom; and
(5)   equity.

Legislation

Legislation is the most important source of law within the Scottish legal system. It **1.12** emanates ultimately from the authority of a legislature and includes Acts of Parliament as well as legislation passed by delegates such as the Scottish Parliament or local authorities. It also includes European Union legislation. Despite its having its own Parliament, arguably the most important legislation in Scotland is still that of the UK Parliament. Despite the Scottish Parliament having law-making powers by virtue of the Scotland Act 1998, the doctrine of the supremacy of Parliament remains in place and the law-making powers of the UK Parliament remain unaffected for Scotland.[5] The doctrine of the supremacy of Parliament also applies to European legislation.

---

[5] Scotland Act 1998, s 28(7). For further discussion of the supremacy of Parliament, see para **3.29**.

UK parliamentary legislation

1.13   Parliamentary legislation is initiated mainly by the Government and tends to introduce changes to society which reflect the policies of a particular Government. Proposals for an Act of Parliament take the form of a Bill and, during the opening ceremony of Parliament, the Queen will generally outline the forthcoming Bills for the year ahead. Bills themselves fall into three distinct categories. Public Bills are the most important and take up the majority of parliamentary time since they deal with matters of important principle and generally affect society as a whole.

1.14   There are two types of Public Bill: Government Bills and Private Members' Bills. Government Bills are introduced by the ruling government of the day and generally reflect current policy or manifesto commitments.[6] The majority of Acts passed by Parliament originate from Government Bills; Private Members' Bills, on the other hand, generally originate from an individual MP. These Bills will more often than not deal with an area which does not receive Government backing or is controversial and they often reflect personally held beliefs of MPs.[7] In some cases, controversial measures for which a Government does not want to take responsibility may be introduced by back-benchers, with the Government secretly or openly backing the measure and ensuring its passage. Such Bills are sometimes known as "Government handout Bills"; the Abortion Act 1967 was passed in such a manner. This type of Bill ensures that back-benchers have more input into the legislative process of Parliament, but the success of such Bills is very limited.[8] Most Private Members' Bills fail to become an Act.

1.15   The second category of Bills is known as Private Bills. These contain proposals which generally affect the interests of specified persons or localities. They are introduced through petition by the persons or organisations who desire the Bill. Private Bills are commonly introduced by local authorities or public corporations and seek to give statutory powers to those bodies which they would otherwise not have. For example, the Liverpool City Council (Prohibition of Smoking in Places of Work) Bill is currently before Parliament and seeks to give Liverpool City Council the power to ban smoking in all places of work within its geographical boundaries. Private Bills follow a slightly different procedure in their enactment from other Bills and there is often very little discussion of such Bills within Parliament.[9]

1.16   The third and final category of Bills is called Hybrid Bills. These are normally Government Bills which specifically affect particular individuals or groups. They are therefore treated in many ways like Private Bills. An example of such a Bill can be found in the Channel Tunnel Bill of 1986, now the Channel Tunnel Act 1987. The Bill was generally public in nature, given that it set out to create the Channel Tunnel, however, certain sections of the Act gave the Government powers of compulsory purchase to buy areas of land in Kent required to build the tunnel. Since these sections specifically affected only Kent landowners, the Bill was hybrid in nature.

---

[6] For example, the Constitutional Reform Act 2005 was introduced as a Government Bill reflecting the Labour Government's enthusiasm for judicial reform.

[7] Recent examples of Private Members' Bills include the Female Genital Mutilation Act 2003 and the Gangmasters (Licensing) Act 2004.

[8] For example, in the 2003–04 session of Parliament, 38 Public Bills received Royal Assent; of these, only five were Bills introduced by back-bench Members.

[9] For a detailed discussion of Private Bill procedure, see further A W Bradley, and K D Ewing, *Constitutional and Administrative Law* (13th edn, 2003), pp 193–194.

Parliamentary stages of Bills. Bills may be introduced in either the House of Commons or **1.17** the House of Lords. However, there are a number of Bills which must always originate in the Commons, such as Money Bills and Bills of constitutional importance. A Bill which originates in the House of Lords will progress through the same stages as those in the House of Commons. The stages of a Bill as it passes through Parliament are as follows:

- **First Reading**
  The first stage consists of a number of formalities where the Bill is announced and its short title is read out. A date is set for the Second Reading of the Bill and from here the Bill will be printed and distributed.

- **Second Reading**
  At this stage, the House will debate the general principles contained in the Bill. At the end of the debate, the motion is put to a vote. It is very rare for a Government Bill to lose a vote, although it is not unheard of. For example, the Shops Bill 1986 was lost at the Second Reading.

- **Committee Stage**
  During the Committee Stage, most Bills are passed over to a Standing Committee which is created for the specific purpose of dealing with the Bill.[10] Standing Committees generally consist of between 18 and 50 MPs and reflect the state of the parties represented in the House of Commons. At this stage, the Bill is subjected to a thorough line-by-line examination and any of its clauses may be amended where necessary.

  A small number of Bills at this stage are passed over to a Committee of the Whole House as opposed to a Standing Committee. During such a Committee, each clause of the Bill is debated on the floor of the House of Commons by all MPs. Such a Committee is used for Bills of constitutional significance, such as the Scotland Bill during 1999. It is also used to pass Bills which require a rapid enactment, such as the annual Finance Bill.

- **Report Stage**
  If a Bill has come from a Committee of the Whole House, then this stage is purely a formality. However, for the majority of Bills, this stage will involve a review of any amendments made during the Committee Stage. All members of the House have an opportunity to debate at this stage, making it rather more democratic than the Committee Stage where the scope for debate is rather limited. There is no vote at this point.

- **Third Reading**
  Here, the House examines the final version of the Bill. The Bill is debated in principle and a vote taken. This stage is usually very brief since no major amendments may be made.

A key problem with the legislative process of the Commons is the amount of time it takes. The more amendments a Bill receives, the longer it will take to pass through Parliament. Consequently, many Bills are subject to what is called a "guillotine" motion. Such a motion will quickly bring the debate on a Bill to an end, allowing it to proceed more quickly. Since 1999, the Commons has also used a new procedure known as the "programme" motion. Using this motion, a programme or timetable is put before the House, agreeing the amount of time allocated to stages of a Bill and dates for progression.

---

[10] A new Standing Committee is appointed for each Bill and will disband after it has completed its work.

- **Lords Stages**

  Once the Commons stages have been completed, the Bill is sent to the House of Lords, where the whole procedure is repeated. The Lords stages are similar in many ways to those of the Commons, except for a few key differences. The Committee Stage in the Lords always consists of a Committee of the Whole House and there is no use of "guillotine" or "programme" motions which allow for unrestricted debate on the principles of a Bill. It is also possible to table amendments during the Third Reading in the Lords.

  Changes made to a Bill in the House of Lords result in an extra stage in the Commons known as "Lords Amendments Considered". This is necessary in order to approve any amendments made by the Lords.[11] Occasionally, the two Houses will not agree on a Bill. In such circumstances, the Lords can exercise its delaying power and refuse to accept the proposals of the House of Commons.[12] However, this delaying power is limited by the Parliament Act 1911, as amended by the Parliament Act 1949, which states that the Lords can delay a Bill only for up to one year. Using the Parliament Acts, the House of Commons can then submit a Bill for Royal Assent without the consent of the House of Lords. Thus, the power of the House of Lords to block legislation permanently is curtailed.[13] Unless the House of Commons invokes the Parliament Acts, then both Houses of Parliament must always agree in order for the final Bill to progress.

- **Royal Assent**

  This is the final stage of a Bill, where the Crown must formally assent to the Bill in order for it to become an Act of Parliament and pass into law. In modern times this has become something of a formality since the UK is a constitutional monarchy and the sovereign is bound to assent to any Bill, except in extraordinary circumstances. The last time assent was given by the Crown in person was in 1854 and assent has not been refused since 1707 when Queen Anne refused to consent to the Scottish Militia Bill.

Reading a statute

1

1.18   # Murder (Abolition of Death Penalty) Act 1965   2

1965 CHAPTER 71   3

An Act to abolish capital punishment in the case of persons convicted in Great Britain of   4
murder or convicted of murder or a corresponding offence by court-martial and, in

---

[11] The Commons will generally accept around 90% of Lords amendments since most are non-controversial.

[12] A recent example of this can be found in the Sexual Offences (Amendment) Bill, now the Sexual Offences (Amendment) Act 2000 (c 44).

[13] For a useful analysis of the Parliament Acts, see the decision in *Jackson* v *Attorney-General* [2005] 3 WLR 733.

connection therewith, to make further provision for the punishment of persons so convicted.

[8th November 1965] **5**

6

Be it enacted by the Queen's most Excellent Majesty, by and with the advice and consent of the Lords Spiritual and Temporal, and Commons, in this present Parliament assembled, and by the authority of the same, as follows:—

8   **1.**—(1) No person shall suffer death for murder, and a person convicted of murder shall, subject to subsection (5) below, be sentenced to imprisonment for life.

Abolition of **7**
death penalty
for murder.

9   (2) On sentencing any person convicted of murder to imprisonment for life the Court may at the same time declare the period which it recommends to the Secretary of State as the minimum period which in its view should elapse before the Secretary of State orders the release of that person on licence under section 27 of the Prison Act 1952 or section 21 of the Prisons (Scotland) Act 1952.

1952 c. 52.
1952 c. 61.

(3) For the purpose of any proceedings on or subsequent to a person's trial on a charge of capital murder, that charge and any plea or finding of guilty of capital murder shall be treated as being or having been a charge, or a plea or finding of guilty, of murder only; and if at the commencement of this Act a person is under sentence of death for murder, the sentence shall have effect as a sentence of imprisonment for life.

(4) In the foregoing subsections any reference to murder shall include an offence of or corresponding to murder under section 70 of the Army Act 1955 or of the Air Force Act 1955 or under section 42 of the Naval Discipline Act 1957, and any reference to capital murder shall be construed accordingly; and in each of the said sections 70 there shall be inserted in subsection (3) after paragraph (*a*) as a new paragraph (*aa*)—

1955 c. 18.
1955 c. 19.
1957 c. 53.

"(*aa*) if the corresponding civil offence is murder, be liable to imprisonment for life".

(5) In section 53 of the Children and Young Persons Act 1933, and in section 57 of the Children and Young Persons (Scotland) Act 1937, there shall be substituted for subsection (1)—

1933 c. 12.
1937 c. 37.

"(1) A person convicted of an offence who appears to the court to have been under the age of eighteen years at the time the offence was committed shall not, if he is convicted of murder, be sentenced to imprisonment for life, nor shall sentence of death be pronounced on or recorded against any such person; but in lieu thereof the court shall (notwithstanding anything in this or in any other Act) sentence him to be detained during Her Majesty's pleasure, and if so sentenced he shall be liable to be detained in such place and under such conditions as the Secretary of State may direct."

10

2. No person convicted of murder shall be released by the Secretary of State on licence under section 27 of the Prison Act 1952 or section 21 of the Prisons (Scotland) Act 1952 unless the Secretary of State has prior to such release consulted the Lord Chief Justice of England or the Lord Justice General as the case may be together with the trial judge if available.

Release on licence of those sentenced for murder.
1952 c. 52.
1952 c. 61.

3.—(1) <u>This Act may be cited</u> as the Murder (Abolition of Death Penalty) Act 1965.

(2) The enactments mentioned in the Schedule to this Act are hereby repealed to the extent specified in the third column of that Schedule.

(3) This Act, except as regards courts-martial, shall not extend to Northern Ireland.

(4) This Act shall come into force on the day following that on which it is passed.

Short title, repeal, **11**
extent and
commencement.

4. This Act shall continue in force until the thirty-first day of July nineteen hundred and seventy, and shall then expire unless Parliament by affirmative resolutions of both Houses otherwise determines: and upon the expiration of this Act the law existing immediately prior to the passing of this Act shall, so far as it is repealed or amended by this Act, again operate as though this Act had not been passed, and the said repeals and amendments had not been enacted:

Duration.

Provided that this Act shall continue to have effect in relation to any murder not shown to have been committed after the expiration of this Act, and for this purpose a murder shall be taken to be committed at the time of the act which causes the death.

SCHEDULE   **12**
ENACTMENTS REPEALED

Section 2.

Chapter	Short Title	Extent of Repeal
33 Hen. 8. c. 12.	The Offences with the Court Act 1541	Section 2, so far as relates to the punishment of persons found guilty of murder.
25 Geo. 2. c. 37.	The Murder Act 1751	In section 9 the words from "or rescue", where secondly occurring, to "during execution".
4 Geo. 4. c. 48.	The Judgment of Death Act 1823	In section 1 the words "except murder".
24 & 25 Vict. c. 100.	The Offences against the Person Act 1861.	Section 1 (but without prejudice to the operation of sections 64 to 68). In section 71 the words "otherwise than with death".
31 & 32 Vict. c. 24	The Capital Punishment Amendment Act 1868.	The whole Act, except as applied by any other enactment.
50 & 51 Vict. c. 35.	The Criminal Procedure (Scotland) Act 1887.	In section 55 the words from "in cases in" to "conviction, or". In section 56 the words from "except on conviction" to "1829".
3 & 4 Eliz. 2. c. 18.	The Army Act 1955.	In section 70(3)(*a*) the words "or murder" (and the words added by the Homicide Act 1957). In section 125(2) the words "and any rules made under section seven of that Act."

3 & 4 Eliz. 2. c. 19.	The Air Force Act 1955.	In section 70(3)(a) the words "or murder" (and the words added by the Homicide Act 1957). In section 125(2) the words "and any rules made under section seven of that Act."
5 & 6 Eliz. 2. c. 11.	The Homicide Act 1957.	Sections 5 to 12. In section 13, in subsection (1) the words from "and" to "Part III", and subsection (2). Section 15. Schedule 1.
5 & 6 Eliz. 2. c. 53	The Naval Discipline Act 1957.	In section 42(1), in paragraph (a) the words from "or" to "1957" and in paragraph (b) the word "other". In section 80(2) the words "and any rules made under section seven of that Act".

KEY

1. The *Royal seal* is simply to show that, by the Royal Assent having been given, the Act is one associated with Her Majesty. Bills, as proposals for Acts which are not yet passed, have no Royal seal. On a lighter note, it is also there for decoration!

2. The *short title* gives a broad indication of the scope of the Act. The word "Scotland" in brackets means that the Act applies to Scotland only. This is often shortened to a capital letter "S", full stop. Ideally the short title should be prosaic, but often it is political or emotive. For example, the Tenants' Rights etc (Scotland) Act 1980 was essentially a Housing Act; why was it not named so?

3. The *chapter number*. This means that the Act was the 71st passed in 1965. The system is straightforward and was adopted by the Acts of Parliament Numbering and Citation Act 1962. Prior to that, the reference was to the session of Parliament in which the Act was passed, the session being numbered according to the length of reign of the existing monarch, for example the Factories Act 1961 (9 & 10 Eliz II c 34).

4. The *long title* states in more detail the objectives of the Act, but still in fairly general terms (the phrase ". . . and for connected purposes" is often used). The long title will also state whether the Act is a consolidating or codifying Act, if either. A consolidating Act is one that repeals or re-enacts the provisions of a number of statutes dealing with the same subject into a single Act, for example the Sale of Goods Act 1979. A codifying Act brings all the earlier law (both statutes and precedent) together into one Act, often with changes to the pre-existing law, for example the Legitimation Act 1968.

5. The *date of Royal Assent* is the date upon which the provisions of the Act come into effect unless otherwise stated elsewhere in the Act. This is known as the date of commencement.

6. The *enacting formula* is a standardised formula which verifies the statute as a true Act of Parliament. It shows that the House of Commons, the House of Lords and the Queen must all be consulted and must approve it. Since the Parliament Acts of 1911 and 1949, the House of Commons has been able to override the will of the House of Lords. If the Lords makes amendments to a Bill, or rejects it completely, then, provided that the House of Commons can

1.19

pass its own version of the Bill twice in one parliamentary session, this will become law; the European Parliamentary Elections Act 1999 was passed in such a way. These Acts have a slightly different enacting formula and include "... as prescribed by section 4(1) of the Parliament Act 1911 as amended ...".

7. A *marginal note* performs many functions, such as indicating the general scope or purpose of a section (as in this Act where the note reads "Abolition of death penalty for murder", showing the effect of s 1 of the Act), or citing the reference to another Act. For example, in this Act, s 1(2) refers to the Prisons (Scotland) Act 1952, and the marginal note cites "1952 c 61".

8. A *section* is the main form of division in an Act, here s 1. It is indicated in citations by a small letter "s" followed by a full stop.

9. A *subsection* is the next level of division below a section. It is shown by numerals in brackets, for example "s 1(2)".

At this point the reader should also be aware of the existence of the *paragraph* and the *sub-paragraph*, not shown on the Murder (Abolition of Death Penalty) Act 1965. A paragraph is the third level of division below a section and is shown by lower-case letters in brackets, for example s 3(1)(a) of the Scotland Act 1998, illustrated below:

"3. – (1) The Presiding Officer shall propose a day for the holding of a poll if –
(a) the Parliament resolves that it should be dissolved and, if the resolution is passed on a division, the number of members voting in favour of it is not less than two-thirds of the total number of seats for members of the Parliament, or
(b) any period during which the Parliament is required under section 46 to nominate one of its members for appointment as First Minister ends without such a nomination being made."

A sub-paragraph is the fourth and lowest division below a section. It is shown by lower-case Roman numerals, for example s 2(1)(c)(i) of the Prevention of Terrorism (Temporary Provisions) Act 1989, illustrated below:

"2. – (1) Subject to subsection (3) below, a person is guilty of an offence if he –
(a) belongs or professes to belong to a proscribed organisation,
(b) solicits or invites support for a proscribed organisation other than support with money or other property; or
(c) arranges or assists in the arrangement or management of, or addresses, any meeting of three or more persons (whether or not it is a meeting to which the public are admitted) knowing that the meeting is—
   (i) to support a proscribed organisation;
   (ii) to further the activities of such an organisation; or
   (iii) to be addressed by a person belonging or professing to belong to such an organisation."

10. An *amending provision* is part of an Act which amends the law in a pre-existing Act by deleting, inserting or substituting certain words, phrases or paragraphs.

11. The *short title, extent and commencement* section contains a number of sub-sections which have a variety of purposes. Here, s 3(1) contains the short title of the Act. This states how the Act may be referred to in other Acts, case reports and textbooks. It accordingly follows that two Acts in the same year

will not be called the same thing, as this would cause unnecessary confusion. If the same title is used, the use of the words "(No 2)" in brackets can be employed, for example the Education and Education (No 2) Acts 1986.

The territorial extent of the Act can be found in s 3(3). This determines whether the Act, and if so which parts of it, applies to specific areas of the UK. The most usual areas are Northern Ireland, England and Wales, and Scotland. If no extent is mentioned, the Act is assumed to extend in entirety to the whole of the UK.

The commencement subsection can be seen in s 3(4). Here, the most common form of commencement is used, ie that the Act will come into force on the day of Royal Assent, or one or more specified days thereafter (here, it is on the following day). An Act may also come into force on a specific date, such as 22 June 2006. The date will be specifically mentioned within the section in such cases. It is also possible for an Act to come into force when a commencement order is made by a subordinate person or body (usually a Secretary of State) if the Act expressly allows for this. Finally, an Act or a provision of it may come into force upon the coming into effect of another Act.

12. A *Schedule* can be used in a variety of ways. Here, it is used to show what parts of old legislation are to be repealed (got rid of!) by the passing of the new Act. Repeals can be of the whole Act, any part, section, subsection, paragraph, sub-paragraph, phrase or even single word, or any combination of them. Schedules may also be used to give more detail to an Act, for example detail as to membership of bodies in Sch 7 to the Local Government etc (Scotland) Act 1994. They can also provide guidance as to the interpretation of a provision within the Act, for example Sch 2 to the Unfair Contract Terms Act 1977. If legislators wish to show the form of something (for example, the ballot paper in the referendum held under the Scotland Act 1978) they may use an Appendix instead of a Schedule.

Subordinate legislation. It is common for Parliament, through an Act, to confer on Ministers or other executive bodies the power to make rules and regulations which have the force of law and are thus properly called legislation. The phrase "subordinate legislation" covers every exercise of such power and is sometimes also known as "delegated legislation". The power to enact this kind of legislation comes from an authorising or "parent" Act which will be an Act of Parliament. There are many types of subordinate legislation but the most common are statutory instruments and Orders in Council. More than 3,000 of these are passed every year and they have a number of advantages and uses:

1.20

- Parliament has time to concern itself only with the broad principles of Acts. Detailed regulations and rules should be dealt with by the administration. The Road Traffic Acts are a good example. The Road Traffic Act 1972 empowered the Secretary of State to make regulations for the use of vehicles on public roads; such detail cannot possibly be set out in an Act of Parliament. Thus subordinate legislation can save parliamentary time.
- Subordinate legislation allows the knowledge and experience available outside Parliament to be utilised through appropriate consultation. For example, in

issuing regulations under the Dangerous Dogs Act 1991, the Secretary of State must consult with the British Veterinary Association.

- In times of emergency, it is impossible to pass an Act of Parliament quickly enough to deal with the situation. Subordinate legislation can be passed rapidly and allows responsiveness to emergencies. For example, the Secretary of State for the Environment could restrict the movement of livestock if there was an outbreak of Foot and Mouth Disease.
- Subordinate legislation is also used to give effect to Acts of Parliament. Often an Act of Parliament will state that all, or some, of the Act is to come into force on a date to be set by the Secretary of State. This is done using a statutory instrument known as a "commencement order".

1.21   *Statutory instruments.* Statutory instruments are also known as "Regulations" or "Rules" and the power to make them will be delegated to a Minister by an Act of Parliament. Most statutory instruments are "laid" before Parliament. However, they are not scrutinised to any great extent. If the authorising Act states that an instrument is to be passed using the *negative* procedure, then it will come into force in 40 days unless either House of Parliament resolves that it should be annulled. This is a fairly weak form of control.

1.22   The second method of laying an instrument before Parliament involves the *affirmative* procedure. Under this method, the instrument requires parliamentary approval before it can come into force. This is achieved through a 90-minute debate in Parliament. If a resolution to pass the instrument is not achieved then it will be taken back and amended in order for re-submission. This is obviously a slightly stronger form of control than the negative procedure.

1.23   Many statutory instruments have no laying requirement at all. This is not uncommon and regularly applies to commencement orders.

1.24   *Orders in Council.* Orders in Council refer to the Privy Council which advises the Queen on matters of constitutional importance. There are two types of Order in Council: those made under the authority of the Royal Prerogative, and those which are delegated to Ministers through an Act of Parliament. The first is an Order which is made without requiring the consent of Parliament. Such Orders are usually reserved for matters of constitutional importance, such as the dissolution of Parliament. They are made by the Privy Council with the authority of the Queen; although the Queen's assent today is purely formal and in reality is exercised by Ministers on her behalf. The second type of Order is authorised by an Act of Parliament and cannot be made without parliamentary approval. Such an Order was used to transfer powers from the UK Ministers to the Scottish Parliament under the devolution settlement.

1.25   Orders in Council do not really differ in status from that of statutory instruments but are considered through custom and convention to be more dignified and are therefore used for matters of constitutional importance.

1.26   *Control of subordinate legislation.* Challenge in the courts is not possible for Acts of Parliament, but it is for subordinate legislation. This is because the legislative powers of the UK Parliament are unlimited, whereas those of Ministers and subordinate bodies are not. There are two main grounds of challenge in the courts:

(1) that the content or substance of the legislation is *ultra vires* the parent Act. (In other words, it goes beyond the powers authorised by the Act); and

(2) that correct procedures have not been followed in the making of the legislation.

Scottish parliamentary legislation

Legislative competence. On 1 July 1999, the Queen officially opened the Scottish Parliament. The Scotland Act 1998 (SA 1998) created the Scottish Parliament by devolving various powers from the UK Parliament and handing them over to the Scottish Parliament.[14] Of those devolved powers, arguably the most important is the power to make law. The Scotland Act states that the ". . . Parliament may make laws, to be known as the Acts of the Scottish Parliament"[15] but the power to make such laws is not unlimited.   **1.27**

The Scottish Parliament is a creature of statute and can only pass laws in areas where it has legislative competency. This is because the UK Parliament has not passed all of its law-making powers to the Scottish Parliament. The Scotland Act 1998 does not state which powers have categorically been given to the Scottish Parliament since the Scotland Act subscribes to the retaining model of devolution. Under this model, everything is devolved to the Scottish Parliament except a number of specific areas which are "retained". These retained areas are listed within the Scotland Act and dictate the legislative competence of the Scottish Parliament.   **1.28**

The legislative competence of the Scottish Parliament is clearly spelled out in s 29 of the Scotland Act: **1.29**

- the Scottish Parliament may not legislate for another territory;
- the Scottish Parliament may not legislate on a matter reserved to the UK Parliament by virtue of Sch 5;
- the Scottish Parliament may not legislate in breach of the restrictions contained in Sch 4;[16]
- Acts of the Scottish Parliament must be compatible with the Human Rights Act 1998 and the European Communities Act 1972; and
- the Scottish Parliament may not remove the office of Lord Advocate.

In terms of Sch 5 to the Scotland Act, there are a number of areas which are known as "reserved" areas and here the Scottish Parliament has no power. The reserved areas are split into both "general" and "specific" reservations.[17] General reservations deal with subjects such as defence, social security and foreign affairs. These are areas where the law generally needs to be uniform across the UK or must be retained in order to fulfil international obligations. Specific reservations are very detailed and provide particular named areas where the Scottish Parliament has no power. The list is long and includes such areas as abortion; space exploration; interference with time zones; and xeno-transplantation.   **1.30**

---

[14] For more discussion on Scottish devolution, see para **3.77**.

[15] SA 1998, s 28(1).

[16] Schedule 4 states that particular statutes of constitutional note cannot be amended or repealed by the Scottish Parliament, eg the Acts of Union 1707, the European Communities Act 1972 and SA 1998.

[17] See SA 1998, Sch 5, Pts I, II.

1.31   **Bills and parliamentary stages**. Like Acts of the UK Parliament, Acts of the Scottish Parliament must begin as Bills. A Bill may be introduced by a member of the Scottish Executive, a Committee of the Scottish Parliament, or an individual MSP. Prior to the introduction of a Bill, a member of the Scottish Executive must make a statement that the provisions of the Bill are within the legislative competence of the Parliament.[18] The Presiding Officer must also consider the provisions and make a similar statement to the Parliament as to whether or not the Bill is competent.[19]

1.32   There are four main categories of Bill which can be brought before the Scottish Parliament. These are Executive Bills, Committee Bills, Members' Bills and Private Bills. As a general rule, there is extensive consultation and pre-legislative scrutiny on a Bill before it is introduced to the Parliament. All Bills on introduction must be accompanied by a Financial Memorandum setting out estimates of the administrative and compliance costs of the Bill. Furthermore, all Government Bills must be accompanied by explanatory notes summarising the provisions of the Bill, and a Policy Memorandum which sets out the policy objectives of the Bill. The parliamentary process that a Bill follows will vary depending on the type of Bill but the most common procedure is that used for Executive Bills which consist of three stages:

- **Stage 1**: the Bill is referred to the relevant subject committee, known as the "lead committee", for consideration of its general principles. The lead committee can take evidence at this stage and other committees with an interest in the Bill may also be involved in putting forward their views, for example the Finance Committee. The lead committee prepares a report which is submitted to the Parliament where a debate and vote are held on the principles of the Bill;
- **Stage 2**: after a period of at least 2 weeks, the Bill is sent to one or more committees to receive more detailed line-by-line consideration. The lead committee will generally draw together the observations of any other committee involved at this stage. It is also possible for a Bill to be sent to a Committee of the Whole Parliament. At this stage, amendments may be proposed and made to the Bill;
- **Stage 3**: following a further 2-week period, the amended Bill returns to the Parliament for further consideration and amendment. The Parliament must decide whether the Bill in its final form should be passed and at least a quarter of all MSPs must vote.

1.33   Following the final vote in the Parliament there must be a 4-week period before the Bill is submitted for Royal Assent. This time gap allows certain Law Officers, namely the Advocate General, the Lord Advocate and the Attorney-General, to have a role in the scrutiny of Bills. During this period, if any of the Law Officers doubts whether any provision is within the legislative competence of the Scottish Parliament, then they may refer the issue to the Judicial Committee of the Privy Council (JCPC).[20] This power may be similarly exercised by a Minister of the UK Parliament.[21] If the JCPC finds that

---

[18] SA 1998, s 31(1).
[19] SA 1998, s 31(2).
[20] SA 1998, s 33.
[21] SA 1998, s 35.

the Bill is outwith the legislative competence of the Parliament, then the Bill must be returned to the Parliament in order for amendments to be made. If the amended Bill is then subject to no further challenge, the Presiding Officer submits it to the Queen for Royal Assent.

Committee Bills. Committee Bills are seen as an innovation of the Scottish Parliament   **1.34** and a modern addition to the law-making process. The White Paper *Scotland's Parliament*[22] suggested that legislation should be initiated by committees of the Scottish Parliament, in keeping with the spirit of giving more MSPs a greater role in the legislative process of the Parliament. Committee Bills allow a committee of the Parliament to conduct inquiries into an area of law where it is perceived that change is required. The committee may then submit a report on this to the Parliament. With the agreement of the Parliament, the Scottish Executive then has 5 days to decide whether or not to support the report and propose legislation. If the Executive does not itself agree to bring forward legislation in line with the committee's proposals, then the Parliament may decide to adopt the Bill and bring forth draft legislation. The draft Bill would then be introduced to the Parliament and be subject to a general debate on its principles. If approved in principle, then the Bill would generally follow the same procedure outlined for an Executive Bill. The first Committee Bill was introduced by the Justice 1 Committee in 2001 and was enacted as the Protection from Abuse (Scotland) Act 2001.

Members' Bills. These are similar to Private Members' Bills within the UK Parlia-   **1.35** ment. Individual MSPs are entitled to bring forward proposals for legislation before either the Parliament or a relevant committee. If an MSP submits proposals to a committee, then the committee may hold an inquiry in order to assess whether the legislation is required. If the committee decides to proceed with the proposals then the Committee Bill procedure will be used. Alternatively, if an MSP submits proposals to the Parliament, then they must have the support of at least 11 other MSPs. After lodging the Bill with the Parliamentary Clerk, if the Bill receives 11 signatures within 1 month, then it will proceed following the Executive Bill procedure. One of the most high-profile Members' Bills was the Protection of Wild Mammals (Scotland) Bill introduced by Lord Watson which subsequently received Royal Assent in 2002.

Private Bills. Private Bills may be introduced by a person, body or association in order   **1.36** to gain powers in a specific area. They may be introduced to the Parliament on any sitting day. Private Bills generally follow the Executive Bill procedure, however, during Stage 1, the committee may require additional information and may ask the proposer to advertise the Bill in order to allow for any objections. The Committee must then prepare a report which deals with the need for such legislation and incorporates any public objections. The first Private Bill introduced in the Parliament was the Robin Rigg Offshore Wind Farm (Navigation and Fishing) (Scotland) Bill which received Royal Assent in 2003.

---

[22] *Scotland's Parliament* (Cm 3658, July 1997).

1.37   **Subordinate legislation of the Scottish Parliament**. The Scotland Act 1998 conveys
powers to make subordinate legislation upon Scottish Ministers, Ministers of the Crown
and Her Majesty in Council.[23] This is necessary for the same reasons that the UK Parliament
requires power to enact statutory instruments and Orders in Council. Statutory instruments
of the Scottish Parliament are known as Scottish statutory instruments or SSIs. Although
Scottish Ministers normally make subordinate legislation only in areas where the Parliament has legislative competence, provisions exist which also allow them to legislate in areas
where the Parliament has no competence. The Scotland Act 1998 allows a UK Minister to
transfer functions, by Order in Council, to Scottish Ministers and these functions may then
be exercised in so far as they relate to Scotland.[24] There are some restrictions placed upon the
power to make subordinate legislation. Such legislation cannot create serious criminal
offences,[25] and it is also subject to the same principles of challenge as UK subordinate
legislation, for example the *ultra vires* doctrine.

Byelaws

1.38   As well as subordinate legislation emanating from both the UK and Scottish Parliaments, there exists another form of subordinate legislation which is known as a byelaw.
Byelaws are rules made by an authority subordinate to Parliament for the regulation,
administration or management of a certain district and/or property. In Scotland,
byelaws are made by local authorities and certain other public bodies such as railway
authorities. However, the vast majority of byelaws are enacted by local authorities by
virtue of the Local Government (Scotland) Act 1973.[26] The 1973 Act states that local
authorities may make byelaws for the good rule and government of their area. A
common example is the "anti-drinking" byelaw adopted by most Scottish local
authorities which bans the consumption of alcohol within certain public areas. Such
byelaws must satisfy a number of conditions. They must be within the authority of the
authorising statute and must not be contrary to the general law of the land. In addition,
they must be certain in their enactment and not unreasonable. Byelaws are capable of
being challenged in court as *ultra vires*[27] if they fail to adhere to these conditions and
have not been made by following the prescribed procedure.

1.39   Byelaws have the same effect as any other law, provided that they are validly enacted.
Before being deemed valid, a byelaw must be confirmed by a relevant Scottish Minister.
Prior to confirmation, the local authority must inform members of the public of its
intention to legislate. This is done by printing a notice in the local newspaper and
informing the public where copies of the draft byelaw can be obtained. This procedure
allows citizens to lodge any relevant objections. Such objections must be taken into
account by the Scottish Ministers who then have the power to confirm, modify or refuse
the byelaw. Once a byelaw has been confirmed, it must be publicised in the area
concerned. Local authorities are also obliged to keep a register of byelaws for their
area in order to allow public inspection.

---

[23] SA 1998, Pt IV. For a detailed overview of subordinate legislation in the Scottish Parliament,
see J McFadden and M Lazarowicz, *The Scottish Parliament: An Introduction* (3rd edn, 2003),
Chapter 5.
[24] SA 1998, s 63.
[25] SA 1998, s 113(10).
[26] ss 201–204.
[27] See further J McFadden, *Local Government Law in Scotland: An Introduction* (2004), Chapter 4.

European legislation

European law has become increasingly important in the UK. As a result of its member- **1.40**
ship of the European Union, the UK has agreed to be bound by European law. The
European Communities Act 1972 ensures the applicability of European law in the UK
and states that all directly effective EU legislation creates an enforceable right within the
UK and must be enforced by all courts and tribunals. It also states that all UK law must
be applied subject to European law. Therefore, European law overarches our system of
national law and, if there is any conflict, it is European law which prevails.

These provisions are fairly revolutionary in that they fundamentally undermine the **1.41**
concept of parliamentary sovereignty and the supremacy of the UK Parliament. The
implications of the European Communities Act 1972 were discussed in great detail in
the case of *R* v *Secretary of State for Transport, ex parte Factortame (No 2)*.[28] On appeal, it
was affirmed by the House of Lords that an Act of Parliament contradicting EU
legislation could not be enforced in the courts of the UK. Furthermore, since EU law
had to be enforced, courts were entitled to issue orders to such effect. In effect, the 1972
Act allows European legislation to take precedence over that of the UK. There have been
many positive effects of this principle, and some areas of UK law have been fundamentally changed for the better due to the influence of European law.[29]

Sources of European law. There are two main sources of European law. These are **1.42**
primary legislation and secondary legislation. Primary legislation consists of the
Treaties which originally established the European Economic Community (EEC) and
subsequently amended and altered its constitution. Since the EEC was created in 1957 it
has greatly developed and expanded in its form and membership, becoming the
European Community (EC) and now the European Union (EU). Upon joining
the EU, Member States agree to be bound by the provisions of the Treaties. It is
through the authority of the Treaties that secondary legislation is created. Some of the
key European Treaties are as follows:

- the *Treaties of Rome 1957* led to the creation of the European Economic
  Community and the European Atomic Energy Authority;
- the *Treaty of Accession 1972* marked the entry of the UK to the EEC and further
  enlargement through the membership of Ireland and Denmark;
- the *Maastricht Treaty 1992* created the European Union;
- the *Amsterdam Treaty 1997* set new objectives for the European Union;
- the *Treaty of Nice 2001* saw the creation of the EU Charter of Fundamental
  Rights.

Secondary legislation consists of Regulations, Directives and Decisions. European **1.43**
Regulations are of general application and become law within all Member States
automatically. Member States do not have to pass any national legislation to apply

---

[28] [1990] 3 CMLR 375.
[29] For example, under UK law, separate legal protections used to exist for full-time and part-time
workers. These were held to be discriminatory under EU law and so abolished. Also, female
employees of the armed forces who became pregnant used to be instantly dismissed. This too was
held to be discriminatory and abolished.

the Regulations and they supersede any national law. Such Regulations are described as having "direct effect" within the Member States.

1.44   European Directives, on the other hand, state objectives to be achieved by Member States and it is up to each individual state to enact or amend national legislation in order to comply. A Directive does not, therefore, have direct applicability. There is normally a time limit within which a Directive must be implemented. If a Directive is sufficiently clear and specific, and if the time limit for implementation has elapsed, then the Directive will have direct effect. This means that a citizen can rely on the Directive to challenge the failure of the UK Government to comply.

1.45   Decisions are issued by the European Commission. The Commission is the administrative body of the EU and is responsible for all aspects of decision-making within the EU. The Commission ensures that Member States uphold their obligations to implement EU laws. Failure to implement obligations can result in enforcement proceedings being taken against a Member State. This involves the Commission investigating an alleged breach and issuing a reasoned opinion or decision on the matter. Decisions are binding upon the state to whom they are addressed and may also be issued to a public body, a private company or an individual.

Judicial precedent

1.46   Judicial precedent is the most important source of law after legislation. It is sometimes also known as case law, or common law. Precedent is not created by Parliament; instead, it emanates from the decisions of judges in cases heard before them. As such, precedent can often be difficult to find and interpret since it must be extracted from the written judgment of cases. With legislation, many drafters are involved in creating the most precise wording and form possible to avoid any ambiguities. However, judges will often produce their decisions in various styles, and some more clearly than others. Nonetheless, when a precedent is extracted from a case it forms part of the body of law in that area and can be regarded as authoritative. The relationship between precedent and legislation is an important one and worthy of note. Since legislation is the most important source of law, its position is supreme. Through the doctrine of the supremacy of Parliament, legislation cannot be altered by any kind of judicial precedent. Conversely, it is possible for legislation to alter precedent. For example, Parliament may decide to legislate for an area which has been traditionally governed by common law and the law of precedent. In England and Wales, for example, the Theft Act 1968 codified the common law of theft. This meant that the Theft Act superseded the pre-existing common law in that area.

The rules of precedent

1.47   Judicial precedent operates under the principle of *stare decisis* which literally means "to stand by decisions". This principle means that a court must follow and apply the law as set out in the decisions of higher courts in previous cases. In this way a consistent body of precedent can be created and applied with some certainty. But not all precedents are binding, and there are a number of rules which are applied by the judiciary in ascertaining the status of a precedent.

1.48   If a precedent is to be followed by a judge in a current case, then first it must be "in point". This means that the question of law answered in the previous case must be the same as the question before the current judge. It is not the facts of the case which must be similar but the actual point of law being dealt with in relation to those facts. In deciding whether a precedent is "in point", a judge needs to identify the *ratio decidendi* of the original decision. The *ratio* is the point of law which led to the decision. Sometimes judges will make it clear what the reason for the decision was in a case, by clearly stating so. More often, however, they will not and thus finding the *ratio* of a precedent can be a difficult task. There may also be statements made in a case which are *obiter dicta*, meaning "things said by the way". These do not form part of the reasoning for the decision or part of the *ratio*. They are often hypothetical questions or issues which illustrate how different facts in the case could lead to a different decision. *Obiter* remarks are never binding; they are merely persuasive on a judge. Their degree of persuasiveness will depend upon the authority of the judge who made the remarks.

If a precedent is not "in point" then it becomes merely "persuasive". A precedent **1.49** which is persuasive is not binding upon a judge and it may be distinguished. If a judge decides to distinguish a precedent then he is not bound to follow it. This leads to the development of the law in dealing with new situations. On the other hand, if a precedent is "in point", then it may be binding and the judge will be obliged to follow and apply the *ratio* of that decision. Yet this is ultimately dependent upon the position of the court within the hierarchy.

Precedent and the court hierarchy

It is not simply enough that a precedent be "in point" in order for it to be binding. The **1.50** relationship between the court where a precedent originated from and that of the court making the current decision is also crucial. As a general rule, in Scots law, a court will only be bound to follow the precedent of a court of higher status.[30] Decisions from courts with lower status are, as a rule, only persuasive. Precedents from courts outwith Scotland can also be considered but, apart from decisions of the House of Lords, none of these precedents is binding. On matters of European law, all UK courts are bound by precedents of the European Court of Justice. Here follows a brief overview of the principles of *stare decisis* in operation:

Criminal courts:
- The *district court*, being the lowest criminal court, is bound by the decisions of **1.51** the High Court of Justiciary (both as an appeal and as a trial court).
- The *sheriff court* is bound by the decisions of the High Court of Justiciary (both as an appeal and as a trial court).
- The *High Court of Justiciary (trial court)* is bound by the decisions of the High Court of Justiciary sitting as an appeal court. A decision of one Lord of Justiciary in the trial court does not bind another Lord of Justiciary in the trial court.
- The *High Court of Justiciary (appeal court)*, being the highest and most authoritative of the criminal courts, is not bound by its own precedents. However, any precedent which was questioned would have to be reviewed by a larger number of judges. A Full Bench of judges could easily overrule a precedent set by three appeal court judges.

---

[30] For the position of courts within the Scottish court hierarchy, see Chapter 2.

Civil courts:

1.52

- The *sheriff court*, being the lowest civil court, is bound by the decisions of the Inner House of the Court of Session and by the decisions of the House of Lords in Scottish appeals. A decision by one sheriff does not bind another sheriff, although sheriffs are bound by the sheriffs principal of that sheriff-dom. A decision by a sheriff principal does not bind another sheriff principal.
- The *Court of Session (Outer House)* is bound by the decisions of the House of Lords in Scottish appeals and by decisions of seven or more judges.[31] Lords Ordinary are also bound by decisions of the Inner House of the Court of Session. The decision of a Lord Ordinary in the Outer House does not bind another Lord Ordinary in the Outer House.
- The *Court of Session (Inner House)* is bound by the decisions of the House of Lords in Scottish appeals. Either Division, or an Extra Division of the Inner House, is bound by its own previous decisions. Any precedent called into question can be overruled by a Full Bench of judges.
- The *House of Lords* sits as a final court of appeal in Scottish civil matters. Decisions of the House of Lords are binding on all Scottish civil courts. The House normally considers itself to be bound by its own precedents but may depart from them when circumstances dictate.[32]

Institutional writings

1.53   Institutional writings, also known as authoritative writings, are the works of writers who first brought together the principles of Scots law into legal texts. These institutional writers lived mostly during the 17th and 18th centuries but their work has proved to be highly influential in the development of Scots law. Although their influence has dwindled somewhat in modern times, a statement made by an institutional writer will settle the law if there is no statute or judicial precedent covering the area in question. Some of the most important institutional writers are as follows:

- *James Dalrymple, Viscount Stair* (1619–95) is probably the most well known of all the institutional writers. Former Lord President of the Court of Session, his *Institutions of the Law of Scotland* was first published in 1681. Stair's work was based upon the principles of custom, feudal and Roman law, and Biblical law.
- Professor John Erskine (1695–1768) was responsible for producing *An Institute of the Law of Scotland*. Second only to Stair in terms of influence, this work was highly authoritative and set out the principles of Scots common law prior to the impact of judicial precedent and legislation.
- *Baron David Hume* (1757–1843) is famous for his treatise on Scots criminal law. His *Commentaries on the Law of Scotland respecting the Description and Punishment of Crimes* was first published in 1797 and still has relevance today in many aspects of criminal law in Scotland.

---

[31] *Munro's Trustees* v *Munro* 1971 SC 280.
[32] See Lord Chancellor's Practice Note at [1966] 3 All ER 77.

Custom

While custom was historically a very important source of law, it plays a far lesser role **1.54** today and is unlikely to be recognised in terms of creating new principles of law. Most older customs became embodied in the works of institutional writers and from there were incorporated into law by the courts as part of the common law. In modern, well-developed legal systems, custom has also been superseded by increasing amounts of parliamentary legislation. Nonetheless, it is still technically possible for custom to be accepted as a new source of law. In order for this to happen, four conditions must be fulfilled. First, the custom must be an exception to the general law but still be generally consistent with it. Second, there must have been a long acquiescence with the custom for it to be generally accepted as law. Third, it must be definite and certain and, finally, it must be fair and reasonable.

Equity

The use of the term "equity" in Scots law means justice, fairness and reasonableness. It **1.55** refers to the equitable power of the Court of Session and the High Court of Justiciary to provide a remedy in the interests of justice where otherwise there is none. This power is known as the *nobile officium* and is not often used by the courts. The *nobile officium* power of the Court of Session allows the law to operate in circumstances where otherwise a technicality would prevent it. In the case of *Ferguson, Petitioner*,[33] an electoral registration officer wrongly deleted the names of prospective voters from the draft electoral register. There was no common law or statutory remedy available which would allow the names to be placed back on the register. Therefore, in the interests of justness and fairness, the court invoked the *nobile officium* and ordered the names to be reinstated in order that the petitioners could vote in an imminent election.

The *nobile officium* power also allows the High Court of Justiciary to declare certain acts **1.56** to be criminal in nature where previously they were not. This is known as the declaratory power of the High Court of Justiciary. In the case of *Khaliq* v *HM Advocate*,[34] a shopkeeper was convicted of selling "glue-sniffing kits" to children. The named offence was unknown to Scots criminal law but the High Court decided that it was behaviour of a type which was harmful and should be criminalised. This power is seldom used today.

---

[33] 1965 SC 16.
[34] 1984 JC 23.

ESSENTIAL FACTS

1.57

- Law can be categorised as either public law or private law. Public law deals with the operation of government and the regulation of the relationship between government and citizens. Private law is concerned with the regulation of relationships between individual citizens and/or companies and organisations.

- The law may also be described as civil law or criminal law. The main difference is that each has a different court structure for its regulation. Criminal law deals with the punishment of criminal behaviour while civil law deals with disputes arising between private individuals, where the conduct of one party has caused unjustified loss to another.

- Legislation is the most important source of law. It consists of Acts of the UK Parliament, Acts of the Scottish Parliament, European Community legislation and various forms of delegated legislation.

- The UK Parliament is the supreme law-making body in the UK. UK legislation begins as a Bill and must then pass through the scrutiny of the House of Commons and the House of Lords. A Bill must then be submitted for Royal Assent before it can become an Act of Parliament. Such Acts are commonly known as statutes.

- The Scottish Parliament has devolved power to enact legislation for Scotland by virtue of the Scotland Act 1998. Its law-making power is limited in that certain areas are "reserved" to the UK Parliament. The Scottish Parliament may not pass any laws in these areas.

- Subordinate legislation arises when Parliament confers the power to make laws on Ministers or other delegated bodies. The product of exercising such power is sometimes also known as "delegated legislation". There are many types of subordinate legislation but the most common are statutory instruments, Orders in Council and byelaws. All subordinate legislation is subject to the *ultra vires* doctrine and the control of the courts.

- European legislation has become increasingly important in the UK as a result of its membership of the European Union. The European Communities Act 1972 ensures the applicability of European law in the UK and states that all directly effective EU legislation creates an enforceable right within the UK and must be enforced by all courts and tribunals. There are two main sources of European legislation: primary and secondary. Primary legislation consists of the founding Treaties of the EU, whereas secondary legislation consists of Regulations, Directives and Decisions issued under the authority of those Treaties.

- Judicial precedent or "common law" is the second most important source of law in the UK. Utilising the rules of precedent and the doctrine of *stare decisis* (standing by decisions), court decisions become a source of law by building up a body of binding decisions. Superior courts generally bind inferior courts within the court hierarchy but decisions become binding only if a case is "in point" and a previously decided *ratio decidendi* is the same as the *ratio* in the present case. The *ratio* is the legal principle upon which a case is decided. Hypothetical comments made in a decision are said to be made "by the way" or *obiter dicta*. They are not binding upon future cases and are merely persuasive.

- Institutional writings, also known as authoritative writings, are the works of writers who first brought together the principles of Scots law into legal texts. The institutional writers lived mostly during the 17th and 18th centuries but their work has proved to be highly influential in the development of Scots law. Their influence has dwindled in modern times with the growth of legislation and judicial precedent.
- Custom was historically a very important source of law but there is little scope for it today in the creation of new legal principles. For this to happen, four conditions must be fulfilled. First, the custom must be an exception to the general law but still be generally consistent with it. Second, there must have been a long acquiescence with the custom for it to be generally accepted as law. Third, it must be definite and certain and, finally, it must be fair and reasonable.
- Equity in Scots law relates to justice, fairness and reasonableness. It refers to the equitable power of the Court of Session and the High Court of Justiciary to provide a remedy in the interests of justice where otherwise there is none. This power is known as the *nobile officium* and is not often used by the courts.

2 SCOTTISH LEGAL SYSTEM

The purpose of this chapter is to give the reader a detailed overview of the Scottish court structure and of the people who work within the legal profession in Scotland. As discussed in Chapter 1, Scots law can be described in terms of both civil law and criminal law and each has a different court structure for its regulation. A useful starting point is to examine the civil and criminal court structures in some detail.
2.1

SCOTTISH CIVIL COURT STRUCTURE

The civil courts in Scotland are the sheriff court, the Court of Session and the House of Lords. Civil cases are known as litigation and are adversarial in nature. They involve a judge considering evidence submitted by all parties to the case and then issuing a judgment based upon the "balance of probabilities".[1]
2.2

THE SHERIFF COURT

The majority of civil litigation in Scotland is dealt with by the sheriff court. This is the lowest of the civil courts and deals with a wide range of civil cases. Scotland is divided into six sheriffdoms based upon the groupings of the old local government areas. The current sheriffdoms are:
2.3

- Lothian and Borders;
- South Strathclyde, Dumfries and Galloway;
- Glasgow and Strathkelvin;
- North Strathclyde;
- Tayside, Central and Fife; and
- Grampian, Highland and Islands.

Each sheriffdom has a sheriff principal who has the general duty of securing the speedy and efficient disposal of business within the courts of the sheriffdom. The sheriff principal is a full-time judge and is assisted by a number of sheriffs. Sheriffs and sheriffs principal are required to be solicitors or advocates of at least 10 years' standing and are appointed by the Queen on the recommendation of the First Minister after consultation with the Lord President.
2.4

Each sheriffdom is divided into several sheriff court districts. There are currently 49 such districts and each is staffed by as many sheriffs as are required to deal with the
2.5

---

[1] See para **1.5** for an explanation of the differing standards of proof in civil and criminal law.

volume of litigation for each court. The largest sheriff court in Scotland is Glasgow. This is the busiest court in Europe and has in excess of 23 sheriffs.

Jurisdiction

2.6   In civil actions, the sheriff court is both a court of first instance and a court of appeal. Its jurisdiction is wide and encompasses actions ranging from debt recovery to breach of contract, and divorce. The sheriff court has exclusive jurisdiction over certain matters. This is known as *privative* jurisdiction, and an example includes actions which involve a sum of money less than £5,000. In terms of deciding geographically where an action should be raised, the general rule is that a case should be heard by the court which has jurisdiction over the defender. This rule is embodied in the Latin maxim *actor sequitur forum rei* – meaning "the pursuer follows the court of the defender". The defender must either be resident within the relevant sheriffdom or have a place of business there. Cases coming before the sheriff court are categorised according to their monetary value. There are three different types, namely *small claims*; *summary causes*; and *ordinary causes*.

Small claims

2.7   The small claims procedure was introduced by the Law Reform (Miscellaneous Provisions) (Scotland) Act 1985. The procedure deals with actions for payment worth no more than £750[2] and was created to assist citizens in resolving minor disputes. It is relatively informal in nature and seeks to make the court process more user friendly by relaxing the normal rules of evidence and procedure. The normal rules about court expenses are also relaxed and generally the procedure seeks to encourage individual citizens to raise or defend small claims with little assistance. Cases are heard before a sheriff sitting alone and the pursuer does not require legal representation.

2.8   The unique feature of a small claim is the preliminary hearing at which it is determined whether the action requires to go to a full hearing or whether it can be dealt with there and then. Both the pursuer and the defender must advise the sheriff of the points which are in dispute between them and the sheriff must take a note and deliberate on these. The hearing is relatively informal and strict rules of evidence do not apply, allowing self-representation.[3]

2.9   An appeal against the decision of a sheriff in a small claim is made to the sheriff principal only and must be based upon a point of law.

Summary cause

2.10   The summary cause was introduced to provide citizens with an efficient and cheap means of procedure. It is used for cases with a monetary value of over £750 up to a limit of £1,500 and its jurisdiction is exclusive and final in such cases. Actions are heard by a single sheriff who is assisted by a sheriff clerk in terms of administrative

---

[2] Proposals to raise this limit to £1,500 are currently being considered by the Scottish Parliament. See para **2.23** below for further discussion.

[3] Nonetheless, legal representation still remains commonplace within small claims and can seriously affect the likelihood of success. It should be noted that legal aid is not available for small claims.

functions. A summary cause does not normally involve written pleadings, unlike an ordinary cause.

An appeal against the decision of a sheriff in a summary cause is made to the sheriff **2.11** principal on a point of law. A further appeal can be made with leave to the Inner House of the Court of Session and then to the House of Lords.

Ordinary cause

This procedure is used for actions over £1,500, with no upper limit upon the value of the **2.12** claim. It is the most expensive and time-consuming procedure within the sheriff court and can be heard by a sheriff, sheriff principal or an assessor. Ordinary actions are conducted by way of formal written pleadings, which are full and detailed. An ordinary cause may be remitted to the Court of Session if the case is of sufficient complexity or importance and any of the parties to the case have requested so.

An appeal from a sheriff in an ordinary cause can be made to the sheriff principal, and **2.13** then to the Inner House of the Court of Session. A further appeal to the House of Lords can be made on a point of law only. Alternatively, an appeal can be made directly to the Inner House of the Court of Session, essentially usurping the sheriff principal. This is likely to happen when the issue being dealt with is one of importance and therefore requires a decision from a more authoritative court or where both parties to the case are determined to appeal against the sheriff principal, regardless. However, an appeal to the Inner House is expensive, as an advocate or solicitor-advocate is required for repre-sentation. Thus, in order to avoid escalating costs, most parties are content with an appeal to the sheriff principal.

THE COURT OF SESSION

The Court of Session was established in 1532 and sits only in Parliament House, **2.14** Edinburgh. It is a supreme court which has jurisdiction over the whole of Scotland and has both original and appellate jurisdiction. It generally deals with civil actions which involve very large sums of money[4] or important points of law which require a more authoritative judgment than that of a sheriff. Judges of the Court of Session are officially known as either Senators of the College of Justice or Lords of Council and Session and there are currently 32 such judges. The most senior Court of Session judges are the Lord President and the Lord Justice-Clerk, in order of seniority. They are appointed by the Queen on the nomination of the Prime Minister from a recommendation of the First Minister. The remaining judges are appointed by the Queen on the recommendation of the First Minister following consultation with the Lord President. The judges can be sheriffs or sheriffs principal of at least 5 years' standing, or advocates or solicitor-advocates with at least 5 years' right of audience in the Court of Session. All Court of Session judges are also judges within the High Court of Justiciary where the Lord President becomes known as the Lord Justice-General.

The Court of Session is divided into two distinct parts, namely the Outer House and **2.15** the Inner House. The names of these two parts do not have any technical explanation – merely a historical and geographical one. In centuries past, the most senior judges

---

[4] For example, £100,000 or more.

would sit in an inner chamber of Parliament House while more inexperienced judges would sit in other "outer" chambers of the building. When a party to an action was unhappy with a decision emanating from a judge in an outer chamber then it was common for an appeal to be made to the more experienced inner chamber judges. Thus the Inner and Outer House distinctions were created.

Outer House

2.16   The Outer House is a court of first instance, meaning that cases can be heard there for the first time. Cases are normally heard before a single judge but it is possible in some cases to seek a jury trial within the Outer House. This is rare, however, and is limited to cases such as an action for defamation or damages for personal injury. If a jury is used in such cases it consists of 12 members of the public selected at random from the electoral role.

2.17   The jurisdiction of the Outer House extends to all kinds of civil action except those which are excluded by statute or privative to another court. It is the only court in Scotland which can hear actions for judicial review of administrative action. This is known as the controlling power of the Court of Session and is used widely to review acts of persons and bodies who have been given delegated power from Parliament, for example local authorities and other government bodies. Decisions from the Outer House can be appealed to the Inner House of the Court of Session.

Inner House

2.18   The Inner House is primarily a court of appeal for civil actions raised in either the sheriff court or the Outer House. It also has some first instance jurisdiction but in extremely limited circumstances, for example an appeal against certain tribunals. The Inner House has two divisions, namely the First Division and the Second Division. Each has equal authority and jurisdiction. The First Division consists of the Lord President and three senior Lords of Session, while the Second Division comprises the Lord Justice-Clerk and three other Lords of Session. In practice, only three of the four judges actually sit in each division and it would only be in extraordinary circumstances that a Full Bench of four would sit.

2.19   In order to deal with heavy workloads, the Lord President may appoint any three judges to convene an Extra Division of the Court of Session. Also, in important or complicated cases, the First and Second Divisions may combine to form a more authoritative court of seven judges. Final judgments of the Inner House may be appealed to the House of Lords.

THE HOUSE OF LORDS

2.20   The House of Lords is an appellate court and is the final court of appeal in Scottish civil cases. It will normally only hear appeals on important or complex questions of law, and sometimes fact. There are 12 Lords of Appeal in Ordinary who hear appeals and they are commonly known as "Law Lords". In recent years, it has become customary to have at least two Law Lords who are of Scottish origin.[5] The quorum for hearing appeals is

---

[5] In that they have Scottish qualifications and have been prolific in practice within Scotland throughout their career.

three judges, but they are regularly heard by five and sometimes, in the most important cases, by seven Law Lords. It is a convention that at least one Law Lord should be of Scottish origin when hearing a Scottish civil appeal case, although this is not always possible and is subject to circumstance.

In an appeal from the Inner House of the Court of Session, the appellant must petition the House of Lords, "praying" that the decision of the Inner House be altered. A decision of the House of Lords is not an operative judgment since it must be returned to the Court of Session where a decree from the Inner House will apply that judgment. Decisions of the House of Lords are ultimately binding upon all lower civil courts but the House itself is not bound by its own decisions and may depart from them when appropriate. **2.21**

CIVIL JUSTICE REFORM

Recently, a number of changes have been introduced which will have a significant impact upon the existing Scottish civil court structure. Of these probably the most significant are changes to the jurisdictional limits within the sheriff court and, more importantly, the creation of an entirely new court which will be known as the Supreme Court. **2.22**

DEVELOPMENTS IN THE SHERIFF COURT

In July 1998 the Scottish Courts Administration issued a consultation paper[6] which sought views on increasing the jurisdictional limits in the sheriff court. A number of reforms were put forward which were aimed at making the small claims procedure more accessible and which it was hoped would reduce the volume of ordinary causes. Thus, the Justice and Home Affairs Committee of the Scottish Parliament announced that small claim limits, fixed at £750 since 1988, are to be increased to £1,500 and summary cause limits are to be raised to £5,000. Consequently, ordinary causes will be reserved for more expensive actions exceeding £5,000. In addition, personal injury claims are to be specifically excluded from the small claim procedure. At the time of writing, these changes are awaiting approval by the Scottish Parliament. **2.23**

A SUPREME COURT FOR THE UNITED KINGDOM

In recent years there have been mounting calls for the creation of a new, independent Supreme Court, separating the highest appeal court from the House of Lords and removing the Law Lords from the legislature. On 12 June 2003 the Government announced its intention to do so and, in late 2004, the Constitutional Reform Act 2005 received Royal Assent. **2.24**

The Government believes that the new Supreme Court will reflect and enhance the independence of the judiciary from both the legislature and the executive. The decision to create the Supreme Court does not imply any dissatisfaction with the previous performance of the House of Lords as the UK's highest court of appeal; indeed, its **2.25**

---

[6] Scottish Courts Administration, *Proposals to Increase Jurisdiction Limits in the Sheriff Court* (1998).

judges have conducted themselves with the utmost integrity and independence throughout the years. However, the Government believes that the time has come to establish a new court regulated by statute as a body separate from Parliament. This will allow the UK to adhere more rigidly to the doctrine of the separation of powers and will allay fears of potential conflict with the Human Rights Act 1998 and the right to a fair trial.

2.26   The Supreme Court will be a United Kingdom body, legally separate from the courts of England and Wales, which will take over the judicial functions of the Law Lords in the House of Lords and from the Judicial Committee of the Privy Council. The Supreme Court will be the final court of appeal in all matters under English law, Welsh law (to the extent that the Welsh Assembly makes laws for Wales that differ from those in England) and Northern Irish law. It will also be a court of record for appeals from the Court of Session in Scotland (there is no right of appeal beyond the High Court of Justiciary for criminal cases except in so far as devolution issues arise). The new Supreme Court is not based upon the US model and will have no power to overturn legislation.

2.27   The court will be located in a building separate from the Houses of Parliament and, after a lengthy survey of suitable sites, including Somerset House, the location for the new court will be Middlesex Guildhall, in Parliament Square, Westminster, which is currently a Crown Court. The court is expected to hold its first hearing in 2008.

SCOTTISH CRIMINAL COURT STRUCTURE

2.28   The criminal courts in Scotland are the district court, the sheriff court and the High Court of Justiciary. Criminal cases are known as prosecutions and are adversarial in nature. There are two types of criminal procedure in Scotland, namely *summary* procedure and *solemn* procedure. Summary procedure is used for more minor cases such as breach of the peace or speeding, whereas solemn procedure is used for more serious offences such as assault or murder. The major difference between the procedures is that summary cases are heard by a judge sitting alone whereas solemn cases involve a trial before a jury of 15 members of the public as well as a judge. The standard of proof required in a criminal trial is "beyond all reasonable doubt", making it much higher than that of the civil courts.[7]

2.29   All criminal prosecutions in Scotland are taken through the system of public prosecution which is embodied in the Crown Office and Procurator Fiscal Service (COPFS). The most senior public prosecutor is the Lord Advocate who is assisted by the Solicitor General and around 15 Advocates Depute. At sheriff court and district court levels, prosecutions are normally undertaken by the procurator fiscal or a depute. Reports of offences are made chiefly by the police to the COPFS where it must be considered whether there is enough evidence and whether it is in the public interest to bring forth a prosecution. The procedure for bringing prosecutions is contained in the Criminal Procedure (Scotland) Act 1995.[8]

---

[7] See further paras **1.5** and **1.6**.

[8] For a discussion of the criminal justice system, see further D McFadzean and K Scott, "Scottish Criminal Justice and the Police" in D Donnelly and K Scott (eds), *Policing Scotland* (2005).

DISTRICT COURT

The district court was created by the District Courts (Scotland) Act 1975. There are **2.30** currently 30 district courts in Scotland which roughly correspond with local authority areas. The district court is the lowest of the criminal courts and deals only with minor criminal matters, thus utilising only summary procedure. The district court is a lay court and is presided over by lay members known as justices of the peace (JPs). JPs are partially appointed by local councils, who may appoint up to one quarter of their members as justices. The remainder are upstanding members of the community who have been recommended by local committees for appointment by the Scottish Ministers. Any JP who sits on the bench of a district court is assisted by a legally qualified clerk of court[9] who will act as a legal assessor and give advice to the justice. In Glasgow, work is shared by JPs and legally qualified stipendiary magistrates. Such magistrates are unique to Glasgow and are not found in any other district courts. They are appointed by local authorities from among legally qualified practitioners in the area.

The sentencing powers of the district court reflect the minor nature of the offences it **2.31** deals with. A justice of the peace has the power to impose a prison sentence of up to 60 days and/or a fine of up to £2,500.[10] A stipendiary magistrate has the power to impose a prison sentence of 3 months (or up to 6 months in cases which involve a previous conviction of theft or dishonesty, or personal violence) and/or a fine of up to £5,000.

An appeal from a decision of the district court can be made to the High Court of **2.32** Justiciary only.

SHERIFF COURT

The jurisdiction of the sheriff court covers most criminal offences committed within the **2.33** sheriffdom except for those which are privative to other courts.[11] Thus, many cases which come before a district court could also be brought before the sheriff court. The decision on whether a case should ultimately be dealt with in the sheriff court is made by the procurator fiscal. As with civil actions before the sheriff court, cases are heard by either a sheriff principal or a sheriff, with or without a jury depending on what procedure is being used.

Summary procedure

This is used for the most minor offences and cases are heard by a sheriff sitting alone. **2.34** The decision on whether a minor offence should be brought before the sheriff court rather than the district court is made by the procurator fiscal and is based upon issues such as seriousness, sentencing and expediency. The sentencing powers of a sheriff under summary procedure are the same as those for a stipendiary magistrate, namely 3 months' imprisonment (or up to 6 months' for those with a previous conviction of theft or dishonesty, or personal violence) and/or a maximum fine of £5,000. The court also

---

[9] The Clerk of Court must be qualified as a solicitor or an advocate.
[10] Note that some statutory offences will have a prescribed level of punishment to which the court must adhere.
[11] Eg parking offences must be dealt with by the district court, and murder or rape must be tried by the High Court of Justiciary.

has the power to order disqualification from driving and in practice deals with most road traffic-related cases where disqualification or endorsement is involved.

Solemn procedure

2.35 Solemn procedure is used to deal with more serious offences such as robbery or assault. The sheriff will sit with a jury of 15 persons who will decide on the guilt of the accused. Three verdicts are available to a jury in Scotland, namely guilty; not guilty; and not proven. This last verdict has the same effect as an acquittal in that the accused is freed without sentence. It is regarded by many as a wholly unsatisfactory verdict since it indicates that the jury thought the accused was not entirely innocent but because there was insufficient evidence they could not convict "beyond all reasonable doubt". If the accused is found guilty, the sheriff has the power to impose a prison sentence of up to 3 years and/or an unlimited fine. It should be noted that the sheriff court also has the power to remit a case to the High Court of Justiciary for sentence, should it believe that its own powers are unduly restrictive.

Appeals

2.36 Appeals from the sheriff court may be taken, with leave, to the High Court of Justiciary for both summary and solemn cases. Unlike the civil jurisdiction of the sheriff court, it should be noted that there is no right of appeal from a sheriff to the sheriff principal in criminal matters.

HIGH COURT OF JUSTICIARY

2.37 Established in 1672, the High Court of Justiciary is the highest criminal court in Scotland and is both a court of first instance and an appellate court. It is presided over by the Lord Justice-General, the Lord Justice-Clerk and the Lords of Session as Lords Commissioners of Justiciary. It has jurisdiction over all crimes committed in Scotland except those which are privative to other courts or are excluded by statute. The High Court has exclusive jurisdiction with respect to a small number of offences which are known as the "Crown crimes", namely murder, rape, treason and incest.

Court of first instance

2.38 As a trial court, the High Court of Justiciary sits in Edinburgh but also has the power to go out on circuit as required. As a circuit court, the High Court can sit in locations throughout Scotland, using the local sheriff court as its base. While there are a number of towns which have regular sittings, such as Kilmarnock and Paisley, the circuits are not restricted to these towns and a sitting may be held wherever it is deemed convenient. Glasgow has a permanent sitting of the High Court because of the exceptionally high number of cases emanating from that area.[12]

2.39   The judges of the High Court of Justiciary are the same as those in the Court of Session, although they are known as "Lords Commissioners of Justiciary" in their criminal capacity. They sit alone, with a jury of 15 members of the public who decide

---

[12] Approximately half of all High Court cases originate from the Glasgow area.

upon the guilt of the accused. In particularly difficult or important cases, it is possible for three judges to sit; however, this is very rare and has occurred in only a handful of cases in the last century. The sentencing powers of the High Court are unlimited in terms of both imprisonment and fine. However, there are certain offences which have a sentence prescribed by statute. For example, by virtue of the Murder (Abolition of Death Penalty) Act 1965, any person convicted of murder must receive a sentence of life imprisonment.

Appeals from the High Court of Justiciary as a court of first instance can be made to **2.40** the High Court of Justiciary sitting as the Court of Criminal Appeal.

Court of Criminal Appeal

The High Court of Justiciary is also the highest court of criminal appeal in Scotland and **2.41** all criminal appeals must be heard before it. It should be noted that there is no right of appeal in Scottish criminal cases to the House of Lords.[13] Appeals from courts of summary criminal jurisdiction consist of appeals from the sheriff or district court against conviction, sentence or both. For appeals against conviction, the court consists of three or more judges and the determination of any question is according to the majority of members of the court sitting. Each judge is entitled to pronounce their own opinion. A lesser quorum of two judges is competent to hear appeals against various sentences. Appeals under solemn proceedings have similar grounds and procedure for those narrated above for summary. They are brought by way of a written note of appeal stating all of the grounds of appeal, ie conviction, sentence or both.

The court has wide powers of disposal for an appeal against conviction or sentence. It **2.42** can allow an appeal and quash a conviction, or it may amend a verdict, or modify a sentence. It also has the power to authorise the Crown to conduct new proceedings. It is worth noting that the Crown also has the right of appeal, albeit on a point of law against acquittal or sentence.

COURTS WITH SPECIAL JURISDICTION

THE EUROPEAN COURT OF JUSTICE

The European Court of Justice (ECJ) has jurisdiction over issues relating to matters **2.43** covered by the European Treaties. When such an issue arises in a case before a UK domestic court, the direction of the ECJ must be sought, or if a decision already exists on the issue then the precedent of the ECJ must be applied. Essentially, it is the job of the ECJ to ensure that European law is applied by Member States. Cases can be brought by individuals or can be referred to the ECJ from national courts for rulings on matters affecting the validity or interpretation of European law.

THE JUDICIAL COMMITTEE OF THE PRIVY COUNCIL

Historically, the Judicial Committee of the Privy Council was of little specific relevance **2.44** to Scotland. The role of the Privy Council was to advise the monarch, to review

---

[13] *Macintosh* v *Lord Advocate* (1876) 3 R (HL) 34.

decisions of certain professional bodies such as the General Medical Council, and to act as a final court of appeal from the colonies of the British Empire and from Common-wealth countries.[14] However, since the setting up of the Scottish Parliament in 1999, the Privy Council has had an increased profile in the administration of justice. The Scotland Act 1998 states that the Judicial Committee shall have the power to determine the legislative competence of a Bill of the Scottish Parliament prior to Royal Assent.[15] It also has the power to act as court of last resort in determining "devolution issues". Schedule 6 to the Scotland Act defines "devolution issues" as:

- a question as to the functions of the Scottish Executive, the First Minister or the Lord Advocate;
- whether the exercise of a function is within devolved competence;
- whether the exercise of a function is compatible with European law or the European Convention on Human Rights; and
- any other question regarding whether the exercise of a function is within devolved competence or any other question relating to reserved matters.

2.45   The Privy Council also hears appeals against devolution issues which arise in the lower courts, ie in Scotland the Inner House of the Court of Session or the High Court of Justiciary.[16] Decisions as to devolution issues are binding upon the lower courts.

STATUTORY TRIBUNALS

2.46   Although not technically courts, statutory tribunals are worthy of note and play an important supplementary role to the work of the courts within the UK. From the Second World War onwards, there has been an explosion in the size and complexity of the Welfare State in Britain. As a result, the state has become involved in more areas of everyday life than ever before. Consequently, this has led to a massive increase in the number of complaints and disputes which arise from the application of rules and regulations by various organs of the state. These disputes could be settled using the existing courts, however, the court system already struggles to cope with ever increas-ing litigation in other areas. As a result, Parliament decided to create special bodies, known as tribunals, for resolving certain categories of dispute between citizens and the state. It also created a number of tribunals with jurisdiction over disputes between citizens, for example in the area of employment law. Most tribunals are set up by statute and the powers and scope of the tribunal are contained either within the statute or in regulations issued under the authority of the statute.

2.47   Today, there are around 2,000 tribunals in the UK. They cover a wide range of disputes and include immigration appeals, employment tribunals, disability living allowance tribunals, and benefit appeals, among many more.[17] The position of tribunals

---

[14] Few countries retain this link but there are still some who use the Privy Council as their final court of appeal, eg Mauritius and the Bahamas.
[15] Scotland Act 1998, s 33.
[16] Scotland Act 1998, s 98 and Sch 6.
[17] For a list of the key statutory tribunals, see H R W Wade and C F Forsyth, *Administrative Law* (9th edn, 2004), Chapter 24.

within the justice system was clarified in 1958 by the Franks Committee[18] and the recommendations of the Committee were embodied in the Tribunals and Inquiries Act 1958, now consolidated in the Tribunals and Inquiries Act 1992. The Franks Report was instrumental in the development of the modern tribunal system and stated that all tribunals should be open, fair and impartial, meaning that they should be free from government interference, have clear and consistent procedures and should be held publicly, giving clear and reasoned decisions. Tribunal proceedings differ greatly from those of a court in that they are very informal. Hearings tend to be held in office buildings, with proceedings being inquisitorial rather than adversarial, and a party to an action may represent themselves.[19]

Appeals from tribunals differ according to the governing legislation for each one. **2.48** There are no hard and fast rules as to the routes of appeal, however, many statutes convey a right of appeal to the sheriff court and then to the Inner House of the Court of Session. Where a right of appeal is given to a sheriff and the statute gives no indication about review of the sheriff's decision then it is presumed that the sheriff's decision is final.

LAW PERSONNEL

The Scottish legal system consists of a number of different offices and appointments, **2.49** including judges, solicitors, advocates and the police. The purpose of the following sections is to give a general overview of the key members of the legal profession.

SOLICITORS

Solicitors were previously known as "writers" or "law agents" and today are **2.50** sometimes known simply as "lawyers". They are members of an ancient profession within Scotland, and have a varied professional role within the legal system. Their work involves representing clients in the lower civil and criminal courts,[20] giving all kinds of legal advice, drafting wills and agreements and providing conveyancing services, among other things. Solicitors can work on their own as a sole practitioner, with other solicitors as a partnership, or for large multi-partner companies, or local authorities. All solicitors must have a practising certificate which is renewable each year.

The requirements for becoming a solicitor and the regulations as to how they may **2.51** carry out their practice are to be found in the Solicitors (Scotland) Act 1980 (as amended). In order to become a solicitor in Scotland, an individual must have successfully completed an LL.B. degree from a recognised institution[21] as well as the

---

[18] *Report of the Committee on Administrative Tribunals and Inquiries* (Cmnd 218, 1957).
[19] It should be noted that legal aid is unavailable for tribunals with the exception of the Employment Appeals Tribunal and the Lands Tribunal for Scotland. However, a person can seek financial help for the costs of preparing a case under the advice and assistance scheme ABWOR (Advice by Way of Representation).
[20] Solicitors may not make an appearance within any of the Supreme Courts, namely the Court of Session, the High Court of Justiciary, the House of Lords and the Judicial Committee of the Privy Council. This is because they have a limited "right of audience" and are restricted to practice within the lower courts only.

Diploma in Legal Practice. From here, a potential solicitor must secure a legal traineeship with a firm of solicitors or other body such as a local authority. The traineeship lasts for two years where the individual will generally receive training and experience in specialist areas of law as well as sitting further examinations such as the Professional Competence Course. On completion of the traineeship, an individual may then be admitted to the Law Society of Scotland as a solicitor and will receive their first practising certificate.

2.52   As a profession, solicitors are regulated and governed by the Law Society of Scotland. All practising solicitors must be a member of the Society. It has a number of key functions which include setting the education, training and admission requirements for the profession, ensuring that professional standards and discipline are maintained and administering the Guarantee Fund[22] which is available to compensate clients if they have suffered financial loss through a dishonest solicitor. By far the most controversial function of the Law Society of Scotland is that of maintaining standards and discipline. The profession is essentially self-regulating, with all complaints handled by the Society free from government interference or regulation. This system has been criticised over the years as being biased and lacking openness and transparency. Consequently, calls have been made for complaints against solicitors to be handled by an independent investigator. In response, the Scottish Parliament is currently reforming this area with the co-operation of the Society.[23]

SOLICITOR-ADVOCATES

2.53   Until 1993, solicitors had no right of audience before the supreme courts. Despite being intimately involved in the preparation of a case, they would not be allowed to appear within any of the superior courts and would have to pass this work on to an advocate. This would also result in increased legal fees for the solicitor's client. In an attempt to erode the monopoly held by advocates in this area, the Government decided to extend rights of audience to certain solicitors. In order to gain extended rights of audience in either the civil or criminal courts, a solicitor must have a minimum of 5 years' experience in court practice. They must then undertake a course of specialised training and examinations provided by the Law Society of Scotland in order to prove that they are worthy of the right of audience. On completion of the training, a panel of five solicitors will then examine the application and make a recommendation to the Law Society.

2.54   A solicitor-advocate gains the same rights of audience as an advocate but is not allowed to work as a junior to a Queen's Counsel. The creation of solicitor-advocates was not welcomed by the Faculty of Advocates and it has issued a ban on working with solicitor-advocates in an attempt to preserve its monopoly.

---

[21] The LL.B. degree is offered by a number of Scottish universities subject to accreditation by the Law Society of Scotland. The Law Society also allows graduates of other disciplines to complete its own examinations in law in order to qualify.

[22] All solicitors must contribute to the Guarantee Fund as well as being covered by a master policy of professional indemnity covering acts of negligence.

[23] See *Reforming Complaints Handling, Building Consumer Confidence: Regulation of the Legal Profession in Scotland* (Scottish Executive, 2005).

ADVOCATES

An advocate is a specialist court practitioner who is a member of the Faculty of **2.55** Advocates. They have rights of audience in all Scottish courts and, unlike solicitors, they must work independently. Advocates are not allowed to enter into partnerships, however they do subscribe to an agency known as Faculty Services Ltd which is a company set up by the Faculty of Advocates to assist advocates with administrative work such as collecting fees and receiving instructions from clients. There are currently around 420 practising advocates in Scotland who may be instructed by solicitors and certain other organisations to appear on their behalf in the supreme courts. They are specialist pleaders but may also provide written or verbal advice on the legal merits of a case. This is known as "counsel's opinion" and is used regularly as a means of settling a case outside of court.

To become an advocate, a candidate must have at least a second class LL.B. honours **2.56** degree, or a second class honours degree in another subject plus an ordinary LL.B. degree, or an ordinary LL.B. degree with distinction as well as a Diploma in Legal Practice. Candidates are known as "intrants" and must go through a matriculation process for admission to the Faculty of Advocates. Intrants must then successfully complete the Faculty's training requirements which includes a process known as "devilling" where an intrant will undertake their training and examinations under the supervision of a senior advocate known as a "devil-master". It is a difficult process to become an advocate since the intrant must pay for all of their expenses, entry fees and equipment and essentially be unsalaried during the training process which takes around one and a half years. Newly qualified advocates become known as "junior counsel" and after many years' practice they may apply to become a Queen's Counsel; this is known as "taking silk".

Advocates, like solicitors, are essentially self-regulating. The Faculty of Advocates **2.57** sets its own education and admissions requirements and is free from government interference. The Faculty is also responsible for the maintenance of standards and discipline within the profession and deals with its own complaints. However, this system is currently under review by the Scottish Parliament and it is likely that advocates will be subject to the same new regulatory regime as solicitors.

LAW OFFICERS FOR SCOTLAND

The Law Officers for Scotland are the Lord Advocate, the Solicitor-General for Scotland, **2.58** and the Advocate-General for Scotland. The Law Officers assist with the handling of government affairs and advise and represent the Crown in civil cases. The Lord Advocate is head of the system of criminal prosecutions and investigation of deaths in Scotland. He decides whether a prosecution should take place and has control over the Procurator Fiscal Service. He can also issue direction to the police in the investigation of crimes. The Lord Advocate and the Solicitor-General may personally prosecute an offence themselves, however it is rare for them do so and in practice advocates-depute are appointed to prosecute on their behalf.

The Lord Advocate and the Solicitor-General for Scotland are appointed by the Queen **2.59** on the recommendation of the First Minister and approval of the Scottish Parliament. Both Law Officers are members of the Scottish Executive. The Advocate-General for Scotland is a special office created by virtue of the Scotland Act 1998. The

Advocate-General is responsible for advising the UK Government on matters of Scots law and the propriety of the Scottish Parliament within its devolved spheres of power.

2.60

Diagram 1: Scottish civil courts

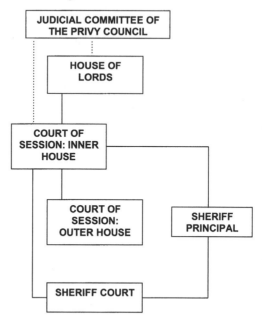

 = direct right of appeal

.... = higher standing but no direct right of appeal

2.61

Diagram 1: Scottish criminal courts

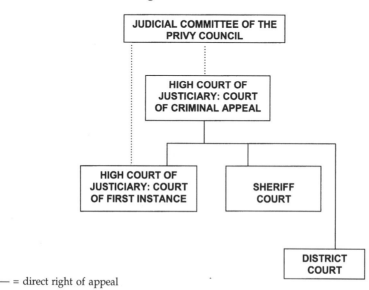

——— = direct right of appeal

.... = higher standing but no direct right of appeal

ESSENTIAL FACTS

- The Scottish court hierarchy has two separate court structures for dealing with the civil and criminal law.

2.62

THE CIVIL COURT STRUCTURE

- Sheriff courts are organised into six sheriffdoms and 49 sheriff court districts. They have a wide civil jurisdiction and are presided over by sheriffs and sheriffs principal. There are three main procedures within the sheriff court, namely the small claim, the summary cause and the ordinary cause.
- The Court of Session sits in Edinburgh and consist of the Inner House and the Outer House. The Outer House is a court of first instance and its jurisdiction extends to all kinds of civil action except those which are excluded by statute or privative to another court. Cases are normally heard before a single judge but it is possible in some cases to seek a jury trial, although this is rare. The Inner House is primarily a court of appeal and is split into two divisions which hear appeals from the Outer House and the sheriff courts.
- The House of Lords is the highest court in the UK and is the final court of appeal in Scottish civil cases. It will normally only hear appeals on important or complex questions of law, and sometimes fact. There are 12 Lords of Appeal in Ordinary who hear appeals and they are commonly known as "Law Lords".

THE CRIMINAL COURT STRUCTURE

- District courts are the lowest courts within the hierarchy and have jurisdiction over minor crimes. They are presided over by lay justices of the peace, except in Glasgow where there are also qualified stipendiary magistrates. A justice of the peace has the power to impose a prison sentence of up to 60 days and/or a fine of up to £2,500. A stipendiary magistrate has the power to impose a prison sentence of 3 months (or up to 6 months in cases which involve a previous conviction of theft or dishonesty, or personal violence) and/or a fine of up to £5,000.
- Sheriff courts deal with more serious criminal offences and utilise either summary or solemn procedure depending upon the severity of an offence. Under summary procedure, a sheriff hears a case alone and has the same sentencing powers as a stipendiary magistrate. Under solemn procedure, a sheriff decides on the law while a jury of 15 members

of the public decide on the facts and the guilt or innocence of an accused. A solemn sheriff has the power to impose a prison sentence of up to 3 years and/or an unlimited fine.

- The High Court of Justiciary is the highest criminal court in Scotland. It is a circuit court and deals with the most serious crimes such as murder, rape and treason. Cases are heard before a Lord Commissioner of Justiciary sitting with a jury of 15. The sentencing powers of the High Court are unlimited in terms of both imprisonment and fine.
- The High Court is also an appellate court when it sits as the Court of Criminal Appeal. A panel of three or more judges may hear appeals from the High Court itself, the sheriff courts and the district courts.

EUROPEAN COURT OF JUSTICE

- The European Court of Justice has jurisdiction over issues relating to matters covered by the European Treaties.
- Cases can be brought by individuals or can be referred to the ECJ from national courts for rulings on matters affecting the validity or interpretation of European law.

JUDICIAL COMMITTEE OF THE PRIVY COUNCIL

- By virtue of the Scotland Act 1998, the Judicial Committee of the Privy Council has the power to determine the legislative competence of a Bill of the Scottish Parliament. It also has the power to act as court of last resort in determining "devolution issues".
- The Privy Council also hears appeals against devolution issues which arise in the lower courts, ie in Scotland the Inner House of the Court of Session or the High Court of Justiciary.

LAW PERSONNEL

- There are many professionals who work within the Scottish legal system, including members of the judiciary, advocates, solicitor-advocates and solicitors.
- Solicitors practise widely in diverse areas of law and generally represent clients in the lower civil and criminal courts. They are regulated by the Law Society of Scotland and all solicitors must be enrolled as members.
- Advocates are specialist court practitioners who are members of the Faculty of Advocates. They are regulated by the Faculty and have rights of audience in the superior Scottish courts. Advocates may also issue "counsel's opinion" on particular points of law.

3 CONSTITUTIONAL LAW

Every civilised country in the world has a constitution, a set of rules which govern the structure and functions of government and the relationships between the state and its citizens. Constitutional law is concerned with the study of these rules. In the case of most countries, the constitution takes the form of a written document which contains the most important rules. Such constitutions tend to have a higher status than ordinary laws and are usually more difficult to amend than ordinary laws. A law which contravenes the constitution can be declared invalid. The constitution of the United Kingdom, however, is very unusual in that it is not contained in a single document, easily accessible to the citizens of this country. **3.1**

Scotland is not a separate state, but it has its own legal system and, since 1999, it has had its own Parliament. Constitutional law in Scotland differs in some respects from that of the UK as a whole and is dealt with in a separate section at the end of this chapter. **3.2**

WHERE TO FIND CONSTITUTIONAL LAW

ACTS OF PARLIAMENT

There are several sources of constitutional law in the UK. The first of these is *Acts of Parliament* or *statute law*. Acts which are of constitutional significance have no special status and are passed in the normal way. Examples of constitutional statutes include the Acts of Union 1706 and 1707 which abolished the separate Parliaments of England and Scotland and created the Parliament of Great Britain. More modern examples include the Scotland Act 1998 which re-established a Scottish Parliament, and the Human Rights Act 1998 which enshrines our citizens' right in law. **3.3**

COMMON LAW OR CASE LAW

The second source is *common law* or *case law*. This is law which is made by the judges, either by filling gaps in the law where no statute exists, or by interpreting the words of a statute where the meaning is not entirely clear. **3.4**

An example of the former is the case of *Burmah Oil Co v Lord Advocate*.[1] The Burmah Oil Company's oil installations in Singapore had been destroyed in 1942 by the British forces, to prevent them falling into the hands of the Japanese. When the war was over, the company sued for compensation which the Government did not want to pay. The judges decided that the company had a right at common law to compensation. (This **3.5**

---

[1] 1964 SC (HL) 117.

case illustrates the sovereignty of Parliament – see below – as Parliament passed the War Damage Act 1965 which *retrospectively* removed the right to compensation where property had been damaged in such cases.) An example of the interpretation of statute law is *Fox* v *Stirk*[2] which involved the meaning of "resident" in the Representation of the People Act 1969. Fox was a student who wanted to be able to vote in the constituency where his hall of residence was situated, rather than in the one where his family home was. The court agreed that the intention of Parliament in passing the Act was to include students as "residents" at their university addresses.

THE ROYAL PREROGATIVE

3.6   Special mention should be made here of the *Royal Prerogative* which is derived from the common law. It has been described as "the residue of discretionary power which at any given time is legally left in the hands of the Crown". It dates back to the time when the monarch held power and could do whatever he or she wished. Nowadays, however, "the Crown" normally means the Government Ministers rather than the Queen, although the Queen still exercises some prerogative powers, such as choosing the Prime Minister and dissolving Parliament. Examples of Ministers' use of prerogative power include declaring war, making treaties and pardoning convicted criminals. The destruction of the Burmah Oil Company's installations described above was carried out under prerogative powers.

EUROPEAN COMMUNITY LAW

3.7   Since the UK joined the European Community in 1973, after the passing of the European Communities Act 1972, European Community law has become a source of UK constitutional law. EC law includes Treaties, Regulations, Directives and Decisions. As long as the UK remains a member of the EC, EC law has primacy. This means that where a UK law is in conflict with EC law, EC law prevails.

CONVENTIONS

3.8   Conventions are rules of political behaviour which are regarded as binding by those who administer the constitution. They are, however, "non-legal" rules, as the courts will not enforce them although they recognise their existence. They are not written down in any formal sense but evolve over a period of time. They are obeyed by those involved out of political self-interest, because, of the political repercussions and damaging publicity which would result from a breach.

3.9   An example of a convention is that the Queen will not refuse to grant Royal Assent to a Bill, although in law she has the power to do so. Another convention is that a government which loses a vote of confidence in the House of Commons is expected to resign and ask the Queen for a general election to be held.

3.10   The Cabinet and the office of Prime Minister are based on convention as they were not established by Act of Parliament but evolved over the centuries.

---

[2] [1970] 2 QB 463.

THE LAW AND CUSTOM OF PARLIAMENT

Parliament has the right to regulate its own procedures and a body of law and custom has **3.11** grown up over the centuries of Parliament's existence. Its rules are contained in its Standing Orders, in various resolutions passed by either the House of Commons or the House of Lords and in rulings by the Speaker who presides over the House of Commons.

AUTHORITATIVE WRITINGS

Where there is no relevant statute or case law, the judges may resort to authoritative **3.12** writings, books and articles by leading constitutional lawyers, historians or political scientists. Examples of these are the works of Walter Bagehot and A V Dicey, two 19th-century constitutional lawyers both of whom are mentioned below. These are, of course, not legally binding, as they are not law.

CHARACTERISTICS OF THE UK CONSTITUTION

Since there is no single document called "the constitution", the UK constitution is sometimes **3.13** described as "unwritten". However, this is inaccurate. Much of the constitution is indeed found in written documents and thus it is better to describe the constitution as *"uncodified"*.

The UK constitution is also very *flexible* in that Parliament can change any law by a **3.14** simple majority vote.

All law-making power stems from the Parliament of the UK and thus the UK **3.15** constitution is described as *unitary*, as opposed to federal, where law-making power is divided between central government and state or provincial governments. Although the UK Parliament has devolved some law-making powers to the Scottish Parliament, the Northern Ireland Assembly and the Welsh Assembly, the doctrine of the sovereignty of Parliament (see below) means that a subsequent UK Parliament could take these powers back. This is not the case in federal states where the powers of the states or provinces are protected by the written constitution.

In the UK, the head of state is the Queen, not an elected president, and thus the **3.16** constitution is *"monarchical"* as opposed to "republican" or "presidential".

THE PRINCIPAL ORGANS OF GOVERNMENT

The principal organs of government in any state are the legislature, the executive and **3.17** the judiciary.

For the UK, the *legislature* is the body which settles policy and makes law and consists **3.18** of the Members of Parliament, ie Members of the House of Commons and Members of the House of Lords.

The *executive* is the body which directs general policy and executes the laws made by **3.19** the legislature. However, if the executive is strong and the legislature weak, the executive has a powerful role in making policy which the legislature passes into law. In the UK the executive consists of the Prime Minister, the Cabinet, the other Government Ministers and civil servants. Included in the executive are police officers, members of the armed forces and members of public bodies established by the Government, such as quangos, executive agencies and service authorities.

3.20   The *judiciary* is the body of professional judges whose function is to settle disputes by interpreting and applying the law.

3.21   The Queen is Head of State and technically is head of each of the three organs of government.

DOCTRINES OF THE CONSTITUTION

THE RULE OF LAW

3.22   The rule of law is a rather nebulous concept which does not have any readily definable content. Basically, it means that matters should be regulated not by force but by law and by certain fundamental principles such as justice, morality, fairness and due process. The powers of the state are conferred by law and do not include a general power to act outside the law in the interest of the state. The Government is not above the law.

3.23   The classic case on the rule of law is the case of *Entick* v *Carrington*.[3] In this case, the court ruled that a general warrant executed by a Secretary of State for entry into Entick's house and the seizure of his books and private papers was contrary to law and amounted to trespass. The court did not accept the Secretary of State's argument that the power of seizure was essential to government.

THE SEPARATION OF POWERS

3.24   In its pure form, the doctrine of the separation of powers means that the powers of the organs of government, legislative, executive and judicial, should be exercised by separate institutions. There should be no overlap of membership or function and one organ should not seek to dominate the others. The reason for this is to avoid the concentration of power in too few hands, as this could lead to tyranny.

3.25   However, the doctrine is not strictly observed in the UK. For example, in terms of membership overlap, the Prime Minister and Ministers who are key members of the executive are also members of the legislature, either in the House of Commons or in the House of Lords. Also, although the two Houses of Parliament together form the supreme law-making body in the UK, the judges make law when they decide cases, either by interpreting Acts of Parliament or by "filling the gaps" where no relevant Act exists. Government Ministers can also make law in the form of statutory instruments.

3.26   However, the separation of the judiciary from the executive and the legislature is fairly strictly observed in the UK and there are a number of rules which aim to ensure their independence. So, for example, members of the judiciary are disqualified by the House of Commons Disqualification Act 1975 from standing for election as members of the House of Commons.

3.27   In addition, they hold office during "good behaviour" and it is extremely difficult to sack a judge. In England, there is a complicated procedure to be followed, involving both houses of Parliament. This is to protect them from being dismissed for political reasons.

3.28   However, the judges who sit in the Appellate Committee in the House of Lords (the Law Lords) take part in the law-making business of Parliament. This breaches the doctrine of the

---

[3] [1765] 19 State Tr 1029.

separation of powers in terms of membership overlap. Another major breach of the doctrine has been the office of Lord Chancellor. He was head of the judiciary in England and Wales, a senor member of the Cabinet and a member of the House of Lords. Thus he was a member of each of the three organs of government. This anomaly was rectified by the Constitutional Reform Act 2005. This Act removes the Law Lords from the House of Lords and appoints them to a new Supreme Court, separate from the Houses of Parliament. This will come into effect in 2008. The role of the Lord Chancellor in relation to the judiciary is modified and a new office of Secretary of State for Constitutional Affairs has been established.

THE SOVEREIGNTY OF THE UK PARLIAMENT

A very important doctrine of the constitution and one which separates the UK from most other states is the sovereignty or supremacy of Parliament. This means that Parliament has no *legal* restrictions on what laws it can pass. In other states the written constitution sets legal limits on what laws the legislature can pass and if the legislature oversteps these limits, a court can declare its laws to be invalid. **3.29**

The most famous definition of parliamentary sovereignty is that of a 19th-century constitutional lawyer called A V Dicey. In his view: **3.30**

(1) Parliament is the supreme law-making body and can make or unmake laws on any subject;

(2) no Parliament can be bound by the laws passed by its predecessors, nor can any Parliament bind its successors as to the form or content of future legislation;

(3) no person or body, including a court of law, can successfully challenge the validity of an Act of Parliament.

Examples of point (1) above include: **3.31**

- the Parliament Acts of 1911 and 1949 which reduced the powers of the House of Lords over legislative proposals of the House of Commons from veto to delay;
- the War Damage Act 1965 which had *retrospective* effect and overturned the award of compensation made by a court to the Burmah Oil Company whose property had been destroyed by British forces to prevent it falling into enemy hands during the Second World War;
- the Abdication Act 1936 which removed King Edward VIII from the throne and changed the line of succession to that of his brother who became King George VI, the father of Queen Elizabeth II.

However, there are *practical* and *political limits* on what laws Parliament can pass. For example, it is inconceivable that Parliament would pass a law which stated that all blue-eyed babies were to be strangled at birth. In addition, Parliament can make effective laws only for the territory it controls (although it can make a law whereby a person committing a particular offence abroad may be tried in the UK courts).

In relation to point (2), if provisions of a later Act of Parliament contradict provisions of an earlier Act, the later Act prevails and is taken to repeal the contradictory provisions in the earlier Act. In the case of *Ellen Street Estates Ltd* v *Minister of Health*,[4] the court **3.32**

---

[4] [1934] 1 KB 590.

decided that it was impossible for Parliament to enact in the Housing Act 1919 that its provisions in relation to compensation for property which had been compulsorily purchased could prevail over contradictory provisions in the Housing Act 1925. This is called the doctrine of implied repeal.

3.33   However, again, there are practical and political limits to this rule. The UK Parliament has passed many Acts granting independence to former colonies. No one expects Parliament to pass Acts to take back the independence, on the basis that, once freedom is conferred, it cannot be revoked.

3.34   However, occasionally, Parliament will insert a section into an Act which seems to be intended to bind a future Parliament. For example, s 1 of the Northern Ireland Act 1998 states that Northern Ireland shall not cease to be part of the UK without the consent of the people of Northern Ireland voting in a poll held for that purpose. Because of the sovereignty of Parliament, this cannot prevent a future Parliament from passing an Act without holding such a poll. However, it might be political suicide to do so.

3.35   An example of point (3) above is the case of *British Railways Board* v *Pickin*.[5] Pickin alleged that Parliament had been misled when considering a Private Bill promoted by British Railways Board and had used the wrong procedure in passing the Act. The court rejected Pickin's challenge, stating that if errors in procedure had occurred, it was for Parliament alone to correct them. The court could not question the validity of any Act.

Parliamentary sovereignty and European Community law

3.36   The UK joined the European Community (EC) in 1973, after passing the European Communities Act 1972. The laws of the EC are binding on all the Member States. This means that EC law prevails over inconsistent UK law. There is no problem in the case of Acts inconsistent with EC law passed before 1973, as the doctrine of implied repeal, discussed above, means that the European Communities Act 1972 repeals the earlier inconsistent Acts.

3.37   The difficulty occurs when an Act passed *after* the UK joined the EC is inconsistent with EC law. The UK courts will try to interpret the Act as widely as possible, to avoid inconsistency. If this cannot be achieved, EC law must be applied, rather than the UK Act. This principle was made clear by the House of Lords in the case of *R* v *Secretary of State for Transport, ex p Factortame*[6] when it set aside provisions of the Merchant Shipping Act 1995 as being incompatible with the EC Common Fisheries Policy.

3.38   The only way to reconcile this with the doctrine of parliamentary sovereignty is to say that the limitation on legal sovereignty has been undertaken voluntarily by the UK and remains only so long as the UK decides to remain a member of the EC.

THE UNITED KINGDOM PARLIAMENT

3.39   Parliament consists of three elements:

- the monarch;
- the House of Lords (an unelected body);
- the House of Commons (an elected body).

---

[5] [1974] AC 765.
[6] [1991] AC 603.

THE MONARCH

The Queen plays a formal role in the work of Parliament. By convention, she must give **3.40**
Royal Assent to Bills which have been passed by the House of Commons and the House
of Lords to enable them to become Acts and therefore law. She also summons
Parliament after each general election and dissolves it at the end of its term of up to
5 years. Each term is divided into sessions lasting approximately a year and the Queen
opens each session, normally in November, by making a formal speech from the throne
in which she indicates the Government's programme of laws for the forthcoming
session. The speech is written for her by Government Ministers.

THE HOUSE OF LORDS

Until 1999, the majority of members were hereditary peers (about 750) who had **3.41**
inherited their peerages from (normally) their fathers. Under the House of Lords Act
1999, most of the hereditary peers lost the right to sit in the House of Lords.

The composition of the House of Lords now is: **3.42**

- 92 hereditary peers;
- around 600 life peers appointed by the Queen on the advice of the Prime
  Minister under the Life Peerages Act 1958;
- 26 spiritual peers who are the senior archbishops and bishops of the Church of
  England:
- 12 Law Lords. These are senior judges and they will lose the right to sit in the
  House of Lords when the new Supreme Court comes into being in 2008.

Powers and functions of the House of Lords

Members of the House of Lords have an important role to play in the law-making **3.43**
process. Normally, an Act of Parliament must be passed by both the House of Lords and
the House of Commons and receive the Royal Assent.

Until 1911, the law-making powers of the Lords were equal to those of the Commons, **3.44**
although the Lords accepted that they should not initiate or amend Bills relating to finance as
that was the prerogative of the elected House. However, they claimed the power to *reject*
financial legislation. Attempts to reject the then Government's Finance Bill led to the Lords'
power of veto being reduced to one of delay for a period of 2 years under the Parliament Act
1911. This was reduced to a period of 1 year by the Parliament Act of 1949. This means that
certain Acts of Parliament can be passed without the consent of the House of Lords. A recent
example is the Hunting Act 2004. However, the consent of the Lords is still required for a Bill
to prolong the length of a parliamentary term beyond 5 years, for Private Bills, subordinate
legislation and for Bills which start in the House of Lords.

The House of Lords also has the following functions: **3.45**

- the provision of a forum for debate in matters of public interest;
- the revision of Bills sent up by the House of Commons;
- the initiation of some Bills;
- the consideration of subordinate legislation;
- scrutiny of the work of the executive;

- Select Committee work;
- the final court of appeal for all civil cases in the UK and for criminal cases in England and Wales. This function will transfer to the new Supreme Court in 2008.

THE HOUSE OF COMMONS

3.46   The House of Commons consists of 646 men and women known as Members of Parliament or MPs. They are elected by the system known as "first past the post" under which the person who secures the largest number of votes is the winner, even if the majority of the voters have voted for other candidates. General elections are normally held every 4 or 5 years. The maximum life of a Parliament is 5 years.

The right to vote in a parliamentary election

3.47   People entitled to vote are residents of the UK who are:

- British citizens;
- commonwealth citizens;
- citizens of the Irish Republic;
- 18 years of age or over;
- registered in the register of parliamentary elections.

3.48   People who are not entitled to vote are:

- aliens (generally, foreigners);
- minors (under 18);
- members of the House of Lords;
- prisoners;
- offenders detained in a mental hospital;
- undischarged bankrupts
- persons guilty of certain electoral offences.

Disqualification from membership of the UK Parliament

3.49   The following are not entitled to sit as Members of Parliament:

- aliens;
- people under 21;
- members of the House of Lords;
- people suffering from a mental illness;
- undischarged bankrupts;
- persons guilty of certain electoral offences;
- people sentenced to a term of imprisonment of more than a year;
- persons guilty of treason;
- members of foreign legislatures outside the Commonwealth (excluding the European Parliament and Ireland)
- holders of certain public office, eg judges, members of the armed forces or the police, civil servants, members of certain public bodies and tribunals.

Functions of the House of Commons

The two main functions of the House of Commons are to pass Acts of Parliament and to scrutinise the work of the executive (the Government) and hold Ministers to account.   **3.50**

Passing Acts of Parliament

A proposal for an Act is called a Bill. There are three types of Bill. The most common is a   **3.51**
Public Bill which applies to members of the public generally. Most Public Bills are initiated by the Government but some may be initiated by backbench MPs. The latter are called Private Members' Bills. These should not be confused with *Private Bills* which apply to a particular area or, less commonly, to particular persons and which are normally initiated by local authorities or public bodies. A *Hybrid Bill* is one which affects particular persons but also the public generally. An example of a Hybrid Bill was the Channel Tunnel Bill which applied to certain landowners in the south-east of England, but which also enabled the construction of the Channel Tunnel which is a public route. For the various parliamentary stages of Bills, see para **1.17**.

Parliamentary questions

Ministers are expected to answer questions from MPs on a rota basis for about an hour   **3.52**
every day, from Mondays to Thursdays. Prime Minister's Question Time takes place every Wednesday and lasts for 30 minutes. The questions are put down in advance by backbench MPs.

The main purpose of Question Time should be to extract information or to press for   **3.53**
action. However, questions are also used to embarrass the Government, by airing a sensitive matter, to publicise a national or local issue, or to score a political point. Sometimes a question is "planted" by a Minister with a backbencher of the same party, to enable the Minister to make an announcement. Question Time has become something of a ritual and is not a very effective method of scrutinising the work of the Government.

MPs may also put down questions for written answer. These are generally more   **3.54**
serious attempts to gain information.

Debates

There are various opportunities for MPs to take part in debates. The general debate at   **3.55**
the Second Reading of a Bill has already been mentioned in Chapter 1. In addition, the Opposition parties are allocated certain times for debates on subjects of their own choosing.

Also, at the end of each parliamentary day, there is a short debate, called an   **3.56**
adjournment debate. Backbench MPs who wish to use this opportunity take part in a ballot and choose the subject to be debated.

There is also a procedure called an Early Day Motion. This is a written motion which   **3.57**
may be tabled by any MP, requesting a debate on virtually any subject "at an early day".

Finally, there are Emergency Debates. Any MP may apply to the Speaker (the   **3.58**
Chairman) of the House to raise an urgent matter for debate. One successful example was the debate on the deployment of British soldiers in Afghanistan.

Select Committees

3.59   Some Select Committees relate to the running of the House of Commons or to the procedures employed. Others are departmental Select Committees whose task is to investigate and report on the working of a government department and their associated public bodies and agencies. These Select Committees offer the best opportunity for MPs to scrutinise the work of the Government.

3.60   The Committees have the power to send for persons, papers and records, to sit despite the House being adjourned, to meet in different places and to appoint specialist advisers.

3.61   There are too many Select Committees to list here, however, the current list can be accessed via the House of Commons website.[7] The Select Committees are established for an entire parliamentary term and members can develop considerable expertise in the subject-matter of their committees. Their reports have increased the amount of information about the workings of government. Members, to some extent, put aside their party-political ties and unite to scrutinise the work of Ministers and civil servants, though if their reports are debated by the full House of Commons, these ties may reassert themselves.

Control of financial matters

3.62   Constitutionally, Parliament has control over taxation and expenditure. Taxation and expenditure policies originate in the Treasury and the Chancellor of the Exchequer presents his Budget to the House of Commons, usually in the spring each year. Parliament must pass an annual Finance Act following the Budget but changes in the rates of taxes can become effective as soon as the House of Commons passes a resolution to that effect. Expenditure plans require to be approved in an annual Appropriation Act.

3.63   Scrutiny of public expenditure is carried out by the Public Accounts Select Committee which examines reports of audits carried out by an officer of the House of Commons, the Comptroller and Auditor General, head of the National Audit Office. The Committee is chaired by a member of the Opposition and the members generally act in a non-partisan manner. The reports of this Committee are very influential.

THE GOVERNMENT OF THE UNITED KINGDOM

3.64   The Government of the UK consists of the monarch, the Prime Minister, the Cabinet and other Ministers of the Crown. The Queen is the titular head of the Government and all Government acts are carried out in her name but her role is largely a formal one.

THE MONARCH

3.65   Britain has a constitutional monarchy, a king or queen whose role is constrained by rules of the constitution. Succession to the throne is governed by the Act of Settlement 1700. The monarch must be a Protestant; Roman Catholics and those married to Roman Catholics are disqualified. Succession is also governed by the rule of male primogeniture. This means that the first-born male child will succeed in preference to an older daughter. When the

---

[7] http://www.parliament.uk/parliamentary_committees/parliamentary_committees16.cfm

monarch dies, succession is automatic. If the monarch is under 18, or becomes too ill to carry out his or her constitutional duties, a regent must be appointed under the Regency Acts 1937–53. This will normally be the adult who is next in line to the throne.

The monarch may adopt whatever title he or she wishes. The title adopted by the   **3.66** present Queen, Elizabeth II, when she became Queen in 1952 was challenged by some Scots on the grounds that she was not the second Queen Elizabeth of Scotland (*MacCormick* v *Lord Advocate*[8]) but the challenge was unsuccessful.

The monarch and certain members of his or her family are funded from the Civil List,   **3.67** a fund provided by Parliament.

According to Walter Bagehot, a 19th-century constitutional lawyer, the monarch has the   **3.68** right to be consulted by her Ministers and the right to encourage and to warn them. The Queen is kept fully informed of the business of government and meets the Prime Minister on a regular basis. Since she has been on the throne since 1952, she has accumulated vast experience of political matters but she remains above party politics.

The monarch is said to have a number of "personal prerogatives" or powers. These are: **3.69**

- the appointment of a Prime Minister, normally the leader of the party which has won the largest number of seats at a general election;
- the dissolution of Parliament, on the advice of the Prime Minister;
- the dismissal of Ministers (this has not happened in the UK since 1835);
- giving the Royal Assent to Bills (a formality);
- the conferring of various honours, such as the Order of the Thistle.

The extent to which the monarch exercises her own discretion in these matters (apart from the conferring of certain honours) is a matter for debate.

THE PRIME MINISTER AND THE CABINET

The office of Prime Minister has developed by convention rather than by Act of   **3.70** Parliament. The Prime Minister is the most powerful member of the Government. He or she is appointed by the Queen who invites the leader of the political party which wins the largest number of seats at a general election to form a Government. Although in the past there have been Prime Ministers who were members of the House of Lords, nowadays the Prime Minister must, by convention, be a member of the democratically elected House of Commons.

The Prime Minister chairs the Cabinet which consists of around 20 of the most senior   **3.71** Ministers. In theory, the Prime Minister is "first among equals" but a strong individual can dominate the Cabinet. The Prime Minister effectively appoints members of the Cabinet and all other Ministers. He or she can ask them to resign or move them to other posts.

The Prime Minister controls the machinery of government and decides on the   **3.72** distribution of work between departments.

Members of the Cabinet are drawn mainly from the House of Commons but some   **3.73** come from the House of Lords. Each member holds a major government post. By convention, the Chancellor of the Exchequer, the Home Secretary, the Foreign Secretary and the Defence Secretary are always included in membership.

---

[8] [1953] SC 396.

3.74   The main functions of the Cabinet are the determination of government policy, the general scope of legislation to be enacted by Parliament, control of the executive and the co-ordination of the activities of government departments.

Ministerial responsibility

3.75   The term "ministerial responsibility" has two aspects – individual responsibility and collective responsibility. "Responsible" here means answerable to Parliament. Individual responsibility means that a Minister is responsible for the acts and omissions of his or her department. So a Minister is required to come before the House of Parliament of which he or she is a member to answer questions and explain the actions taken within his or her department. The departments of modern government are huge and it is impossible for any Minister personally to oversee the work of every civil servant in the department. Even so, Ministers should not attempt to put the blame for any act or omission on to a civil servant unless the civil servant has acted contrary to the Minister's wishes. The acceptance of responsibility by a Minister does not mean that he or she must inevitably resign over a failure in his or her department. Resignation will depend on how the Minister is viewed by the Prime Minister and by his or her colleagues in Parliament.

3.76   Collective responsibility means that Ministers, whether members of the Cabinet or not, are expected to support the policies of the Government, at least in public. If a Minister cannot publicly support a particular policy, he or she is expected to resign. Thus, expressions of differing opinions within the Cabinet should be kept private. However, leaks about controversial issues happen frequently and nowadays there is pressure for the workings of government to be made more open.

THE SCOTTISH PARLIAMENT

BACKGROUND

3.77   Prior to 1707, Scotland was a separate state from England and had its own Parliament. For various reasons, mainly economic, the Parliaments of England and Scotland were united into the Parliament of Great Britain by the Acts of Union of 1706 and 1707. The union was never very popular with the Scottish people and during the 19th and 20th centuries demand grew for some form of Scottish Home Rule.

3.78   A Scottish Constitutional Convention was formed in 1989 which published various documents culminating in 1995 in *Scotland's Parliament: Scotland's Right* which advocated a Scottish Parliament with legislative powers over a wide range of domestic issues.

3.79   The Labour and Liberal Democrat Parties both strongly supported the work of the Scottish Constitutional Convention and when the Labour Party won the general election in May 1997, the new Government announced its plans to establish a Scottish Parliament with limited tax-raising powers. These plans were endorsed by the Scottish people in a referendum held in September 1997 and the UK Parliament passed the Scotland Act in 1998.

3.80   The form of government which the Scotland Act established is known as legislative devolution. This means that the UK Parliament has voluntarily transferred some of its law-making powers to the Scottish Parliament without relinquishing its own sovereignty.

ELECTING THE SCOTTISH PARLIAMENT

There are 129 Members of the Scottish Parliament, known as MSPs. They are elected by **3.81** the form of proportional representation known as the Additional Member System. This combines the traditional "first past the post" system, involving single-member constituencies, with an additional element which tops up political parties' representation by allocating regional seats on the basis of a second vote cast not for an individual but for a political party. It is also possible for individuals without any political affiliation to stand as candidates. At each general election, 73 constituency members and 56 regional MSPs are elected, the latter divided equally among eight regions. The way the regional list works enables representatives of the smaller political parties, such as the Green Party and the Scottish Socialist Party, to win seats.

The two categories of MSPs have equal status in law. **3.82**

The rules regarding the right to vote in Scottish Parliament elections are similar to **3.83** those for the UK Parliament, but extended to include members of the House of Lords and to citizens of the European Union who are resident in Scotland.

The rules regarding membership of the Scottish Parliament are also similar to the **3.84** rules for the UK Parliament, again extended to members of the House of Lords and to European citizens resident in the UK.

Unlike the UK Parliament, which has a maximum term of 5 years, the Scottish **3.85** Parliament has a fixed term of 4 years and ordinary general elections are held on the first Thursday of May.

THE POWERS OF THE SCOTTISH PARLIAMENT

In passing the Scotland Act 1998, the UK Parliament voluntarily transferred certain law- **3.86** making powers to the Scottish Parliament without relinquishing its sovereignty. This means that the Scottish Parliament is not independent and is not free to make law in any area it chooses.

In any system of government where law-making powers are divided between two **3.87** levels, the powers of each level must be set out in a written document, to minimise the possibility of one level trespassing into the territory of the other. The UK Parliament chose to adopt the *retaining* model and thus the powers which the UK Parliament retains or reserves to itself are listed in the Scotland Act. These are called "reserved matters". It is therefore to be understood that everything not listed is within the powers of the Scottish Parliament and these are called "devolved matters".

The UK Parliament retains the power to legislate on devolved matters but a con- **3.88** vention has arisen that it will not do so without the consent of the Scottish Parliament.

Reserved matters

The lists of reserved matters are contained in Sch 5 to the Scotland Act 1998. There are a **3.89** number of general reservations. These include:

- succession to the Crown;
- the union of the Kingdoms of Scotland and England;
- the UK Parliament;
- international affairs;

- defence and the armed forces;
- the civil service.

3.90   Specific reservations include:

- taxation (except local taxes) and control of UK public expenditure;
- immigration and nationality;
- aspects of trade and industry;
- electricity, nuclear energy and most aspects of coal and gas;
- some aspects of transport;
- social security;
- regulation of the professions;
- employment rights and duties;
- abortion, embryology, surrogacy, genetics and medicines;
- regulation of TV and radio broadcasting;
- equal opportunities;
- miscellaneous matters, including weapons of mass destruction; regulation of activities in outer space; timescales and time zones.

Devolved matters

3.91   Broadly speaking, devolved matters include:

- overall responsibility for the NHS in Scotland;
- education and training;
- local government, social work and housing;
- aspects of economic development and transport;
- most aspects of criminal and civil law; the court system; prisons;
- police and fire services;
- protection of animals;
- environmental protection;
- agriculture, forestry and fishing;
- sport and the arts.

3.92   In addition to its law-making powers, the Scottish Parliament has the power to increase or decrease the basic rate of income tax paid by Scottish taxpayers by a maximum of 3 pence in the pound. This power has not been used since the Parliament came into being in 1999.

HOW THE SCOTTISH PARLIAMENT WORKS

3.93   The Scottish Parliament is given a relatively free hand by the Scotland Act 1998 in deciding how it should work. It operates within a comprehensive framework of Standing Orders adopted initially in 1999.

3.94   The Parliament normally sits in Edinburgh from Monday afternoon to Friday lunchtime. Its recesses take account of the school holidays in Scotland.

3.95   The Parliament can meet in plenary session, ie all the MSPs together, or in committees. In plenary sessions MSPs have opportunities to debate issues and to question Ministers in much the same way as happens at Westminster.

However, in most of the world's parliaments, much of the detailed work is dealt with **3.96** in committees rather than in plenary session and in the Scottish Parliament the committees play a significant role in proceedings.

Committees

The committees of the Scottish Parliament combine the roles of the Standing and Select **3.97** Committees found in the UK Parliament, with broad remits covering the consideration and scrutiny of both policy and legislation. There are two types of committee: Mandatory Committees and Subject Committees.

Mandatory Committees must be set up by the Parliament soon after a general election **3.98** and they remain in existence for the entire parliamentary session. The Mandatory Committees are:

- Procedures Committee;
- Standards Committee;
- Finance Committee;
- Audit Committee;
- European and External Relations Committee;
- Equal Opportunities Committee;
- Public Petitions Committee; and
- Subordinate Legislation Committee.

Subject Committees are established to deal with a specific subject or group of related **3.99** subjects. The Subject Committees in existence in 2006 are:

- Communities;
- Education;
- Enterprise and Culture;
- Justice (two committees established because of the workload);
- Environment and Rural Development;
- Health;
- Local Government and Transport.

Each committee has a membership of between five and 15 members, including the **3.100** convener and vice-convener. Places are allocated to reflect the balance of seats held by the different political parties in the Parliament. Committees may appoint external advisers to assist them in their work. They normally meet in public and although committees may sit anywhere in Scotland, the vast majority of committee meetings are held in the Parliament's headquarters in Edinburgh.

The Committees have been described as the Parliament's powerhouse. They play a **3.101** very active role in the Parliament's business, gathering information, scrutinising policy, holding inquiries and scrutinising proposals for legislation. Committees can and have made important changes to Bills and can, themselves, initiate Bills.

The Parliamentary Bureau

The Parliamentary Bureau consists of the Presiding Officer, who chairs plenary meet- **3.102** ings of the Parliament, and a representative of each party with five or more MSPs.

Parties with fewer than five MSPs and independent members can combine to form a group for the purpose of appointing a representative to the Bureau. The main function of the Bureau is to recommend the Parliament's business programme. It also recommends the establishment, remit, membership and duration of committees and sub-committees.

THE LAW-MAKING POWERS OF THE SCOTTISH PARLIAMENT

3.103 Section 28 of the Scotland Act 1998 gives the Scottish Parliament its power to make laws. The procedure followed shows some similarities to the procedure used by the UK Parliament. A proposal for legislation, a Bill, is normally considered by a committee and by the full Parliament. At the end of the process a Bill must receive the Royal Assent and then becomes an Act of the Scottish Parliament (an "asp").

3.104 However, there are some important differences. First, the Scottish Parliament has no second chamber, equivalent to the House of Lords, to scrutinise and amend Bills. Secondly, s 29 of the Scotland Act sets limits on the Scottish Parliament's legislative powers or "legislative competence".

3.105 The limits are as follows. The Scottish Parliament cannot pass a valid law which would:

- form part of the law of any country other than Scotland;
- be incompatible with the European Convention on Human Rights or European Community law;
- relate to reserved matters;
- modify any of the protected enactments set out in Sch 4 to the Scotland Act 1998, such as the Acts of Union of 1706 and 1707;
- remove the Lord Advocate from his position as head of the system of criminal prosecution and investigation of deaths in Scotland.

3.106 The provisions of any Bill thus have to be scrutinised very carefully to make sure that they are within the legislative competence of the Scottish Parliament. Consultation with interested parties will normally take place before a Bill is introduced. On introduction, both the Presiding Officer and the MSP who is in charge of the Bill must each provide a written statement that they consider the Bill to be within the Parliament's powers.

3.107 Within 4 weeks of the Bill passing through the parliamentary process, the Lord Advocate, the Attorney-General and the Advocate General for Scotland (Law Officers of the Scottish and UK Parliaments), may refer the Bill to the Judicial Committee of the Privy Council to decide whether the Bill is within the legislative competence of the Scottish Parliament. If they do so, the Presiding Officer cannot submit the Bill for Royal Assent until this has been decided. In addition, Secretaries of State in the UK Parliament may make an order prohibiting the Presiding Officer from submitting a Bill for Royal Assent if they think that any provision is outwith the powers of the Scottish Parliament.

BILLS IN THE SCOTTISH PARLIAMENT

3.108 There are three types of Public Bills, namely Executive Bills; Committee Bills; and Members' Bills. The Scottish Parliament may also pass Private Bills but these are relatively uncommon. For the procedures for passing Bills, see para **1.17**.

THE SCOTTISH GOVERNMENT

The Government of Scotland is generally known as the Scottish Executive. It consists of **3.109** the First Minister, Scottish Ministers and the Scottish Law Officers (the Lord Advocate and the Solicitor-General. The main rules relating to the appointment of the Scottish Executive are contained in the Scotland Act 1998.

The First Minister is normally the leader of the party able to command the support of **3.110** a majority of MSPs. The Additional Member System used to elect the Members of the Scottish Parliament does not usually result in one political party having an overall majority, so a candidate for the post of First Minister must have the support of MSPs of more than one party. The post must be filled within 28 days of a general election.

The First Minister nominates a team of Ministers and Junior Ministers from among the **3.111** MSPs but, unlike at Westminster, the team must be approved by the Parliament before the names are submitted to the Queen for appointment. They may be removed from office by the First Minister and must resign if they lose the confidence of the Parliament. The Ministers, about ten in number, but not the Junior Ministers, are members of the Scottish Cabinet.

RELATIONS BETWEEN THE SCOTTISH AND UK PARLIAMENTS

The Sewel Convention

As we have seen, the UK Parliament retains the power to legislate in the areas devolved to **3.112** the Scottish Parliament. It was always envisaged that there might be occasions when it would be more convenient all round for the UK Parliament to do so. However, the UK Government made it clear from the outset that it expected that a convention would arise that this would only happen with the consent of the Scottish Parliament. The convention is known as the Sewel Convention, after a Government Minister in the House of Lords called Lord Sewel, and the motions put to the Scottish Parliament seeking agreement for the UK Parliament to legislate became known as Sewel Motions. (These have recently been renamed Legislative Consent Motions.) In fact, Sewel Motions have been passed much more frequently than was originally envisaged. This has aroused criticism that the decision-making powers of the Scottish Parliament are being undermined.

Liaison arrangements

The UK Government and the Scottish Ministers have entered into a memorandum of **3.113** agreement which sets out how the two should work together at both political and official levels. This agreement is not legally binding and cannot be enforced in the courts. It is a statement of principles, binding in honour only. However, it is of great practical significance. There are also concordats which set out detailed working arrangements between the two administrations. In addition, there are bilateral concordats between the Scottish Executive and the individual UK government departments.

There is also a Joint Ministerial Committee made up of the Prime Minster, the Scottish **3.114** and Northern Irish First Ministers, the First Secretary of the Welsh Assembly and the Secretaries of State for Scotland, Northern Ireland and Wales.

The office of the Secretary of State for Scotland

The office of the Secretary of State for Scotland has a long history, dating back to the **3.115** time before the Union of the Scottish and English Parliaments in 1707. The government department of the Scottish Office was established in 1885 and was responsible for the administration of government policies in Scotland until the modern Scottish Parliament was elected in 1999. The Secretary of State for Scotland had a seat in the Cabinet.

3.116   When the Scottish Parliament assumed its powers in 1999, most of the powers of the Secretary of State were transferred to the Scottish Executive and the role of the Secretary of State was diminished. The Scottish Office was renamed the Scotland Office. In 2003, the role of the Secretary of State was altered significantly. Although the post remained, it was added to the responsibilities of another member of the Cabinet who represents a Scottish constituency. In 2003, the Scotland Office was abolished as a separate department and taken under the umbrella of a new Department of Constitutional Affairs headed by its own Secretary of State.

THE SCOTTISH PARLIAMENT AND THE COURTS

3.117   As we have seen, the doctrine of the sovereignty of the UK Parliament means that no Act of Parliament can be declared invalid by the courts. The Scottish Parliament, however, is a creation of the UK Parliament and is not a sovereign body. This means that its Acts may be successfully challenged in the courts as being *ultra vires* or beyond the powers of the Scottish Parliament. Similarly, actions of the Scottish Executive can be challenged as being beyond the authority granted to the Executive by the Scotland Act 1998.

3.118   These challenges are called "devolution issues" and can arise in any court or tribunal, in civil or criminal cases. Schedule 6 to the Scotland Act sets out in great detail how such issues are to be handled.

3.119   Most of the cases in which devolution issues have been raised so far have been criminal cases where it has been alleged that the Lord Advocate has brought a prosecution which is in some way incompatible with the European Convention on Human Rights.

3.120   One such case which had significant repercussions is *Starrs* v *Ruxton*.[9] Starrs was being tried before one of the temporary sheriffs appointed by the Lord Advocate on year-long contracts. Article 6(1) of the ECHR guarantees "a fair and public hearing . . . before an independent and impartial tribunal established by law". It was successfully argued for Starrs that a temporary sheriff on a short-term contract might not be independent and impartial as he or she could be influenced in his or her decision-making by the desire to avoid unpopularity with the Lord Advocate. The decision in this case led to the removal of temporary sheriffs from the Bench in Scotland.

3.121   A few cases have involved challenges to the validity of provisions of Acts of the Scottish Parliament.

3.122   An early case concerned the very first Act passed by the Scottish Parliament. This was *Anderson* v *Scottish Ministers*.[10] After Anderson was convicted of culpable homicide, he was kept under a restriction order in the State Mental Hospital under the Mental Health (Public Safety and Appeals) (Scotland) Act 1999. He argued that s 1 of the Act was incompatible with Art 5 of the ECHR (which concerns the right to liberty) and was therefore outside the legislative competence of the Scottish Parliament. However, the Privy Council, which is the highest court of appeal in devolution issues, held that the Act was not incompatible with Art 5 of the ECHR as it contains exceptions which allow for the detention of people of unsound mind.

---

[9] [2000] SLT 42.
[10] [2003] AC 602.

Another case was *Adams* v *Scottish Ministers*.[11] The Act which was being challenged **3.123** was the Protection of Wild Mammals (Scotland) Act 2002 which made fox hunting with dogs illegal. Adams was a manager of foxhounds. He, along with others who participated in fox hunting, argued that the ban on fox hunting breached Art 8 of the ECHR (respect for private and family life) and Art 11 (right to freedom of peaceful assembly and association with others). If these were breaches then provisions of the Act were outside the legislative competence of the Scottish Parliament and therefore invalid. The court was not convinced of these arguments and held that the Act was valid.

So far, there has not been a successful challenge to the validity of an Act of the Scottish **3.124** Parliament.

ESSENTIAL FACTS

The UK Parliament **3.125**

- The constitution of the UK is to be found in Acts of Parliament; decisions of judges; Royal prerogative powers; European Community law; conventions; the law and custom of Parliament; and authoritative writings.
- The constitution of the UK is uncodified (not found in a single written document); unitary, not federal; flexible, and monarchical.
- The principal organs of government are the legislature, the executive and the judiciary.
- The doctrine of the separation of powers means that the powers of the organs of government, legislative, executive and judicial, should be exercised by separate institutions. However, the doctrine is not strictly observed in the UK except in relation to the independence of the judiciary.
- The sovereignty of Parliament means that the UK Parliament has no *legal* restrictions on what laws it can pass.
- No UK Parliament can be bound by the laws passed by its predecessors nor can any UK Parliament bind its successors as to the form or content of future legislation.
- No Act of the UK Parliament can be successfully challenged in the courts.
- Since the UK joined the European Community, EC law prevails over inconsistent UK law but only as long as the UK remains a member of the EC.
- The UK Parliament consists of the monarch; the House of Lords and the House of Commons. The maximum life of a UK Parliament is 5 years.
- An Act of Parliament normally requires the consent of the House of Commons and the House of Lords and the assent of the Queen.
- Most residents of the UK aged 18 years or over are entitled to vote in UK elections and most aged 21 years or over are also entitled to stand for election. Members of the UK Parliament are elected by the system known as "first past the post".

---

[11] [2004] SC 665.

- Important functions of Parliament are the scrutiny of the executive and the control of taxation and expenditure.
- The Government of the UK consists of the monarch, the Prime Minister, the Cabinet and other Ministers of the Crown.
- The Prime Minister is appointed by the Queen and is normally the leader of the party which has won the largest number of seats in a general election. The Prime Minister is the most powerful member of the Government and, by convention, is a member of the House of Commons.
- Ministerial responsibility means that Government Ministers must be answerable to Parliament for the actions of their departments.

The Scottish Parliament

- The Scottish Parliament was established in 1999 by the Scotland Act 1998.
- The Scottish Parliament is elected by the form of proportional representation known as the Additional Member System.
- The rules relating to the right to vote and to stand for election to the Scottish Parliament are similar to those for the UK Parliament but include members of the House of Lords and EU citizens resident in Scotland.
- The UK Parliament has devolved certain law-making powers to the Scottish Parliament, but the Scottish Parliament cannot make law in the areas which the UK Parliament has reserved to itself.
- The Scottish Parliament has the power to increase or decrease the basic rate of income tax paid by Scottish taxpayers by a maximum of 3 pence in the pound.
- The role of committees in the Scottish Parliament is more significant than the role of committees in the UK Parliament.
- The main function of the Scottish Parliamentary Bureau is to recommend the Parliament's business programme
- The Government of Scotland is generally known as the Scottish Executive and consists of the First Minister, Scottish Ministers and the Scottish Law Officers.
- The First Minister is normally the leader of the party able to command the support of a majority of MSPs.
- The Sewell Convention means that the UK Parliament will not make law in devolved areas without the consent of the Scottish Parliament.
- Various liaison arrangements, which are not legally binding, govern relationships between the UK Parliament and the Scottish Parliament.
- The powers of the office of the Secretary of State for Scotland have been diminished since the Scottish Parliament was established.
- The validity of Acts of the Scottish Parliament may be challenged in the courts.

ESSENTIAL CASES

UK CASES

3.126

- *Burmah Oil Co* v *Lord Advocate* (1964): illustration of the sovereignty of Parliament. The War Damage Act 1965 had retrospective effect and overturned the award of compensation made by a court to the Burmah Oil Co whose property had been destroyed by British forces to prevent it falling into enemy hands during the Second World War.
- *Entick* v *Carrington* (1795): classic ruling expounding the rule of law. A general warrant executed by a Secretary of State for entry and seizure of books and private papers was contrary to law and amounted to trespass.
- *Ellen Street Estates* v *Minister of Health* (1934): if provisions of a later Act of Parliament contradict provisions of an earlier Act, the later Act prevails and is taken to repeal the contradictory provisions in the earlier Act.
- *British Railways Board* v *Pickin* (1974): if errors in the procedure of passing a Bill have occurred, it is for Parliament alone to correct them. The court cannot question the validity of any Act of Parliament.
- *R* v *Secretary of State for Transport, ex p Factortame* (1991): in effect confirms the practical limitations placed upon parliamentary sovereignty by EU membership. The European Communities Act 1972 Act allows European legislation to take precedence over that of the UK.

SCOTTISH CASES

- *Starrs* v *Ruxton* (2000): the removal of temporary sheriffs from the bench in Scotland. Article 6(1) of the ECHR guarantees "a fair and public hearing . . . before an independent and impartial tribunal established by law". A temporary sheriff on a short-term contract was not independent or impartial as he or she could be influenced in his or her decision-making by the desire to avoid unpopularity with the Lord Advocate.
- *Anderson* v *Scottish Ministers* (2003): an unsuccessful challenge that s 1 of the Mental Health (Public Safety and Appeals) (Scotland) Act 1999 was incompatible with Art 5 of the ECHR (which concerns the right to liberty) and was therefore outside the legislative competence of the Scottish Parliament.
- *Adams* v *Scottish Ministers* (2004): an unsuccessful challenge that the Protection of Wild Mammals (Scotland) Act 2002 breached Art 8 of the ECHR (respect for private and family life) and Art 11 (right to freedom of peaceful assembly and association with others), and was therefore outside the legislative competence of the Scottish Parliament.

4 DELICT

The law of delict is concerned with civil wrongs, that is to say, the law governing **4.1** compensation or reparation for damage which one individual inflicts on another. The person injured invokes the law of delict in order to obtain compensation for injury which is caused to him. An obligation is imposed upon the person who injures another to compensate that other person. The obligation which is imposed arises *ex lege* (by law) as opposed to *ex contractu* (that is, by way of contract).

The law imposes a unilateral obligation on the person who committed the wrongful **4.2** act to compensate the person who is injured. That injury may take many forms. It may take the form of physical injury to one's person. This would be the case in relation to injury which is inflicted in a road accident, or an injury which is sustained in the workplace because of the negligence of a fellow road user or a fellow worker, respectively. However, the injury or damage for which I seek reparation may take other forms. I might sustain financial loss because I have relied on negligent advice. For example, if my financial adviser were to suggest that I invest money in the purchase of shares in a newly floated company and the company then goes into liquidation, the consequence of which is that I lose money, my loss would be purely financial. However, the injury for which the law of delict can also be invoked may take more subtle forms. For example, the injury could comprise loss of my reputation or hurt feelings as a result of what has been said or written about me. The law of defamation (which is part of the law of delict) allows one to recover in certain circumstances for such injury. Again, the injury could take the form of my being unable to enjoy the comfort of my house because my next-door neighbour persists in playing his drums all hours of the day. In such circumstances the law of nuisance can provide a remedy.

However, not every human act which causes injury or harm allows one to recover in **4.3** terms of the law of delict. For example, a small corner shop may be put out of business after a large supermarket is built in the vicinity. In this case the courts would not allow one to recover since there is no wrongful act in the eye of the law.

There are a number of theories on the function and role of the law of delict. The **4.4** theories overlap to some extent. Occasionally, judges expressly refer to the theories in their judgments. In the majority of cases they do not.

Some argue that the law of delict operates to control the behaviour of people before they **4.5** perform a particular act which has the potential to cause harm. Therefore, I refrain from drinking before I set out on a journey in my car because I know that if I injure someone I could be sued. I refrain from assaulting you for the same reason. However, it could be argued that in such cases it is not the fear that I may be required to compensate my victim that makes me act in a non-delictual way but rather the fear of sanction under criminal law. I might be sent to jail for drunk driving or for assaulting you! One could also argue that another reason for my refraining from acting in a delictual way is not fear of any form of legal sanction, whether civil or criminal, but rather fear of public opprobrium.

4.6   Another function of the law of delict is based on distributive justice. This is founded on the premise that by spreading the loss from an individual victim to those who benefit from an activity the loss is more easily borne in terms of society as a whole. For example, a public utility which is forced to compensate someone injured in a gas explosion is able to absorb the cost by raising the price of its service among those who benefit from it, in other words, the public. Another example of the principle of distributive justice is seen in the concept of vicarious liability where an employer (who can more easily bear the legal obligation to compensate the victim) is held strictly liable (in other words, liable without fault) for the delicts of his employees. The same principle applies to a situation in which a product injures a consumer. The producer can spread his loss (represented in terms of his obligation to compensate the victim) by raising the price of his products. Some are of the view that the requirements of distributive justice can also be satisfied simply by allowing the loss to lie where it falls. In *McFarlane* v *Tayside Health Board*[1] the pursuers were negligently advised that a vasectomy had rendered the husband infertile. The couple relied on that advice and ceased to take contraceptive precautions. A child was born to them and the couple sued the health board for the financial loss which they would incur in bringing up the child. The House of Lords rejected their claim. Lord Steyn was of the view[2] that such losses were those which society (some of whom wanted, but could not have, children, others who have to bring up disabled children) as a whole had to bear. It would not be morally acceptable for the law to transfer the loss in respect of which the pursuer claimed compensation to the health board.

4.7   However, the main function of the law is to compensate the victim for the damage or injury which he has sustained, whether the damage sounds in terms of economic loss or physical injury. Again, the injury for which the pursuer seeks compensation may take less obvious forms. This would, for example, be the case were I to seek compensation from the courts in respect of the sleepless nights which I have endured as a result of the all-night parties which my next-door neighbour has been having for the past several months.

4.8   The law of delict, unlike, for example, the law of evidence or the law of succession, consists of a number of separate delicts. Some delicts, such as assault and intentional interference with contractual relations, comprise intentional acts on the part of the defender. Others, such as negligence, do not. In some delicts, such as the law of nuisance and defamation, there often exists an element of intention and also negligence in relation to the conduct which forms the factual basis of the action. For example, in relation to the law of nuisance, I may intend to carry out building operations on my land the consequence of which is that neighbouring proprietors are inconvenienced by the noise. The reason why this is so is that I have failed properly to ascertain the potential impact of my actions and thus acted negligently.

4.9   There are thus various delicts which are recognised by law. One concentrates on the more important delicts from a practical viewpoint.

4.10   The most important delictual wrong for which pursuers seek compensation from the courts is in relation to negligent conduct on the part of the defender, to which we now turn.

---

[1] [2000] 2 AC 59.
[2] At 82.

NEGLIGENCE

Negligence actions form the vast bulk of civil actions which are brought before the courts, and negligent conduct can take various forms. It can consist of my sustaining an injury on the road by virtue of negligent driving. It could also consist of my sustaining an injury at work by virtue of the negligence of my employer. The negligence which forms the basis of an action could also consist of negligent advice tendered by my financial adviser. **4.11**

What we have to look at here is how the courts have attempted to ascertain whether liability exists by harm caused by negligent acts. We will see that the courts, for policy reasons, are more willing to allow a negligence claim to succeed for certain types of injury than for others. **4.12**

In order to recover for damage which is caused by negligent conduct one requires to establish that: **4.13**

1 the defender owes the pursuer a *duty of care* in law;
2 the *standard of care* which the law demands of the defender has been breached; and
3 the negligent act in question *caused* the requisite injury to the pursuer.

We shall now look at each of these requirements in turn.

(1) THE DUTY OF CARE

In order to ascertain if I am liable in law for the damage which I have caused, the courts have at first to determine whether I owe the injured person a duty of care. **4.14**

During the course of the 19th century, with the advent of road and rail transport and industrialisation in general, negligence actions were increasingly being brought before the courts. By the end of the century the courts had already established that a doctor owed a duty of care to a patient in respect of the treatment which was given to the patient; a road user owed a duty of care to another road user for the former's conduct on the road; and an occupier of land owed, in certain circumstances, a duty of care to those who visited his land. However, the courts had never really worked out a general formula whereby one could establish whether the defender owed a duty of care to the pursuer in a novel situation, that is to say, a situation or circumstances which had not come before the courts before. **4.15**

Judges had indeed made several attempts to work out such a formula but the real breakthrough came with the landmark decision of the House of Lords in *Donoghue* v *Stevenson*.[3] In that case Mrs Donoghue went into a café in Paisley. Her friend bought her an ice cream and ginger beer which had been manufactured by Stevenson. The café proprietor poured some of the ginger beer into her glass and Mrs Donoghue consumed some of the contents. Her friend then poured the remainder of the ginger beer into her glass. As she did so, the remains of a decomposed snail floated out of the bottle. Mrs Donoghue claimed that she suffered nervous shock and gastro-enteritis as a consequence. Mrs Donoghue, of course, did not have a contract with Stevenson, as she bought **4.16**

---

[3] [1932] AC 562.

the ginger beer from the café proprietor. Therefore, in order to succeed, she had to sue Stevenson in the law of delict. The question which the court had to answer was whether the manufacturer of the beer, Stevenson, owed a duty of care to Mrs Donoghue as the consumer. The House of Lords held that a duty of care was owed by the former to the latter. Lord Atkin stated:[4]

> "The rule that you are to love your neighbour becomes in law, you must not injure your neighbour . . . You must take reasonable care to avoid acts or omissions which you can reasonably foresee would be likely to injure your neighbour. Who then is my neighbour? . . . persons who are so closely affected by my act that I ought reasonably to have them in contemplation as being so affected when I am directing my mind to the acts or omissions which are called into question."

In other words, according to Lord Atkin, if one could reasonably foresee that one's conduct could harm the pursuer, a duty of care would arise.

4.17   A good example of the Atkinian foreseeability test being applied is seen in *Beaumont* v *Surrey CC*.[5] In this case a teacher discarded a long piece of elastic in an open bin. The elastic was used in horseplay between pupils and the plaintiff lost an eye. The education authority was held liable since it was foreseeable that such an accident would take place. The Atkinian test was used again in a quite different situation in *Ministry of Housing* v *Sharp*.[6] In this case the clerk of a local land registry issued an erroneous certificate to the purchaser of land in respect of which the claimants had a charge.[7] The consequence of this was that when the land was purchased the claimant automatically lost its interest over the land concerned. The land registry was held liable for the negligence of its clerk on the basis that it was foreseeable that the claimant would suffer such a loss. Several years later the House of Lords used the foreseeability principle to establish liability in *Home Office* v *Dorset Yacht Co*.[8] In that case a party of borstal trainees were working on Brownsea Island in Poole Harbour under the supervision and control of three borstal officers. During the night, seven of the trainees escaped and went aboard a yacht which was anchored nearby. They could not navigate properly, which resulted in a collision and damage to a yacht which was owned by the Dorset Yacht Company who successfully sued the Home Office in negligence. The gist of the House of Lords' holding that a duty of care existed was that such an occurrence was foreseeable if the boys were not properly supervised. Lord Reid stated:[9]

> "the time has come when we can and should say that [Lord Atkin's neighbour principle] ought to apply unless there is some justification or valid explanation for its exclusion."

It can be seen that Lord Atkin is suggesting that the law should impose a duty of care if one can foresee that one's conduct will injure someone else. However, he also states that such a duty should not be imposed if policy reasons dictate the contrary. The scene was

---

[4] At 580.
[5] (1968) 66 LGR 580.
[6] [1970] 2 QB 223.
[7] Ie they had real rights over the land in question.
[8] [1970] AC 1004.
[9] At 1027.

therefore set for the next stage in the development of the law relating to the duty of care: the two-staged approach.

Two-staged approach

The development of the concept of duty of care came with the decision in *Anns v Merton* **4.18** *LBC*.[10] In that case a builder negligently constructed the foundations of a building which was being constructed and the walls began to crack. The owner of the building sued the local authority who were responsible for ensuring that the building works complied with the relevant building control legislation. The House of Lords ruled in favour of the claimant, with Lord Wilberforce enunciating a two-staged approach to the duty of care. In his view, if the court were confronted with a novel situation (that is to say, one which had not already come before the courts) one should approach the concept of duty of care in the following way:

(a) first, if a sufficient relationship of proximity exists between the parties then *prima facie* a duty of care arises; and

(b) secondly, if such a duty does arise, it is then necessary to consider whether there are any considerations which ought to negative, reduce or limit the scope of such duty.

In deciding if there was a sufficiently close relationship, one would still rely on the **4.19** foreseeability test of Lord Atkin in *Donoghue v Stevenson*. If one formed the view that a duty of care arose, one would ascertain if there were any policy grounds for excluding liability. We can see here that such an approach to the duty of care allows a court to extend the boundaries of the law of negligence fairly readily.

However, this expansive approach to the duty of care was relatively short-lived. **4.20** Indeed, there were signs that the courts were beginning to take stock of their somewhat generous approach to the law of negligence in *Governors of the Peabody Fund v Sir Lindsay Parkinson*[11] where the House of Lords held that the finding of a duty of care must depend on all the circumstances of the case. Several years later, in *Yuen Kun-Yeu v Attorney-General of Hong Kong*[12] individuals who had deposited money in a bank sued the Government, for, in effect, failing to regulate the bank properly, resulting in their losing money. The Privy Council was of the view that the law should develop novel categories of negligence incrementally and by analogy rather than by a massive extension of a *prima facie* duty of care restrained only by indefinable considerations which ought to negative or to reduce or limit the scope of the duty or class of person to whom it is owed. In other words, the Privy Council advocated an approach in which more sanctity would be accorded to previously decided cases. If a novel factual set of circumstances were presented before the court it would ascertain if the courts had decided a case which was analogous to the present facts. In any case the law should allow the boundaries of the duty of care to be expanded gradually or incrementally.

The final nail in the coffin, as it were, for the two-staged approach to the duty of **4.21** care came with the decision in *Caparo v Dickman*[13] which concerned an action by

---

[10] [1977] 2 WLR 1024.
[11] [1985] AC 210.
[12] [1987] 2 All ER 705.
[13] [1990] 2 WLR 358.

shareholders against auditors. Caparo claimed that the latter had negligently prepared an audit the consequence of which was that the shareholders had purchased shares, in reliance on the relevant report, and had suffered financially. The House of Lords held that no duty of care was owed by the auditors to the shareholders. A relationship of proximity or neighbourhood was required to exist. The court had also to consider it fair, just and reasonable that the law should impose a duty of a given scope. Foreseeability and proximity were different things. Foreseeability was a necessary but not a sufficient requirement to establish a duty of care in negligence.

4.22   The current approach to the duty of care enunciated in *Yuen Kun-Yeu* and *Caparo* is well illustrated in *Hill* v *Chief Constable of West Yorkshire*[14] in which the mother of one of the Yorkshire Ripper's victims sued the Chief Constable for failure to apprehend the Ripper. It was held that no duty of care was owed even though it was it was reasonably foreseeable that if Sutcliffe, the Ripper, was not apprehended, he would inflict serious injury on members of the public. Lord Keith was of the view that it was against public policy to hold the police civilly liable for failure to apprehend a criminal. He stated:

> "A great deal of police time, trouble and expense might be expected to have to be put into the preparation of the defence to the action and attendance of witnesses at the trial. The result would be a significant diversion of police manpower and attention from their most important function, that of suppression of crime."[15]

Again, in *X* v *Bedfordshire CC*[16] the House of Lords had to decide whether or not to impose common law liability in negligence on liability for failing to take appropriate measures to protect the claimant from, among other things, abuse. It was held that the imposition of a common law duty of care would discourage the due performance of the local authority's statutory duties. Similarly, in *Mariola Marine Corporation* v *Lloyds Registration of Shipping (The Morning Watch)*[17] the plaintiff was a US company which had purchased the *Morning Watch*, a steel-hulled motor yacht, in 1985. The yacht had just been surveyed by a Lloyd's surveyor and had been given a clean bill of health. In fact, the ship had serious defects. The court accepted that it was reasonably foreseeable that Mariola Marine might rely on the survey result. Foreseeability was not enough to establish a duty of care in law. There must also be a sufficient degree of proximity between the defender and the pursuer and it must be just and reasonable to impose on the defender a duty of care to the pursuer. The court also added that there was no universal test to determine whether the necessary proximity existed.

4.23   An interesting case where the modern approach to ascertaining if a duty of care is owed is *P* v *Harrow LBC*.[18] The claimant was sent by the defendant local authority to an independent school for boys with emotional behavioural difficulties. He was sexually abused by the headmaster of the school. There had been no complaints about the school but was the local authority liable? It was held that this was a "no duty" situation. There was no foreseeability that the harm in question would occur and there was no proximity between the local authority and the claimant in terms of

---

[14] [1989] AC 53.
[15] At 63.
[16] [1995] 2 AC 633.
[17] [1990] 1 Lloyds Rep. 547.
[18] *The Times*, 22 April 1992.

the latter's physical safety. It was also against public policy to hold the local authority liable, on the basis that it would make such authorities adopt a defensive approach to their duties of the type which centred round this action. Finally, when one looked at the purpose or intention of the relevant Education Acts under which the local authority had acted, there was no purpose or intention in such legislation that the local authority should be liable. This last factor illustrates the point that in order to ascertain if liability lies in law, account must be taken of the relevant statutes to ascertain whether it was Parliament's intention that the pursuer be compensated at common law. In the last analysis, however, one could argue that this would often seem futile given the fact that Parliament never gave any thought to potential civil suits when drafting the legislation in question.

There are several other cases which one can use to illustrate the modern incremental approach to the duty of care. In *Barrett* v *Ministry of Defence*[19] a naval airman engaged in a bout of heavy drinking at a naval establishment. He became inebriated and then unconscious. He was later found dead, having asphyxiated on his own vomit. It was held by the court that the Ministry of Defence was not liable as it did not owe the deceased a duty of care in law. The fact that it was foreseeable that the claimant would sustain injury if he drank too much was insufficient to ground liability. It was fair, just and reasonable for the law to leave a responsible adult to assume responsibility for his own actions in consuming alcoholic drink. Beldam LJ stated:[20] **4.24**

> "To dilute self-responsibility and to blame one adult for another's lack of self-control is neither just nor reasonable and in the development of the law of negligence an increment too far."

An important question which fell to be answered in the wake of the incremental approach to the duty of care was whether, in determining whether a duty of care applies in law, one should adopt the same approach to claims pertaining to physical injury as one does to economic loss. In *Marc Rich & Co AG* v *Bishop Rock Marine Co Ltd*[21] it was held that the courts should not draw any distinction between the type of damage which the pursuer sustains in terms of the duty of care. A good example of this approach to the duty of care as well as that of the current incremental approach in general can be seen in *Watson* v *British Boxing Board of Control*.[22] This case concerned head injuries which were received by Michael Watson, a professional boxer, in his title fight with Chris Eubank. The fight was regulated by the British Boxing Board of Control (BBBC). Watson claimed that the BBBC had failed to take adequate measures to ensure that he received immediate and effective medical attention should he receive injury during the fight. It was held that there was sufficient proximity between the parties to ground a duty of care in law. Since the BBBC had complete control over the contest it was fair, just and reasonable to conclude that a duty of care existed. In his judgment Lord Phillip MR set store[23] by the following: **4.25**

---

[19] [1995] 1 WLR 1217
[20] At 1224.
[21] [1996] AC 211.
[22] [2001] 2 WLR 1256.
[23] At 1281.

1   Watson was one of a defined number of boxing members of the BBBC.
2   A primary stated object of the BBBC was to look after its boxing members'
    physical safety.
3   The BBBC encouraged and supported its boxing members in the pursuit of an
    activity which involved inevitable physical injury.
4   The BBBC controlled the medical assistance which would be provided.
5   The BBBC had access to specialist expertise in relation to medical care.
6   If Watson had no remedy against the Board, he had no remedy at all.
7   Boxing members of the BBBC including Watson could reasonably rely on the
    former to look after their safety.

The factual duty of care

4.26   What we have been looking at so far in terms of the duty of care is best described as the
notional or nominal duty of care. That is to say, that the courts have analysed a
particular series of facts and determined whether a duty of care is owed by the defender
to the pursuer. However, what also requires to be established is whether *on the very facts
of the case* the conduct of the pursuer actually imperilled or posed a risk to the pursuer.
This is well illustrated in the leading case of *Bourhill* v *Young*.[24] There, a pregnant
fishwife had just alighted from a tram when she heard the sound of a road accident. The
accident had been caused by the negligence of a motor cyclist, John Young, who was
overtaking the tram in which Mrs Bourhill had been travelling. He collided with a car
which was turning right and into his direction of travel. Mrs Bourhill did not see the
accident taking place but, nevertheless, suffered nervous shock. The House of Lords
held that, whereas motorists and cyclists who use the roads owe a duty of care to fellow
road users and pedestrians, on the facts of the case the defender did not owe the pursuer
a duty of care. The former could not reasonably foresee that someone where Mrs
Bourhill was situated when the accident took place would have sustained nervous
shock.

Conclusions on the duty of care – the general part

4.27   What we have been looking at above can best be described as the general part of the
duty of care. There are, however, certain areas where the courts have had to refine
the rules which we have looked at, for a number of reasons, often to reduce the number
of potential claims which could be made. These will now be considered.

Pure economic loss

4.28   The general rule is that there is no liability for causing pure economic loss, in other
words loss which is not prefaced on physical injury or damage. This approach is well
illustrated in *Spartan Steel and Alloys Ltd* v *Martin and Co (Contractors) Ltd*.[25] The
claimants operated a steel factory. The factory obtained electricity by direct cable from
a power station. Martin was a building contractor. It used power-driven tools in
carrying out excavating works. A shovel fractured a cable and the electricity supply

---

[24] 1942 SC (HL) 78.
[25] [1972] 3 All ER 557.

to the factory was shut off, causing a "melt" to be damaged. It was also established that during the time when the electricity was unavailable the claimant could have put more melts through the furnace. The claimant brought an action against Martin in order to recover all damages which had been incurred. It was held that the claimants were only entitled to recover for the loss to the particular melt and not for the economic loss or loss of revenue or productivity which was represented by a loss of other melts which might have been put through the furnace had the power supply not failed. According to Lord Denning MR:[26]

> "if claims for pure economic loss were permitted for this particular hazard there would be no end of claims. Some might be genuine but many might be inflated or even false. A machine might not have been in use anyway, but it would be easy to put it down to the cut in supply. It would be well-nigh impossible to check the claims."

A good illustration of the reluctance of the courts to allow claims which sound in terms of pure economic loss is the previously mentioned case of *McFarlane* v *Tayside Health Board*[27] where the pursuers failed in their action since this loss – the cost of bringing up an unwanted child – ranked simply as pure economic loss.   **4.29**

Negligent statements

If I drive my car negligently on the road or if I conduct myself negligently at work I certainly can injure those who are within the relevant risk area. However, the actual number of people who can be affected is normally likely to be small. That being said, as far as liability for negligent statements is concerned, the potential number of people who could be affected by relying on the statement is limitless. For example, if I were to place an advertisement on the Internet to the effect that one should invest in a new company which proves to be financially unsound, the message could in theory reach hundreds of thousands, if not millions, of people. In the leading case on liability for negligent statements, *Hedley Byrne* v *Heller*,[28] Lord Pearce stated: "Words are more volatile than deeds. They travel fast and far afield. They are used without being expended."[29] The question of liability for unlimited sums of money to an unlimited class of individuals is something that the courts are unwilling to encourage. In effect, the law therefore has to introduce some sort of check in order to cut down the possible number of claimants. This is a policy decision on the part of the courts. In *Hedley Byrne* v *Heller*[30] Easypower, a firm, asked Hedley Byrne do some work for it. In order to ascertain whether Easypower could afford to pay the claimant, it asked its bank, National Provincial, to enquire of Easypower's bank, namely Heller, whether Easypower could afford the services of Hedley Byrne. Heller informed Hedley Byrne that Easypower was financially sound but at the same time expressly disclaimed liability for the accuracy of the information which they imparted. Easypower was not, in fact, financially sound and Hedley Byrne lost money. It therefore sued Heller and the House of Lords held that in the absence of a   **4.30**

---

[26] At 38.
[27] [2000] SCLR 105.
[28] [1964] AC 465.
[29] At 534.
[30] [1964] AC 465.

disclaimer the defendant would have been liable. According to Lord Morris, a duty of care will arise if someone possessed of a special skill undertakes, quite irrespective of a contract, to apply that skill.[31] However, Lord Devlin stated that in order for a duty of care to arise in terms of the making of a negligent statement the relationship between the maker of the negligent statement and the recipient must be equivalent to that existing under a contract. In other words, the relationship must be close. The House of Lords also held that there must be assumption of responsibility on the part of the maker of the statement and also reliance on the part of the recipient. In the previously mentioned case of *Caparo* v *Dickman*[32] Lord Oliver was of the view that in order to be liable for the making of a negligent statement, the necessary relationship between the defender and the pursuer requires to have four features:

4.31
    (1)   the advice is required for a purpose either specific or generally described which is made known to the adviser at the time the advice is given;

    (2)   the defender knows the advice will be communicated to the advisee either individually or as a member of an ascertained class in order that it should be used by the advisee for that purpose,

    (3)   the defender knows that the advice is likely to be acted upon without independent enquiry; and

    (4)   the pursuer acts on the advice.

4.32   It is not sufficient that the defender knows that his advice will be relied on.[33] The law must hold that there is a special relationship between the maker of the statement and the person who relies on the statement. Generally speaking, there will be no liability for statements which are made on a purely social occasion since the maker of the statement implicitly accepts no responsibility for the statement.[34] It is also critical that the defender knows that the pursuer will be likely to rely on the statement without obtaining independent advice.[35] Moreover, it is not essential that the person to whom the statement is made solely relies on the statement and thereby incurs a loss.[36] Finally, it is not necessary that the statement be made directly to the person who sustains the loss in question. The statement can be made to a third party who relies on the statement and acts on it to the detriment of the pursuer.[37]

Psychiatric injury

4.33   According to Professor Fleming in *The Law of Torts*, to treat nervous shock in the same way as equivalent to external injuries from physical impact would open up a wide field of imaginary claims.[38] The law must, therefore, impose arbitrary limitations, such as the requirement that the shock must have resulted from the fear of injury to oneself or, at least, a near relative or witnessing an accident with one's own unaided senses, in order

---

[31] At 502 and 503.
[32] [1990] 2 AC 605.
[33] *Galoo Ltd* v *Bright Graham Murray* [1994] 1 WLR 1360.
[34] *Chaudry* v *Prabhakar, The Times*, 8 June 1988.
[35] *Smith* v *Eric S Bush Ltd* [1989] 2 All ER 514.
[36] *JEB Fasteners Ltd* v *Marks Bloom and Co* [1983] 1 All ER 583.
[37] *Spring* v *Guardian Assurance* [1994] 3 All ER 129.
[38] J Fleming, *The Law of Torts* (9th edn, 1998), p 173.

to reduce the potential number of pursuers. As with the case for liability for negligent statements, foreseeability of injury is by itself incapable of providing a solution as to whether the pursuer should recover.

It is usual for the courts to divide victims of nervous shock into primary victims and **4.34** secondary victims. The courts will normally only allow one to recover in respect of psychiatric injury if one has been subjected to a traumatic event such as a road or an industrial accident. The only exception to this is that, in certain circumstances, one can recover in relation to psychiatric injury which is caused by stress at work.[39]

Primary victims

In order that one can recover as a primary victim of nervous shock, one must physically **4.35** participate or be actively involved[40] in the very events which cause the psychiatric injury. It is not sufficient simply to witness the event.[41] A good illustration of a primary victim of nervous shock can be found in *Dooley* v *Cammell Laird Ltd*.[42] In that case the claimant was operating a crane which was being used to unload a ship. The crane rope snapped and the load which was being carried plummeted into the hold of the ship where the claimant's colleagues were working. He sustained nervous shock as a result and successfully sued his employers.

The leading case on the subject of primary victims of nervous shock is now *Page* v **4.36** *Smith*.[43] In this case the claimant, who was suffering from a condition which was known as chronic fatigue syndrome, was involved in a minor road accident. He was uninjured but his condition became permanent as a result of the accident and he successfully claimed damages in respect of this. The House of Lords refused to draw a distinction between psychiatric injury and physical injury. Essentially, the House of Lords held that notwithstanding the fact that the type of injury which the claimant sustained was not reasonably foreseeable, given the fact that physical injury to the claimant's person was foreseeable, the law should not draw a distinction between these forms of injury as far as liability in negligence was concerned. It sufficed simply that some form of injury was foreseeable.

Secondary victims

What we are looking at here is at a situation where the pursuer suffers nervous shock by **4.37** witnessing some sort of traumatic event.

The leading case on the subject is now *Alcock* v *Chief Constable of South Yorkshire*,[44] where **4.38** the defendant was responsible for the policing of a football match. Overcrowding in part of the stadium was caused by the negligence of the police and 95 people were crushed to death. Many more were seriously injured. Live pictures of the harrowing event were broadcast on television. The claimants were all related to, or were friends of, the spectators

---

[39] See, eg, *Fraser* v *State Hospitals Board for Scotland* 2001 SLT 1051.
[40] *Salter* v *UB Frozen and Chilled Foods Ltd* 2003 SLT 1011.
[41] *Robertson* v *Forth Road Bridge Joint Board* (No 2) 1994 SLT 56. See also *Cullin* v *London Fire and Civil Defence Authority* [1999] PIQR 314.
[42] [1951] 1 Lloyd's Rep 271.
[43] [1996] AC 155.
[44] [1991] 4 All ER 907.

who were involved in the disaster. Some people witnessed the traumatic events from other parts of the stadium. Others saw the events on television. However, all claimants alleged that that they had suffered nervous shock. The House of Lords held that in order to succeed it was necessary for the claimants to show both that the injury which was sustained was reasonably foreseeable and also that the relationship between the claimant and the defendant was sufficiently proximate. As far as the latter was concerned, the relationship between the claimant and the victims had to be one of love and affection. Such a degree of affection would be assumed in certain cases, such as when a parent/child or husband/wife was injured. In other cases, however, the requisite affection would require to be proved. This would be the case in respect of remoter relationships such as cousins. Furthermore, the House of Lords held that the claimant was required to show propinquity (or closeness) in terms of both time and space to the accident or its immediate aftermath. A fairly recent Scottish case in which *Alcock* was followed was *Keen* v *Tayside Contracts*.[45] In that case the pursuer, a road worker, had been instructed by his supervisor to attend the scene of a road accident. The pursuer witnessed badly crushed and burned bodies. He suffered psychiatric injury as a consequence. He sued his employers in essence for having negligently exposed him to such traumatic circumstances. He failed in his action, on the basis that his injury was simply caused by his witnessing a traumatic event. In other words, he ranked in the eye of the law as a secondary victim. He was not related to any of the victims. Therefore his action failed.

Postscript on nervous shock

4.39   One could argue that in its attempt to reduce the number of unmeritorious claims the law has set too high a ceiling in respect of secondary victims of nervous shock. Indeed, the man in the street, told of both the facts and the outcome of the decisions in *Alcock* and *Keen*, may have been very surprised!

4.40   The Scottish Law Commission has recently compiled a report on the law relating to nervous shock.[46] Among its recommendations is that one should abolish the rule that the injury in question requires to be brought about by a sudden assault on the senses, that is to say, by a traumatic event. The Commission also advocated that the distinction between primary victims and secondary victims should be abolished and that victims' claims should be governed by new rules. Furthermore, the Commission also recommended that the rule in the case of *Page* v *Smith*[47] be abolished. The effect of this would be that there would be no liability for unintentionally inflicted psychiatric injury which was not a reasonably foreseeable consequence of the defender's negligence.

The duty of care and affirmative action

4.41   Before concluding discussion of the subject of duty of care, very brief mention should be made of the duty of care and affirmative action. In short, the question which should be asked here is whether I can be sued under the law of negligence for my simply failing to take appropriate action in respect of someone who is in need of help. For example, could I be sued in the law of negligence for failing to shout a warning to someone walking

---

[45] 2003 SLT 500.
[46] Scot Law Com No 196, SE/004/129.
[47] [1996] AC 155.

towards a dangerous cliff? The general rule is that the law refrains from imposing an affirmative duty on the defender. I can stand idly by and watch a baby to whom I am not related drown in a shallow pool of water.[48] However, there are certain situations where the law does require me to take affirmative action. For example, I am under a duty not to allow my land to become a known source of danger to my neighbours.[49]

(2) THE STANDARD OF CARE

Once one has established that the defender owes a duty of care to the pursuer it is **4.42** necessary to ascertain whether the duty of care has been breached. Whether the defender is negligent or not is judged objectively. In other words, no account is taken of individual disabilities or idiosyncrasies, except in relation to children who are judged in terms of the standard of children of the age of the defender. The leading case on this point is *Nettleship* v *Weston*.[50] In that case a learner driver was held to be required to attain the same standard of driving as an ordinary competent driver. This approach may seem harsh but one can appreciate that it would be extremely difficult for the courts to take individual circumstances into account and adopt a subjective approach to the standard of care. In the case of learner drivers, for example, how much higher a standard of care should be demanded of a learner driver who had received ten driving lessons than one who had received only five? Again, if one were to take age into account, how much concession in terms of the standard of care should one make in relation to an 85-year-old driver? These questions would pose the courts great difficulty and it is therefore far simpler to adopt an objective approach to the standard of care.

The courts take into account a number of factors in order to decide whether the **4.43** defender has been negligent. These are now discussed.

The state of current knowledge

The leading case here is *Roe* v *Minister of Health*.[51] In that case the claimant went into hospital **4.44** for a minor operation. He was given a spinal injection. The fluid which was used for the injection was kept in an ampoule, that is, a very small glass container, which, in turn, was kept in a phenol solution. At this time it was not known that phenol could seep into the ampoule through invisible cracks. The claimant was paralysed from the waist downwards. He sued the Minister of Health who was responsible for the hospital concerned. His action failed because the defendant's hospital had not breached its standard of care since it had acted in a way in which any other reasonable hospital would have acted in the situation as the dangers from this type of ampoule were not known at that time.

The magnitude of risk

The greater the risk of injury from the activity which is the subject-matter of the action, **4.45** the greater the amount of precautions which the defender is required to take. In *Blyth* v

---

[48] See Eldridge, *Modern Tort Problems*, p 12.
[49] See, eg, *Sedleigh-Denfield* v *O'Callaghan* [1940] AC 880; *Goldman* v *Hargrave* [1967] 1 AC 645; and *Leakey* v *National Trust* [1980] 1 All ER 17.
[50] [1971] 2 QB 691.
[51] [1954] 2 QB 66.

Birmingham Waterworks Co[52] the defendant water board laid a water main which was 18 inches in depth. One year there was an extremely severe frost which penetrated the ground as far as the water main. The main burst and flooded the claimant's premises. It was held that the water board was not negligent because it had taken reasonable precautions in the circumstances. The modern case on the subject of standard of care is *Bolton v Stone*.[53] In that case the claimant, while standing in a quiet suburban highway outside her house, was struck by a cricket ball. The claimant was situated 100 yards from the batsman and the ball had cleared a 17-foot fence which was situated 78 yards from him. Similar hits had occurred only about six times in the previous 30 years. The House of Lords held that since the likelihood of injury was small, the claimant had not established that the defendant had broken his duty of care towards the claimant.

The risk of serious harm

4.46   Here, one takes into account not the likelihood that an accident will occur but, rather, the seriousness of the injury should an accident occur. The leading case is *Paris v Stepney BC*.[54] There, a one-eyed worker was injured while at work. He claimed that his employers should have provided and also required him to use goggles while he was carrying on work. It was proved that there was no greater a likelihood that an accident would take place to the claimant than to a worker with normal sight. However, the House of Lords held that since the consequences of an injury to the claimant were graver, extra precautions were necessary.

The utility of the defender's activity

4.47   The social utility, or usefulness, of the relevant activity which is the subject-matter of the action is taken into account. The greater the utility, the less likely it is that the court will hold that the relevant standard of care has been breached. The leading case is *Watt v Hertfordshire CC*.[55] The claimant was a fireman. One day, his station received a call that a woman was trapped under a heavy lorry as a result of a road accident. A jack was required to lift the vehicle. The lorry which was designed to carry such a device was not available. Two of the claimant's colleagues threw a heavy jack on to a lorry in which they were to travel. The lorry was not designed to carry a jack. During the journey the jack rolled away from its original position and injured the claimant. It was held that the defendants had not been negligent. In reaching its decision the court took into account the social utility of the journey, namely the rescuing of an injured person. However, simply because the defender is involved in an activity which has some social worth does not automatically exonerate him from the need to take care. This point was decided in *Ward v London County Council*.[56] There, the driver of a fire engine was held to have been negligent in driving through a red traffic light and injuring the claimant. It was held that the defendant could not use the reason that he was involved in a journey of social worth as an excuse for his breach of duty of care.

---

[52] (1856) 11 Ex 781.
[53] [1951] AC 850.
[54] [1950] 1 KB 320.
[55] [1954] 1 WLR 835.
[56] [1938] 2 All ER 341.

The practicality of precautions

The easier it is to take measures to counteract the risk, the more likely it is that the courts **4.48** will hold that the appropriate duty of care has been breached. In *Latimer* v *AEC Ltd*[57] the floor of the defendant's factory was flooded by an exceptionally heavy rainstorm. Oil which was kept in troughs was washed out on to the factory floor. The defendant put sawdust on the floor but there was not enough sawdust to cover the entire factory floor. The claimant, who was working on the floor, slipped and injured himself. He sued the occupier of the factory. It was held that the defendant was not liable since he had taken all appropriate precautions short of closing the factory. However, this decision has been criticised on the ground that commercial profitability was given too much prominence by the court over the personal security of the workers.

Emergency situations

If the defendant is placed in a sudden emergency situation which is not of his own creation, **4.49** his actions must be judged in the light of those circumstances. In *Ng Chun Pui* v *Lee Chuen Tat*[58] it was held that the driver of a coach who had braked, swerved and skidded when another vehicle had cut across his path had acted reasonably in an emergency.

Children

Children are treated as a category apart. In order to ascertain if the defender has been **4.50** negligent, one takes into account what degree of care a child of the particular age of the defender can be expected to take.[59]

It should be briefly mentioned by way of conclusion that the courts have formulated **4.51** special rules to determine whether professional people, such as doctors, have breached the standard of care which the law demands of them.[60]

(3) CAUSATION

Factual causation

Finally, in order to succeed in a negligence claim it is necessary to prove that the **4.52** negligent act in question actually caused the relevant injury or damage which is the subject-matter of the action. There are two main tests which the courts use in order to ascertain whether the defender's conduct caused the loss in question, namely:

(a) the "but for" test; and
(b) the "material contribution" test.

The tests are mutually exclusive. It is also difficult to predict which test will be used by the court.

---

[57] [1953] AC 643.
[58] (1988) 132 SJ 1244.
[59] *Yachuk* v *Oliver Blais Co Ltd* [1949] AC 386; *Gough* v *Thane* [1966] 3 All ER 398.
[60] See F McManus and E Russell, *Delict* (1998), Ch 10.

(a) The "but for" test

4.53   The question which the court asks itself here is: but for the negligent act of the defender, would the pursuer have been harmed? The leading case on the subject is *Barnett* v *Chelsea and Kensington Hospital Management Committee*.[61] In that case Barnett, a night-watchman, called early one morning at the defendants' hospital. He had been deliberately poisoned and was complaining of sickness. The doctor in charge refused to see him and suggested that he should consult his GP in the morning. However, Barnett died before he could visit his GP and his widow sued the hospital in negligence. She failed since it was proved that her husband would have died anyway. No form of medical treatment would have saved him at the time he presented himself at the hospital. In other words, the defendant had not caused Barnett's death.

(b) The "material contribution" test

4.54   As far as this test is concerned, the courts are willing to accept that the defender has caused the relevant damage if his negligent act materially contributes to, as opposed to being the sole cause of, the accident. The test is well illustrated in *Wardlaw* v *Bonnington Castings*.[62] In that case the pursuer's illness was caused by an accumulation of dust in his lungs, the dust in question coming from two sources. The defenders (Wardlaw's employers) were not responsible for one of the sources, but they could have prevented (and were therefore negligent concerning) the other. The dust from the latter source (in other words, the "illegal" dust) was not in itself sufficient to cause the disease but the pursuer succeeded because the "illegal" dust had made a material contribution to his injury.[63]

4.55   It is also important to understand that the pursuer requires to prove that the negligent act of the defender caused his injury on a balance of probabilities.[64]

Departure from the "rules"

4.56   In *Fairchild* v *Glenhaven Funeral Services*[65] it was held that in certain circumstances one could depart from the well-established rules governing factual causation. In that case Fairchild had been employed at different times and for different periods by more than one employer. Fairchild's's employers, E1 and E2, had been subject to a duty to take reasonable care or all practicable measures to prevent F from inhaling asbestos dust. Both E1 and E2 failed to do so and as a consequence F contracted mesothelioma. On the current limits of scientific knowledge, Fairchild was unable to prove on the balance of probabilities that his condition was the result of inhaling asbestos dust during his employment by one or other or both of E1 and E2. However, the House of Lords held that, in certain special circumstances, the court could depart from the usual test of legal causation and treat a lesser degree of causal connection as sufficient, namely that the defendant's breach of duty had materially contributed to causing the disease by

---

[61] [1969] 1 QB 428.
[62] 1956 SC (HL) 26.
[63] See also *McGhee* v *NCB* [1972] 3 All ER 1008.
[64] *Wilsher* v *Essex Area Health Authority* [1988] 1 All ER 871.
[65] [2002] 3 All ER 305.

materially increasing the risk that the disease would be contracted. Any injustice that might be involved in imposing liability in such circumstances was heavily outweighed by the injustice of denying redress to the victim.

Legal causation (remoteness of damage)

The law will not allow the pursuer to recover in relation to injury which is deemed to be too remote. One can illustrate this point by considering the following scenario: I encourage Albert, a young man, to take up rowing. I know that he is short-sighted. Several years later, while he is rowing on a canal, he fails to notice another boat, which is being rowed by Pat, approaching his boat. Albert's boat collides with Pat's boat which is sunk. Pat manages to swim to safety but he is cut by glass which has been dumped by the side of the canal. Could I be sued by Pat for the injury and loss which he has sustained? **4.57**

It is probably true that the accident would never have taken place had I not encouraged Albert to take up rowing. However, Pat would certainly not be able to successfully sue me in the law of negligence because the type of injury which has been inflicted is too remote. The leading case on this issue is *The Wagon Mound*[66] where it was held that in order for the pursuer to be able to recover for injury or damage he has sustained, that loss must be reasonably foreseeable. **4.58**

VICARIOUS LIABILITY

Accidents are often caused by those who are carrying out work for others. For example, an employee who performs his duties negligently may injure a fellow worker or a member of the public. Sometimes, however, an accident occurs while someone, who is not an employee of another person, is carrying out work for that person. For example, a taxi driver who I have commissioned to take me to the railway station may negligently run over a cyclist on his way to the station. The important question one must answer here is whether the injured person, in each of the above cases, can sue the person who is paying the person at the time when the accident took place. In short, subject to several limited exceptions, only an employer can be sued for the delicts (including negligent conduct) which have been committed by his servant (or employee) during the scope of his employment. One who simply pays someone else to carry out work for him on an *ad hoc* basis cannot normally be sued if that person causes injury or damage. One cannot therefore normally be sued for work which is being carried out by an independent contractor. What the courts thus do is to distinguish between an employee and an independent contractor. An employee is employed under a contract of *service* whereas an independent contractor is employed under a contract for *services*. **4.59**

In order to ascertain who is an employee and who is an independent contractor, the courts adopt a variety of tests. The most important are: **4.60**

(1) To what extent, if any, does the person who pays the other have the right to choose who works for him? The right to choose is more consistent with a contract of service.

---

[66] [1961] AC 388.

(2) Are wages or other forms of remuneration paid to the other? The right to receive wages and remuneration is more consistent with a contract of service.

(3) To what extent can the person who is paying control the manner in which the tasks which the other has to perform are carried out? The greater the degree of control, the more likely that the relevant relationship is that of employer–employee. However, given that employees nowadays are carrying out much more technical and esoteric tasks than in the past, this test is losing some of its currency.

(4) The right to "hire and fire" the other is more consistent with a contract of service.

4.61 It is often said that it is easy to recognise a contract of service when one sees it but it is difficult to say where the distinction lies between that and a contract of services. That being said, examples of those who are employed under a contract of service would include a ship's master, a chauffeur, a reporter on a newspaper and a schoolteacher. A taxi driver and a newspaper contributor would, however, be employed under a contract for services.

For which acts of an employee is the employer liable?

4.62 An employer is only liable for acts which are done in the course of the servant's employment. An employer will be liable for the conduct of his employees at the relevant place of employment during the hours for which the employee is employed and also as long as the employee is on the premises concerned within reasonable limits of time of the commencement and conclusion of the shift. In *Bell* v *Blackwood, Morton and Sons*[67] a woman in the employment of a firm of carpet manufacturers was jostled by a fellow employee while travelling down a stair, after the hooter had sounded for the end of the shift. The defenders were held vicariously liable for the conduct of the negligent employee.

"Frolic" on part of employee

4.63 There are a number of cases which concern an employee failing to carry out his duties in the manner which his employer requires. If the employee has gone on "a frolic of his own", this act takes him outside the course of his employment and the employer is not liable for the acts of his employee. If the frolic consists of the employee going on a journey of his own, if the deviation from the normal journey is substantial then the employer would not be liable. In *Storey* v *Ashton*[68] a cart driver completed his employer's work and then went to visit a relative. During the course of the journey the carter injured the claimant. It was held that the employer was not liable for this tort, on the basis that the employee had gone on a frolic of his own. Again, in *Hilton* v *Burton*[69] X, H and Y were building workers who were employed at a building site. H drove them to a café seven miles away, in order to buy tea. X was killed by the negligent driving of H. It was held that H was not acting within the scope of his employment. Again, in *Williams* v *Hemphill*[70] a bus driver, while carrying children, made a detour at the request of some of

---

[67] 1960 SC 11.
[68] (1869) LR 4 QB 476.
[69] [1961] 1 All ER 74.
[70] 1966 SC 259.

the children. The bus was involved in a collision. A passenger was injured. It was held that the driver was still acting within the scope of his employment notwithstanding that the deviation from the route which the bus driver's employers wished the driver to take was fairly substantial.[71]

Certain other forms of conduct can take an employee outside the scope of his **4.64** employment. Essentially, an employer will be vicariously liable for the conduct of his employee if the employee is carrying out incompetently something which he is authorised to do.[72] This principle is neatly illustrated in *Century Insurance Co Ltd* v *Northern Ireland Transport Board*.[73] Here, the driver of a petrol lorry struck a match while filling a tank at the petrol station. There was an explosion and property was damaged. It was held that the employer was liable since the employee was acting within the scope of his employment. He was doing what he was employed to do, albeit in an incompetent way. One could also say that what the driver did was so reasonably incidental to his work that it did not take him outwith the scope of his employment.

In deciding whether a given act on the part of the employee takes him outwith the **4.65** scope of his employment, the courts have recently displayed a generous approach as to which acts on the part of the employee can be regarded as being within that scope. In *Lister* v *Hesley Hall Ltd*[74] L was resident in a boarding house which was attached to a school which was owned and managed by H. W, a warden of the boarding house, without the knowledge of H, systematically sexually abused L. L claimed damages against H. The House of Lords held that there was a sufficient connection between the work which W had been employed to do and the acts of abuse that he had committed for those acts to have been regarded as having been committed within the scope of his employment. H was therefore vicariously liable for the acts of W. Again, in *Mattis* v *Pollock*[75] the defendant (P) owned a nightclub. He employed X as a doorman. X was expected to act aggressively towards customers. X grabbed a member of a group of people who were about to enter the nightclub. X was struck several times and also hit by a bottle. X then escaped to his flat from which he emerged and stabbed M. It was held that P was vicariously liable for the assault since X's act was so closely connected with what the employer either authorised or expected of X that it was fair, just and reasonable to make P vicariously liable for the assault.

DEFENCES

Only very brief mention can be made of the defences which are relevant in a negligence **4.66** action. The most important are those of (1) contributory negligence; (2) consent; and (3) illegality. These will be dealt with in turn.

(1) Contributory negligence

The law allows me to recover for injury which has been negligently inflicted on me **4.67** notwithstanding that I am to some extent the author of my own misfortune. For

---

[71] See also *Smith* v *Stages* [1989] 2 WLR 529.
[72] *Kirby* v *NCB* 1958 SC 514.
[73] [1942] AC 509.
[74] [2001] 2 WLR 1311.
[75] [2003] 1 WLR 2158.

example, if I am cycling along the road and I am knocked over by a car driver who is at fault and receive head injuries, I can still succeed in a negligence action against the driver, notwithstanding the fact that my injuries are more severe by dint of my failure to wear a crash helmet. Under s 1 of the Law Reform (Contributory Negligence) Act 1945 a negligence claim may not be defeated by reason of the fact that the pursuer was negligent. However, the damages which are recoverable fall to be reduced to such extent as the court thinks just and equitable having regard to the claimant's share of responsibility for the damage.

(2) Consent

4.68   Briefly, the law provides that no wrong is done to he who has consented. This is expressed in the Latin maxim *"Volenti non fit injuria"*. Where a person consents to run the risk of injury which is caused by another, he cannot thereafter claim damages in respect of the injury. The defence must be specifically pled. The onus of proof that the pursuer consented rests on the defender. The defence operates as a complete defence. In other words, if the defence succeeds, the pursuer's claim fails *in toto*.

(3) Illegality

4.69   The courts will sometimes prevent the pursuer from recovering damages in respect of the negligent act of another, on the ground that the pursuer has, at the time of the accident, been involved in an illegal act. The defence must be specifically pled. If the defence succeeds it operates as a complete defence, thereby depriving the pursuer of the award of any damages. The defence represents a grey area of the law. It should be stated that it is not every illegal act on the part of the pursuer which will deprive him of the chance of succeeding against the defender. For example, the fact that I am driving my car (in respect of which I do not possess a relevant MOT certificate and which therefore contravenes relevant road traffic legislation) on a public road would not *per se* preclude me from succeeding in a negligence claim against another driver who negligently collided with my car and injured me.

REMEDIES

4.70   The main remedies in the law of delict are interdict, declarator and damages. The last mentioned is the most important as far as negligence actions are concerned. Indeed, the award of damages is the normal form of remedy for a delictual wrong. It is said that money is the universal solvent.[76] The purpose of damages is to restore the pursuer, as far as possible, to the position in which he was before the delictual conduct took place. The amount of damages bears no relation to the degree of fault on the part of the defender. Finally, there is no such thing as punitive damages in the law of delict.

---

[76] *Auld* v *Shairp* (1874) 2 R 191.

ESSENTIAL FACTS

NATURE OF LAW OF DELICT

4.71

- The law of delict is concerned with civil wrongs.
- The person injured invokes the law of delict to obtain compensation for injury caused to him.

NEGLIGENCE

- In order to recover for damage caused by negligent conduct one must establish that the defender owes the pursuer a duty of care in law, that the standard of care has been breached and that the negligent act caused the requisite injury.

DUTY OF CARE

- The duty of care in the law of negligence is determined by the "neighbour" principle. One is liable if one can reasonably foresee that one's conduct will injure the pursuer.
- It must also be proved that in the very circumstances in which the pursuer was injured the defender owed him a duty of care in law.

THE STANDARD OF CARE

- The standard of care which the law demands of the defender is set by the "reasonable man" test.
- In order to determine whether the requisite standard of care has been breached one takes a number of factors into account, including the state of current knowledge, the magnitude of risk, the risk of serious harm, the utility of the defender's conduct and the practicality of precautions.

CAUSATION

- In order to succeed in a negligence claim it is necessary to prove that the negligent act in question actually caused the relevant injury.
- There are two main tests which the courts use in order to ascertain whether the defender's conduct caused the loss in question, namely the "but for" test and the "material contribution" test
- The law will not allow the pursuer to recover in relation to injury which is too remote.

VICARIOUS LIABILITY

- An employer is vicariously liable for acts done in the course of the servant's employment.
- There is no liability for "frolics" on the part of the employee.

DEFENCES

- Damages which are recoverable fall to be reduced to such extent as the court thinks just and equitable having regard to the pursuer's share of responsibility for the damage.
- No damages are recoverable by a person who has consented to the wrong.
- The courts will sometimes prevent the pursuer from recovering damages if the pursuer has been participating in an illegal act when he was injured.

REMEDIES

- The main remedies in the law of delict are interdict, declarator and damages.
- Damages is the most important as far as negligence actions are concerned.

ESSENTIAL CASES

4.72

DUTY OF CARE

Donoghue v *Stevenson* (1932): "The rule that you are to love your neighbour becomes in law, you must not injure your neighbour; and the lawyer's question, Who is my neighbour? receives a restricted reply. You must take reasonable care to avoid acts or omissions which you can reasonably foresee would be likely to injure your neighbour. Who then is my neighbour? The answer seems to be persons who are so closely and directly affected by my act that I ought reasonably to have them in contemplation as being so affected when I am directing my mind to the acts or omissions which are called into question" (per Lord Atkin at 580).

Caparo v *Dickman* (1990): This case concerned an action in negligence against auditors who had negligently prepared an audit of a company the consequence of which was that the shareholders had purchased shares in reliance on the report and had suffered financially. The House of Lords held that no duty of care was owed by the auditors to the shareholders. A relationship of proximity was required to exist. The court had to consider if it was fair, just and reasonable that the law should impose a duty of a given scope. Foreseeability was a necessary, but not a sufficient, requirement to establish a duty of care in law.

Hill v *Chief Constable of West Yorkshire* (1989): The mother of one of the Yorkshire Ripper's victims sued the Chief Constable for failure to apprehend the Ripper. It was held that no duty of care was owed even though it was reasonably foreseeable that if Sutcliffe, the Ripper, was not apprehended, he would inflict serious injury on members of the public.

"A great deal of police time, trouble and expense might be expected to have to be put into the preparation of the defence to the action and attendance of witnesses at the trial. The result would be a significant diversion of police manpower and attention from their most important function, that of suppression of crime." (per Lord Keith at 63).

STANDARD OF CARE

Nettleship v *Weston* (1971): A learner driver was held to be required to attain the same standard of care as an ordinary competent driver.

CAUSATION

Factual causation

Barnett v *Chelsea and Kensington Hospital Management Committee* (1969): Barnett, a nightwatchman, called early one morning at the defendants' hospital, complaining of sickness. He had been deliberately poisoned. The doctor in charge refused to see him and told him to consult his GP in the morning. However, Barnett died before he could consult his GP. His widow sued the hospital in negligence. She failed since no form of medical treatment would have saved him at the time he presented himself at the hospital. The defendant's negligence had not caused Barnett's death.

Remoteness of damage

Overseas Tankship v *Morts Dock and Engineeering Co Ltd* (1961): A ship, the *Wagon Mound*, was taking on furnace oil when the appellants' servants negligently allowed oil to spill into the water. Wind and tide carried the oil about 200 yards to the respondents' wharf where servants of the respondents were repairing a vessel by using welding equipment. A piece of metal fell from the wharf and set on fire cotton waste which was floating on the oil which in turn set the oil alight. The wharf was severely burned. The Privy Council held that one should determine whether any given type of injury was too remote by employing the "foreseeability" test. In other words, one asks whether the type of damage which was sustained by the pursuer was reasonably foreseeable.

VICARIOUS LIABILITY

Century Insurance Co Ltd v *Northern Ireland Transport Board* (1942): The driver of a petrol lorry struck a match while filling a tank at the petrol station. There was an explosion and property was damaged. It was held that the employer was liable since the employee was acting within the scope of his employment. He was doing what he was employed to do, albeit in an incompetent way.

Lister v *Hesley Hall* (2001): L was resident in a boarding house which was attached to a school which was owned and managed by H. A warden of the boarding house, without the knowledge of H, systematically sexually abused L. Held that there was a sufficient connection between the work which the warden was employed to do and the acts which he had committed for those acts to be regarded as having been committed within the scope of his employment.

5 CONTRACT

The law of contract is fundamental to society. It is one of the few areas of law in which most people are involved on a daily basis. From where we live to what we buy, to how we get to work, there are contracts involved in every stage of daily life and business. **5.1**

A contract is a voluntary obligation between two or more parties who have reached agreement on its terms and who have capacity to contract and intend to create certain legally binding obligations between them. Most contracts are bilateral onerous contracts because they are between two parties, each party has certain obligations under it and each contributes something of value to it. For example, in the purchase of a car, there are two parties, one of whom agrees to buy the car for a certain price and the other who agrees to hand over possession and ownership of the car in exchange for that price. A contract is a voluntary obligation because the parties have to agree to be legally bound by it – the purchaser cannot be forced into buying the car. This contrasts with other legal obligations which are imposed by law, such as the duty imposed on a parent to support a child. **5.2**

It is important to know when an arrangement falls into the category of "contract" because it is legally enforceable as such; if one party does not carry out his part of the deal then the other can take certain measures against him, including court action if necessary. Non-contractual agreements, such as agreeing to meet up for a drink in the pub, cannot be enforced in this way. **5.3**

It is also possible to have voluntary obligations which are not bilateral onerous obligations and which are also enforceable. These are gratuitous contracts and promises. A gratuitous contract is a contract in which the parties agree to something which does not necessarily bestow a benefit on one of them. This is demonstrated by the case of *Morton's Trustees* v *Aged Christian Friend Society of Scotland*[1] in which Mr Morton offered a charitable donation to the Society which was accepted by it. The donation was to be paid by instalments but Mr Morton died before all of them had been paid. The court held that there was a legally enforceable contract between Mr Morton and the Society and that his estate had to pay the remainder. A promise is very similar but, unlike a gratuitous contract, it is not reciprocal in nature: there is no need for the promisee to accept a promise and it can bind only the promisor. **5.4**

Examples of promise are found in *Littlejohn* v *Hadwen*[2] in which there was the promise to keep an offer open for a certain period of time and in *Stone* v *MacDonald*[3] in which there was a grant of an option to buy land which was held to be binding as a promise. Reward cases, in which a reward is offered for information or lost property, are usually categorised as promise in Scots law. **5.5**

In studying contract law, there are a number of basic issues to consider: **5.6**

---

[1] (1899) 2 F 82.
[2] (1882) 20 SLR 5.
[3] 1979 SLT 288.

- Formation: when does a contract come into being?
- Problems: certain problems can affect the validity or enforceability of a contract and it is important to be able to identify these problems and their effect on the contract.
- Breach of contract: what happens when one party does not perform his part of the contract?
- Termination: when does a contract (or the obligations under it) come to an end?

FORMATION

5.7 A contract is formed when an offer is met with an acceptance.

OFFER

5.8 An offer must be clear, capable of acceptance, include the intention to be legally bound and be communicated to the other party. That party may be a particular person or the offer may be made to the general public as in the case of *Carlill* v *Carbolic Smoke Ball Company*[4] in which the offer was made by way of an advert to the world at large. A company offered a £100 reward to anyone who bought and used its smoke ball correctly but who nevertheless came down with flu.[5] Unlike many adverts, this one had the characteristics of an offer as it was specific, had been effectively communicated and, importantly, the company showed the seriousness of its intentions by declaring that it had lodged £1,000 in a bank to fund payouts. In commerce, there are many situations which might look like offers but which, in fact, are not. Thus, an offer can be contrasted with an invitation to treat which happens when one party displays goods in a shop window, as in the case of *Fisher* v *Bell*;[6] on self-service shelves in a shop, as in *Pharmaceutical Society of GB* v *Boots Cash Chemists*;[7] or on a website. An offer is not a willingness to negotiate,[8] an invitation to tender, a quotation[9] or putting something up for auction.[10] An offer can be verbal, written or made by action as in the case of a slot machine.[11]

5.9 An offer can be revoked at any time before acceptance unless a time limit has been placed on it, in which case it cannot be revoked without breaching that promise.[12] An offer will lapse if a time limit set for acceptance passes without the contract being concluded or, if no time limit is set, is not accepted in a reasonable period of time.[13]

---

[4] [1893] 1 QB 256.

[5] Note: *Carlill* is an English case and the judgment refers to the offer of the reward as a "promise". However, promise is not recognised in the same way as in Scots law and, therefore, this is a case of contract in English law, requiring offer and acceptance.

[6] [1961] 1 QB 394.

[7] [1953] 1 QB 401.

[8] *Harvey* v *Facey* [1893] AC 552.

[9] However, a very specific quotation may be enough to amount to an offer: *Jaeger Bros Ltd* v *J & A McMorland* (1902) 10 SLT 63.

[10] Section 57(2) of the Sale of Goods Act 1979 makes clear that the offer is made by the bidder and the acceptance by the auctioneer.

[11] *Thornton* v *Shoe Lane Parking* [1971] 2 QB 163.

[12] *Littlejohn* v *Hadwen* (1882) 20 SLR 5.

[13] *Wylie & Lochhead* v *McElroy & Sons* (1873) 1 R 41.

ACCEPTANCE

Acceptance can be verbal, in writing or made by action. It must usually be commu- **5.10**
nicated to the offeror, although the case of *Carlill* shows that this need not always be the
case: Mrs Carlill did not advise the Carbolic Smoke Ball Company that she was accepting
its offer but her actions amounted to acceptance. The offer may state how acceptance is to
be made in order to be valid and the usual rule is that silence from the offeree is not
enough. Although these concepts are straightforward, it can be difficult to tell in a real-
life situation when an offer or an acceptance has been made. For example, the purchase of
a newspaper may take place without verbal or written communication; the seller will not
say "I offer to sell this paper". Indeed, while it is on the shelf, there is no offer, merely an
invitation to treat. Once the purchaser picks it up and takes it to the checkout, there can
be said to be an offer to buy at that stage. That offer can be accepted by the seller simply
by accepting the money for it. In more complex commercial situations, such as the
purchase of a factory or goods, there may be protracted negotiations and pinpointing
when an offer and acceptance have been made can be difficult. In these negotiations, the
offeree may make a qualified acceptance (also known as a counter-offer) which accepts
the offer subject to certain important changes. The effect of this was discussed in *Wolf &
Wolf* v *Forfar Potato Co Ltd*[14] and it was held that a counter-offer cancels the original offer
so that it can no longer be accepted. The ball is then in the original offeror's court to
decide whether to accept the counter-offer or not. Until he does so, there is no contract.

Postal rule

A further complication arises if the contract is being made by post. In that case, the **5.11**
contract is made as soon as the acceptance is posted. The case of *Dunlop, Wilson & Co* v
Higgins and Son[15] held that if a time limit is set on acceptance being made but it is
delayed in the post, the postal rule operates to conclude the contract. However, there
is Scottish authority to suggest that there is no contract if the letter is not merely delayed
but lost.[16] The application of the rule in a case where the letter was incorrectly addressed
was considered in *Jacobsen, Sons & Co* v *Underwood & Son Ltd*[17] and it was held that the
rule did apply to conclude the contract, regardless of this mistake. As acceptance
concludes the contract, it cannot generally be revoked.[18] An acceptance will conclude
the contract.

Once the contract has been formed, it cannot be cancelled except in very limited **5.12**
circumstances. For example, there are short "cooling off" periods for some consumer
credit contracts and distance selling contracts whereby the consumer can cancel within
14 days but unless there is a legal right to cancel then both parties are bound to carry out
their respective obligations under the contract or face the consequences of not doing so.

---

[14] 1984 SLT 100.
[15] (1848) 6 Bell's App 195.
[16] *Mason* v *Benhar Coal Co Ltd* (1882) 9 R 883.
[17] (1894) 21 R 654.
[18] This is subject to the interpretation of the case of *Countess of Dunmore* v *Alexander* (1830) 9 S 190
in which two letters were sent separately but arrived together. Although many academics now
consider that the case is an example of an offer of employment being withdrawn, it was thought
for some time that the first letter was an acceptance of an offer and that the second was a
revocation of acceptance which the court allowed because both letters were delivered together.

CONTRACTUAL TERMS

Written contracts

5.13   Contracts can be concluded in many ways: e-mail,[19] face to face, fax, telephone, post or by the actions of the parties. The vast majority of contracts do not have to be in writing to be valid, other than those listed in the Requirements of Writing (Scotland) Act 1995,[20] but if the parties choose to put the contract in writing then the Contract (Scotland) Act 1997 applies. Under this Act, the written contract is presumed to contain all of the contractual terms and conditions but in cases where the contract does not expressly state this, then evidence from outwith the contract can be examined to find out if there are any other contractual terms.

Incorporation

5.14   The terms of any contract, written or not, will be those incorporated into the contract at the time of formation: contractual terms cannot be incorporated afterwards, except with the consent of both parties. It is important that contractual terms are brought to the attention of the other party. Tickets and notices cause particular problems for incorporation: when does a term on a ticket or a notice form part of the contract? Some tickets are contractual, like rail tickets, and their terms (or terms referred to on them) are contractual. However, incorporation can be prevented by use of tiny print[21] or by referring to terms on the back of the ticket.[22] Other "tickets" can actually be classified as receipts or invoices, issued after the contract has been concluded, and in those cases, the terms on them cannot be contractual.[23] Notices are often not visible until after the contract has been concluded and so any terms on those will not be contractual, as in the case of *Thornton* v *Shoe Lane Parking Ltd* in which the contract to use a car park was concluded at the entry barrier from which the notice denying liability for injury in the car park could not be seen. Similarly, a notice in a hotel room which was seen by the guests only after they had checked in and gone to their room did not form part of the contract in *Olley* v *Marlborough Court Ltd*.[24]

Conditions

5.15   The contractual terms will specify what each party has to do to fulfil his obligations under it and it will also set when these obligations have to be fulfilled. Some obligations will be contingent upon other things happening first: for example, if one party is to pay for goods by instalments then he has an obligation to pay but not until the due dates are reached or goods are delivered.

---

[19] Section 7 of the Electronic Communications Act 2000 makes authenticated electronic signatures admissible in court proceedings to establish the authenticity of the communication.
[20] See below.
[21] *Williamson* v *North of Scotland and Orkney Steam Navigation Co* 1916 SC 554.
[22] *Parker* v *South Eastern Railway Co* (1877) 2 CPD 416: however, in this case, the words "see back" were printed on the front and therefore the terms were incorporated.
[23] *Taylor* v *Glasgow Corporation* 1952 SC 440: receipt for baths was post-contractual.
[24] [1949] 1 KB 532.

PROBLEMS WITH CONTRACTS

Although most contracts are valid and binding as soon as they are formed, there are a number of problems which can render the contract void, voidable or unenforceable. **5.16**

VOID

A contract which is void is so fundamentally flawed that the contract is prevented from being formed at all. The parties may have thought that they had formed a contract and, indeed, may have acted on it but the law deems it to be lacking a vital ingredient and so never a real contract at all. If this happens and the parties have already acted on the "contract" (eg bought and sold goods in exchange for money) then the law of unjustified enrichment can be used to "settle up" between the parties: goods and money will be returned where this is still possible. The return of money is called *repetition* and the return of goods is called *restitution*. If one party has benefited from the void contract in some other way then a payment called *recompense* can be made to cover the other party's loss. **5.17**

VOIDABLE

A voidable contract, unlike a void contract, is not so flawed as to actually prevent it from coming into existence. Instead, the flaw allows one party to challenge the contract which, if accepted by the other party or upheld in court, will result in the contract being set aside ("reduced"). The court will only set aside a contract if the parties can be restored to their pre-contract positions (*restitutio in integrum*) and the parties are not personally barred from seeking to have the contract set aside by having discovered the flaw but affirming the contract anyway. **5.18**

UNENFORCEABLE

An unenforceable contract is not void or voidable but the courts will not uphold it for another reason such as illegality. **5.19**

SUMMARY

Thus, in establishing that a contract has a flaw, it is necessary to know what the effect of that flaw is on the contract: does it render it void, voidable or unenforceable? A contract can be affected by (1) lack of consensus; (2) lack of consent to create legal obligations; (3) lack of capacity; (4) lack of formality; (5) illegality; (6) restrictions on the freedom of contract; and (7) other prejudicial circumstances. **5.20**

(1) LACK OF CONSENSUS

It is essential that both parties have *consensus in idem*; in other words, both are agreeing to the same thing. If they do not agree on the important aspects of the contract then this will prevent the contract from being properly formed at all and it will be void. **5.21**

The Scottish courts apply an objective test in deciding if the parties have consensus. An objective test is one which does not take into account what the parties themselves think but which applies a benchmark test to decide whether consensus has been reached. **5.22**

5.23   Lack of consensus (also known as "dissensus") is illustrated by the case of *Mathieson Gee (Ayshire) Ltd* v *Quigley*[25] in which Mathieson offered to supply plant equipment to clear a pond (ie an offer of hire) and Quigley accepted that by confirming his acceptance to an offer to clear the pond (ie accepting an offer to do something else). The court held that, notwithstanding what the parties themselves thought, there was no consensus and so no contract.

Error

5.24   A lack of consensus may arise out of a mistake or misrepresentation (error). In this case the parties or one of them has made a mistake about an important matter to do with the contract.

Unilateral error

5.25   The general rule is that a mistake made by one of the parties (unilateral error) does not affect the contract even if it is an essential error[26] unless it has been induced by something the other party has said or done (induced error)

Essential error

5.26   An essential error is one which goes to the heart or substantials of the contract and traditionally includes, but is not limited to, error as to subject-matter,[27] identity of the parties,[28] price,[29] quantity, quality or nature of the subject-matter of the contract and error as to the nature of the contract.[30]

Induced error

5.27   Inducement can take three forms: innocent misrepresentation; fraudulent misrepresentation; and negligent misrepresentation. The effect of misrepresentation may make the contract void or voidable. If the error is essential and amounts to lack of consensus then the contract will be void but if it is incidental then the contract will be voidable and so the contract will be reduced only if the criteria for reduction are met.

5.28   *Innocent misrepresentation* happens when one of the parties tells the other a fact about a material aspect of the contract (ie an important aspect of the contract but not necessarily falling into the category of essential error) which is wrong and that misleading information induces the other party to enter into the contract.

5.29   *Fraudulent misrepresentation* happens when the mistake is not made innocently but is made fraudulently; this can include information which the party putting forward knows to be wrong or which he puts forward recklessly.

---

[25] 1952 SC (HL) 38.

[26] This is certainly the case for onerous written contracts, following *Stewart* v *Kennedy* (1890) 17 R (HL) 25, but may not be the case in other contracts where the error leads to lack of consensus or in gratuitous contracts (*Hunter* v *Bradford Property Trust* 1970 SLT 173).

[27] *Raffles* v *Wichelhaus* (1864) 2 H & C 906.

[28] Note, however, that this will only be applicable in contracts where the identity of the parties is crucial, as in *Morrison* v *Robertson* 1908 SC 332; cf *MacLeod* v *Kerr* 1965 SC 253.

[29] *Wilson* v *Marquis of Breadalbane* (1859) 21 D 957.

[30] However, this is only likely to affect the contract if induced.

The difference between the two is shown in the two cases of *Boyd & Forrest* v *Glasgow* **5.30**
& South Western Railway Co[31] which arose out of the same situation. Boyd & Forrest
contracted with the railway company to do some work for a price based on figures
supplied by the railway company. Unfortunately, those figures were wrong because
they had been changed by an engineer (a genuine mistake). This meant that the actual
cost of the work carried out by Boyd & Forrest was hugely more expensive than the
agreed contract price. They claimed fraudulent misrepresentation (1912 action) and,
when no fraud was established, they argued innocent misrepresentation (1915 action)
but although this was proved, restitution was not possible because the route had been
dynamited and could not be restored to its previous state.

If reduction is not possible then there are no further remedies for innocent mis- **5.31**
representation but damages are available for fraudulent misrepresentation under delict.

Negligent misrepresentation can also affect a contract and, in this case, damages are **5.32**
available under s 10 of the Law Reform (Miscellaneous Provisions) (Scotland) Act 1985
which allows the innocent party to claim damages if he cannot have the contract
reduced and has suffered a loss (provided that he can show that the other party owed
him a duty of care).

Bilateral error

If both parties have made a mistake then this is called bilateral error; it can be either **5.33**
common or mutual. A common error is where both have made the same mistake and
mutual error occurs where they have reached different but wrong opinions on a matter
to do with the contract. If the error is essential and amounts to a lack of consensus then
the contract is void.

It should be noted that a clerical error in writing down a contract – an error of expres- **5.34**
sion – is not enough to amount to lack of consensus and a clerical error can be corrected by
application to the court under s 8 of the Law Reform (Miscellaneous Provisions) (Scotland)
Act 1985, provided that third parties are not prejudiced by the correction.

(2) LACK OF CONSENT

It is essential that the parties intend to create a binding legal obligation and so it is **5.35**
necessary to distinguish between social and domestic arrangements which are presumed not to include this consent and business arrangements which are presumed to
include consent to binding legal obligations.

If parties are negotiating a business deal and want to avoid certain pre-contractual **5.36**
negotiations becoming binding as contracts, they have to make it very clear that they do
not intend to be legally bound by such an agreement in order to rebut the presumption
that these "agreements" are contractual and therefore binding.[32]

If parties have reached this type of pre-contractual agreement and it is breached then the **5.37**
law becomes more complex. A breach of pre-contractual agreements cannot be dealt with
by contract law because there is no contract. This problem arose in *Dawson International
plc* v *Coats Paton plc*[33] in which it was held that if one party "breached" this type of

---

[31] 1912 SC (HL) 93 and 1915 SC (HL) 20.
[32] *Stobo Ltd* v *Morrisons (Gowns) Ltd* 1949 SC 184.
[33] 1988 SLT 854.

pre-contractual agreement then, as a matter of *equity*, the "innocent party" could claim back any money spent honouring the agreement if the one who pulled out had assured the "innocent party' that there *was* a contract (even although there was not).

5.38   Family arrangements are presumed not to have this element of consent to create legal obligations, as shown in the case of *Balfour* v *Balfour*,[34] and some other arrangements such as sporting and gaming contracts do not create enforceable legal obligations despite the intentions of the parties because they fall into the category of *sponsiones ludicrae*, a category of illegal contracts.[35] However, the courts have enforced a contract between friends in which one person had agreed to share her bingo winnings with another, in *Robertson* v *Anderson*.[36]

(3) LACK OF CAPACITY

5.39   Both parties to a contract must have the capacity (legal ability) to enter into that contract. A complete lack of capacity on the part of either party will render the contract void. There are different rules for different legal persons: children and young persons, the insane and businesses.

Children and young persons

5.40   The Age of Legal Capacity (Scotland) Act 1991 applies. The age at which full capacity is reached is now 16. Children below 16 years of age have no capacity as a general rule under s 1, although transactions commonly entered into by children are excluded from the no-capacity rule, provided they are concluded on reasonable terms under s 2. This will mean such things as buying sweets and comics in shops, travel on buses and trains and, as they get closer to 16, it will apply to contracts such as after-school work and holiday jobs and the purchase of more expensive items, such as computing or musical equipment.

5.41   Although full capacity is reached at 16, there are further protections for 16- and 17-year-olds. If a person aged 16 or 17 enters into a contract which is a "prejudicial transaction" as defined by s 3 of the 1991 Act then it may be set aside in certain circumstances. A transaction is prejudicial if it (a) is one which an adult, exercising reasonable prudence, would not have entered into in the circumstances of that young person and (b) has caused or is likely to cause substantial prejudice to the young person.

5.42   If a young person makes such a contract then he must apply to the court under s 3 to have it set aside. He has until the day before he reaches his 21st birthday to do this. There are three important restrictions in relation to contracts. A young person cannot apply to the court to have a prejudicial transaction set aside if:

> (1)   the transaction was made in the course of his business trade or profession (s 3(2)(f)); or
>
> (2)   he lied about his age and this fraudulent misrepresentation induced the other party into entering into the contract with him (s 3(2)(g)); or

---

[34] [1919] 2 KB 571.

[35] *Kelly* v *Murphy* 1940 SC 96 and *Ferguson* v *Littlewoods Pools Ltd* 1997 SLT 309. See below for a discussion of illegal contracts.

[36] 2003 SLT 235.

(3)   he ratified the contract after the age of 18 despite knowing his right to ask for
       it to be set aside (s 3(2)(h)).

Only the young person has the right to apply to the court; the other party to the **5.43**
transaction does not. The result of a successful application is that the contract is set aside
and the parties returned to their previous positions, subject to the general law relating to
voidable transactions.

   A third party worried about this can apply to court to have the contract ratified under **5.44**
s 3(3)(j) and the court will decide whether it is reasonable or not.

Adults with incapacity

Many adults suffer from mental health or mental disorder problems such as psychiatric **5.45**
problems and dementia. A number of adults are affected by learning difficulties. Under
the common law, an "insane" person has no contractual capacity, which can have
serious implications for managing his or her affairs.[37]

   The Adults with Incapacity (Scotland) Act 2000 provides a legal framework for
managing the affairs of incapax adults, primarily for financial and medical matters.

Intoxicated persons

The level of intoxication through alcohol or drugs or solvent abuse must be very high in **5.46**
order to result in a loss of capacity.[38]

Corporate bodies

The capacity of a corporate body will be determined by its constitution and any **5.47**
contract which is outwith its powers (*ultra vires*) will be void. However, this rule has
been significantly diluted for registered companies. A registered company is a legal
person in its own right, separate from the shareholders who own it and the directors
who run it. A company has full legal capacity and ss 35, 35A and 35B of the
Companies Act 1985 state that a company has full capacity regardless of any
restrictions contained in its memorandum. Furthermore, a contract made by the
board of directors outwith the company's powers cannot be challenged on grounds
of lack of capacity, provided that the third party is in good faith. The third party
may not have this protection if he knows that the company's power to agree is
restricted by its constitution but the mere fact of knowing this does not automatically mean that he is in bad faith.[39]

---

[37] Note that s 3(2) of the Sale of Goods Act 1979 provides that persons suffering from mental
incapacity must pay a reasonable price for necessaries if sold or delivered to him (necessaries are
defined in the Act as goods suitable to the condition in life of the person and to his actual
requirements at the time of sale and delivery).
[38] *Taylor* v *Provan* (1864) 2 M 1226. Section 3(2) of the Sale of Goods Act 1979 also applies for the
purchase of "necessaries" by the intoxicated.
[39] This is likely to be simplified further when the Company Law Reform Bill is passed and
brought into force. Under the Bill, the only contracts which will be voidable because of lack of
capacity will be those between the company and its directors or connected persons.

Partnerships

5.48 Partnerships (firms) have separate legal personality in Scotland (s 4(2) Partnership Act 1890) which means that the firm can sue and be sued. Contracts can also be entered into by the partners on behalf of the firm which bind the firm, provided that the partner(s) act within the confines of s 5 of the Partnership Act 1890 which sets out their authority.

Unincorporated bodies

5.49 Clubs and associations etc do not have contractual capacity and must contract through their office bearers.

(4) LACK OF FORMALITY

5.50 Most contracts do not have to be in writing but those which do are listed in the Requirements of Writing (Scotland) Act 1995. Section 1 lists, among other things, certain contracts and promises which must be in writing to be valid. These include contracts or unilateral obligations for the creation, transfer, variation or extinction of a real right in land except tenancies or rights to occupy land for less than one year under s 1(7) (unless these are rolling arrangements) and gratuitous unilateral obligations (ie promises) except those undertaken in the course of business. Thus, contracts for buying, selling and leasing property such as houses, farms, factories and offices must be in writing to be valid.

Formal writing

5.51 The writing required is formal writing: the contract must be subscribed by the parties which means that they must sign it at the end of the document. Electronic writing is not yet valid for these purposes.[40] The contract or promise can be made probative (self-proving in a court action) by attestation (ie by being witnessed) (s 3) or by endorsement with a court certificate (s 4). Only one witness is required and he or she must be 16 or over.

Curing lack of formality

5.52 If a contract which should be in writing is not but the parties act on it anyway then the 1995 Act makes provision to cure this problem under s 1(3) and (4) which allow the contract to stand if certain criteria are met. To cure a contract, the following questions need to be asked:

(a) Is the contract one of those listed in s 1(2) which therefore should be in writing?

(b) Has one party with a right under the contract done something (eg started ordering bricks for a new house to be built on the land to be bought under it)

---

[40] There is provision under s 8 of the Electronic Communications Act 2000 to allow Ministers to pass orders permitting electronic writing where a statute does not allow it and a draft order allowing dematerialised digital title deeds should be approved by Scottish Ministers during 2006. However, this draft order does not include contracts.

or not done something (eg not renewed the lease on his current rented home as he expects to move into the new house soon) in reliance on the contract?

(c)   Does the other party know about that?

(d)   Has the other party acquiesced (this could be a positive act of consent or he could acquiesce by seeing what is going on but not telling the other party to stop)?

(e)   Has the first party been affected to a material extent by what he has done/not done (usually, this means – "is he out of pocket?")?

(f)   Would he be affected to a material extent if the other party pulled out now?

If the answer to all of these questions is "yes", then the contract is cured under s 1(3) and (4) and is valid and the parties are personally barred from arguing that it is not. **5.53**

Notarial execution

People who cannot sign contracts because of blindness, paralysis or other difficulty can use the device of notarial execution to subscribe contracts under s 9 of the 1995 Act whereby a solicitor, JP or other party listed in the section reads the contract to that person who confirms that they have agreed to its terms and the solicitor then signs on their behalf. The separate matter of probativity is achieved by witnessing or court certificate as before. **5.54**

(5) ILLEGALITY

The general rule is that illegal contracts ("*pacta illicita*") are unenforceable. However, certain contracts which are illegal under *statute* may be void, voidable *or* unenforceable, depending on the wording of the statute. A contract can be illegal in whole or in part. **5.55**

There is a difference between contracts concluded for an illegal purpose and contracts which are performed illegally: **5.56**

Illegal purpose

If the contract is formed for an illegal purpose then it is unenforceable. This can arise in two situations. First, the illegal purpose may be clear from the contract itself. This was demonstrated in the case of *Barr* v *Crawford*[41] in which the contract was for a bribe to be paid by a pub landlady to members of the licensing board. Secondly, the contract may be for a legitimate purpose on the face of it but the parties know that it is really for an illegal purpose. This is shown in the case of *Pearce* v *Brooks*[42] in which a contract for the hire of a coach to a prostitute to allow her to ply her trade was held to be illegal. **5.57**

As the contract cannot be enforced, it cannot form the basis of any claim between the parties (*ex turpi causa non oritur actio*) and so if one party considers that the other has breached the contract, he cannot sue for breach of contract and the general rule is that the court will not "settle up" between the parties: loss lies where it falls (*ex turpi causa melior est conditio*). However, the court may allow a remedy to one party if it considers that the other party shares more of the blame than him, ie they are not *in pari delicto*. **5.58**

---

[41]   1983 SLT 481.
[42]   (1866) LR 1 Ex 213.

Illegal performance

5.59   Alternatively, the contract may be concluded for a legitimate purpose but one or both of the parties may perform it in a way which breaches a particular law. This occurred in the case of *Dowling & Rutter* v *Abacus Frozen Foods Ltd (No 2)*[43] in which two parties had a contract whereby one, the employment agency Dowling & Rutter, supplied labour to the other, Abacus. That is not an illegal contract in itself. However, Dowling & Rutter supplied illegal immigrants to do the work. The way in which this contract was performed therefore breached immigration legislation. However, Dowling & Rutter did not know that the workers were illegal immigrants and the court held that it was entitled to be flexible in the way in which it decided how this form of illegality would affect the contract and the parties. It decided that an equitable remedy would be to allow the party which had performed the contract illegally – Dowling & Rutter – to recover their fees for the supply of labour. This case would probably have been decided differently had Dowling & Rutter known about their breach of legislation. The important point to note is that illegal performance of a contract does not *automatically* render it unenforceable.

Common law illegality

5.60   Common law does not allow contracts which are contrary to public policy to be enforced. The following categories have all been established as being illegal at common law: criminal contracts; contracts which promote sexual immorality; contracts which interfere with the court system (such as bribing witnesses) or which try to bar one party from seeking legitimate redress through the courts; and gaming contracts.

5.61   A very important category of illegal contracts is restrictive covenants which are also known as restraints of trade. These are commonly used in employment contracts, contracts for the sale and purchase of businesses and solus agreements.

Employment contracts

5.62   These clauses are put into contracts of employment by employers to try to prevent the employee from working within a certain geographical area or with a competitor of the employer for a designated period of time after the employee leaves the service of the employer. The presumption is that these clauses are unenforceable *unless* three criteria are met by the restriction. The criteria are re-stated in *Bridge* v *Deacons*:[44] the restriction must protect the legitimate business interests of the employer; it must be reasonable; and it must be in the public interest.

5.63   If an employee does breach the restrictions placed on him in the contract then the employer can go to court and ask for a court order called an interdict which will prohibit the employee from continuing to work for the rival business. The court will take the following matters into account when deciding whether to enforce the restrictive covenant and grant an interdict.

---

[43] 2002 SLT 491.
[44] [1984] AC 705.

Legitimate business interests. In the case of *Bluebell Apparel Ltd* v *Dickinson*,[45] Bluebell **5.64** manufactured Wrangler jeans and Dickinson, their employee, knew Bluebell's trade secrets and was a manager with them. He left them and went to work for Levi's, a competitor. Bluebell was entitled to protect trade secrets to which Dickinson had been privy during the course of employment with them. The court upheld a restrictive covenant which prohibited him from disclosing the trade secrets to any unauthorised person and from working for any competitor for 2 years after leaving Bluebell's employment. The court will consider the position held by the employee (eg the more senior the employee and the greater access he has to confidential information, the more likely the court is to enforce the restrictive covenant).

Restrictions in geographical area and time limits. The court will look at the location of **5.65** the business and consider whether the geographical limit is reasonable. A business located in a sparsely populated rural area is more likely to get away with stating a larger radius within which the employee should not work than one located in a busy city centre. The cases which demonstrate this are:

Stewart v *Stewart*[46] – a work ban as a photographer within a 20-mile exclusion zone **5.66** around Elgin was reasonable.

Dallas, McMillan & Sinclair v *Simpson*[47] – a restriction prohibiting a former partner in a **5.67** firm from working for 3 years within a 20-mile radius of Glasgow Cross was not reasonable even although the clause actually stated that it was agreed by all of the parties that both the time limit and the geographical limit were reasonable.

The court will look at the type of business and decide if it merits a long ban on **5.68** working for a rival or not. Fast-moving industries prone to technological change and fast-moving markets are unlikely to get away with longer time bans.

Severability. If a contract contains some restrictions which are reasonable and some **5.69** which are not, is the entire restrictive covenant unenforceable? It will depend on whether the different elements are severable, ie capable of being separated out from the others and applied separately. This is an issue of how the clauses are drafted and the court will not redraft the clause but will delete unenforceable parts, leaving any reasonable parts which can stand alone.[48] This has led to the standard practice of drafting restrictive covenants which have different elements in them as separate clauses for each restriction rather than lumping them together in one clause.

Sale and purchase of business

The purchaser of a business will not want the seller to set up a new rival business **5.70** nearby. The purchaser of a business wants to protect the goodwill of the business which he or she has bought and will often want to include a restrictive covenant in the contract for the purchase and sale of the business. The same criteria apply in deciding enforceability as they do to employer – employee contracts but the courts are more likely to enforce such business-to-business contracts because of the greater equality in bargaining

---

[45] 1978 SC 16.
[46] (1899) 1 F 1158.
[47] 1989 SLT 454.
[48] *Mulvein* v *Murray* 1908 SC 528.

position and the fact that legitimate business interest in enforcing the clause will be easier to prove.

5.71   The following two cases illustrate how the courts have treated these clauses:

5.72   *Nordenfelt* v *Maxim Nordenfelt Guns and Ammunition Co Ltd*[49] – a worldwide ban on operating in international arms dealing for 25 years was reasonable because of the specialised nature of the business and the fact that purchasers of guns and ammunition were sovereign states and therefore limited in number.

5.73   *Dumbarton Steamboat Co Ltd* v *Macfarlane*[50] – a 10-year UK-wide ban on operating a carrier's business was not reasonable because the business which had been sold had only operated on the west coast of Scotland and not throughout the UK. There were therefore no UK-wide interests to protect.

Solus agreements

5.74   Solus agreements are made between a wholesaler/distributor and a retailer who agrees to stock only that wholesaler/distributor's brand (usually in return for discounts). A solus agreement may or may not be included in another contract between the parties (the most common being if the wholesaler leases the business premises to the retailer too). These can be enforced if reasonable. In the case of *Esso Petroleum Co Ltd* v *Harper's Garages (Stourport) Ltd*[51] a 21-year-long solus agreement was held to be unenforceable. The Competition Act 1998 also prohibits price fixing and cartels.

(6) RESTRICTIONS ON THE FREEDOM OF CONTRACT

5.75   As the category of illegal contracts shows, there are restrictions on what parties can contract to do. Further restrictions on the freedom to agree terms include restrictions on the use of exclusion clauses and restriction on the use of "unfair terms".

Exclusion clauses

5.76   An *exclusion* clause is an attempt to exclude an obligation for breach of contract or for negligence. A *limitation* clause attempts to limit liability for such a breach. These will be looked at very carefully by the courts. Such a clause will be applied *contra proferens* (against the party trying to rely on that clause) to avoid his trying to escape paying out for those breaches if it is at all ambiguous.[52] Many of these clauses are now subject to the statutory controls of the Unfair Contract Terms Act 1977 and the Unfair Terms in Consumer Contracts Regulations 1999.

5.77   The Unfair Contract Terms Act 1977 ("UCTA") applies to a wide range of contracts but not to all contracts nor to all exclusion clauses. It does apply to sale of goods contracts, contracts for services, employment contracts and contracts which allow others to enter land. It does not apply to insurance contracts, contracts for formation of

[49] [1894] AC 535.
[50] (1899) 1 F 993.
[51] [1968] AC 269.
[52] *W & S Pollock* v *Macrae* 1922 SC (HL) 192 and *Smith* v *UMB Chrysler and South Wales Switchgear Ltd* 1978 SLT 21.

companies and partnerships nor to contracts for real rights in land (eg buying or selling land). It also applies to non-contractual notices.

UCTA does a number of things: **5.78**

(1) it renders clauses which limit/exclude liability for death or personal injury arising out of breach of duty void;

(2) it allows clauses which limit/exclude liability for other losses arising out of breach of duty *if* they are fair and reasonable;

(3) it allows clauses in standard form or consumer contracts which limit/exclude liability for breach of contract *if* they are fair and reasonable;

(4) it allows indemnity clauses (a clause allowing one party to recover monies paid out by him from another party) in consumer contracts *if* fair and reasonable and;

(5) it prohibits sellers of goods from excluding certain implied terms found in the Sale of Goods Act 1979 in contracts with consumers and only allows such exclusions in other contracts *if* fair and reasonable.

Breach of duty

Section 16(1) UCTA states that: **5.79**

"where a term of a contract or a provision of a notice given to persons generally or to particular persons purports to exclude or restrict liability for breach of duty arising in the course of any business or from occupation of any premises used for business purposes of the occupier, that term or provision –
(a) shall be void in any case where such exclusion or restriction is in respect of death or personal injury:
(b) shall, in any other case [eg in respect of financial loss], have no effect if it was not fair and reasonable to incorporate the term in the contract [or to put it in the notice]."

Breach of duty is defined in s 25 as a breach: **5.80**

"(a) of any obligation, arising from the express or implied terms of a contract, to take reasonable care or exercise reasonable skill in the performance of the contract;
(b) of any common law duty to take reasonable care or exercise reasonable skill (but not any stricter duty);
(c) of the duty of reasonable care imposed by section 2(1) of the Occupier's Liability (Scotland) Act 1960."

It will therefore include negligence claims. **5.81**

The definition of what is fair and reasonable for exclusion clauses which try to avoid financial loss is set out in s 24: **5.82**

"regard shall be had only to the circumstances which were, or ought reasonably to have been, known to or in the contemplation of the parties to the contract at the time the contract was made" and in respect of a non-contractual notice "regard shall be had to all the circumstances obtaining when the liability arose."

Limitation clauses

5.83   Section 24(3) also sets out a reasonableness test for clauses which do not exclude liability but which try to limit liability by capping it at a certain level (eg "we accept liability up to £300"). In this type of contract/notice, the reasonableness test allows the following to be taken into consideration in determining if that amount is "fair and reasonable": (a) the resources which the party seeking to rely on that term could expect to be available to him for the purpose of meeting the liability should it arise; and (b) how far it was open to that party to cover himself by insurance. Section 24(4) places the onus of proving that the term/provision is fair and reasonable on the party trying to rely on the exclusion or limitation.

Breach of consumer or standard form contracts

5.84   Section 17 deals with this type of exclusion or limitation clause which attempts to exclude or limit liability for breach of *contract* (rather than the other breaches of duty covered by s 16). Breach of contract is dealt with below. Generally, if one party fails to perform his part of the contract, or performs it badly, then he is in breach of that contract and certain remedies can be taken against him, which can include having to pay damages to the other party. However, one party may try to exclude or limit liability for breach of contract by stipulating in the contract that an obligation which would otherwise be imposed on him is excluded or limiting liability for breach or non-performance in some way. In the case of consumer contracts or standard form contracts then s 17 states that such exclusions or limitations must be fair and reasonable.

5.85   "Consumer contract" is defined in s 25 as a contract in which:

> "(a) one party to the contract deals, and the other party to the contract ('the consumer') does not deal or hold himself out as dealing, in the course of a business, and (b) in the case of a contract such as is mentioned in s 15(2)(a) of this Act [ie of sale of goods or supply of goods], the goods are of a type ordinarily supplied for private use or consumption".

5.86   "Standard form contract" is not defined in UCTA. However, it can include a contract which is one which is not individually negotiated between the parties but which has most of its terms pre-printed with some details such as price and names left blank to be completed by the parties before signature. The case of *McCrone v Boots Farm Sales Ltd*[54] found that conditions of sale could be covered as a standard form contract under s 17.

Unfair terms

5.87   The Unfair Terms in Consumer Contracts Regulations 1999 (SI 1999/2083) also apply to exclusion clauses but have a much wider application than that. Unlike

---

[53] 1981 SLT 103.

UCTA, these Regulations apply only to consumer contracts where the seller deals in the course of business and the consumer is a natural person acting outwith his usual trade or profession. Under the Regulations, a contractual term which has not been individually negotiated shall be regarded as unfair if, contrary to the requirement of good faith, it causes significant imbalance in the parties' rights and obligations arising under the contract, to the detriment of the consumer. This means that if a business puts a term into such a contract which is one-sided and favours the business while prejudicing the consumer then it may be considered unfair under the Regulations.

If a contractual term is deemed to be unfair by the Regulations then it is not binding **5.88** on the consumer under reg 8 but the rest of the contract will stand if it can continue in existence without that offending term.

Some exclusion and limitation clauses are included in a list of terms which are **5.89** considered as unfair. However, the Regulations are much broader than UCTA in scope and deem a much wider range of terms to be unfair, including, for example, any term enabling the seller or supplier to alter the terms of the contract unilaterally without a valid reason which is specified in the contract. Anyone involved in drafting standard trading terms and conditions for businesses which deal with consumers must therefore take these Regulations into account.

(7) OTHER PREJUDICIAL CIRCUMSTANCES

There are other circumstances surrounding the formation of a contract which taint it. **5.90** These are to do with the way in which one of the parties behaved in order to get the other to enter into the contract. These circumstances may render the contract void or voidable. The circumstances include:

Facility and circumvention (voidable)

Vulnerable people may retain capacity but be termed "facile" in law and be taken **5.91** advantage of ("circumvention") by the other party in the contract, as in the case of *MacGilvary* v *Gilmartin*[55] in which a recently widowed mother was taken advantage of by her daughter to sign over the title deeds on a house. The court set aside the transfer.

Undue influence (voidable)

Similarly, a person can abuse their own position of trust, as in a case where a parent **5.92** influences a child to make a decision which is not in his or her interest[56] or in cases of professional advisers who abuse their positions of trust to their own advantage. Such contracts are voidable. This happened in a case in which a professional art adviser built up a relationship of trust with his client, only to use that to have her bequeath four valuable paintings to him in her will.[57]

---

[54] 1986 SLT 89.
[55] *Gray* v *Binny* (1879) 7 R 332.
[56] *Honeyman's Executors* v *Sharp* 1978 SC 223.

Force and fear (void)

5.93   Consensus cannot exist where one party is threatened with or actually assaulted into agreeing to a contract. This is vividly demonstrated in the case of *Earl of Orkney* v *Vinfra*[57] in which the Earl held a knife to his victim in order to convince him to sign over some property to him. This amounted to a lack of consent and the contract was void.

5.94   More subtle measures such as economic pressure have been discussed in the courts[58] and it has been held that as long as no unlawful means are used to back up such financial pressure then it is acceptable. Of course, one would need to look at the relationship between the parties to establish whether such pressure amounted to circumvention or undue influence.

BREACH OF CONTRACT

5.95   Once the parties have formed their contract, each will expect the other to perform his part of it. However, breach of contract arises where one party refuses to perform (repudiation/anticipatory breach), fails to perform (without actually refusing to do so) or performs his part of it but does so defectively. In those circumstances, the party who is not in breach, the innocent party, needs to consider what remedies are available to him. It should be noted that he cannot claim a remedy if he is also in breach, because of the principle of mutuality of contract.[59] The remedies available for breach of contract are: contractual remedies, damages, action for payment, action for specific implement, action for interdict, rescission, retention and lien. There are also specific remedies and actions which can be taken under the Sale of Goods Act 1979 for breaches of sale of goods contracts. Some remedies have to be sought in the courts but others can be taken without court action.

ANTICIPATORY BREACH

5.96   In the case of anticipatory breach, which occurs when the party in breach issues a refusal to perform his obligations *before* the due date for performance, then there are additional choices for the innocent party to make. He has to decide whether to accept the refusal to perform when it is issued. If he does accept the refusal then the contract is repudiated.[60] The innocent party no longer has to fulfil his obligations under the contract and can sue the party in breach for damages for loss arising out of the breach. Alternatively, the innocent party can wait to see if the party in breach is bluffing and will actually perform the contract on the due date and, indeed, he can go ahead and perform his own obligations under it at the proper time, regardless of what the party in breach does.[61] He can ask the court to compel the party in breach to carry out his obligations, using the action of payment, specific implement or interdict as appropriate.

---

[57] (1606) Mor 1648.
[58] *Allen* v *Flood* [1898] AC 1.
[59] *Graham* v *United Turkey Red Co* 1922 SC 533.
[60] W McBryde, *The Law of Contract in Scotland* (2nd edn, 2001, W Green), paras 20–30.
[61] *White and Carter (Councils) Ltd* v *McGregor* 1962 SC (HL) 1.

REMEDIES

The remedies are: **5.97**

Contractual remedies

The contract may contain an interest clause for late payment or a liquidated damages clause which sets an agreed level of damages to paid out for breach of contract without having to resort to court action.[62] The contract should also be checked for any enforceable contractual restrictions on remedies such as an exclusion clause or a limitation clause.

Damages

A claim for damages from the party in breach can be raised in court by the innocent party if   **5.98**
he does not want to insist on performance of the contract but wants monetary compensation for losses arising out of the breach of contract instead. The amount of damages which will be awarded by the court is strictly limited. The loss claimed for must be caused by the breach[63] and must not be too remote. A claim will be too remote if the claim does not fall into the category of general damages or special damages, the tests for which are set out in the important case of *Hadley* v *Baxendale*[64] and discussed in more detail in *Victoria Laundry (Windsor) Ltd* v *Newman Industries*.[65] General damages are those which arise naturally in the ordinary course of things and therefore include matters which the parties are imputed (implied) to know. Special damages are those which should have been in the reasonable contemplation of the parties at the time the contract was concluded and include matters which the parties actually knew about. Thus, in *Hadley* v *Baxendale*, profits lost when a broken mill crank shaft was not replaced quickly enough were not found to be general damages because, in the ordinary course of things, mills carried spare parts and so, in the ordinary course of things, production should not have stopped. They did not fall under special damages because the party in breach had not been told that the crank shaft was needed urgently. In *Victoria Laundry*, there were two losses arising out of the failure to deliver a new boiler on time: anticipated profits from new business which the new boiler could have serviced, and large government contracts. The court held that the lost profits had arisen in the ordinary cause of things and so were recoverable. However, the government contracts did not fall into this category. The court had to decide whether these fell into the category of special damages but as the party in breach did not know about them when the contract was concluded, they did not meet the test for special damages and so could not be recovered. In the case of *Balfour Beatty (Construction) Ltd* v *Scottish Power plc*,[66] the court had to decide how much one business could be expected to know about another as this would determine what fell into the category of "ordinary course of things" and what would require special knowledge of the circumstances. It was held that "It must

---

[62] Note that these will only be enforced if a fair assessment of likely losses arising from breach. Punitive clauses are not enforceable: *Dingwall* v *Burnett* 1912 SC 1097.
[63] *A/B Karlshamns Oljefabriker* v *Monarch Steamship Co Ltd* 1949 SC (HL) 1.
[64] (1854) 9 Exch 341.
[65] [1949] 2 KB 528.
[66] 1994 SC (HL) 20.

always be a question of circumstances what one contracting party is presumed to know about the business activities of the other. No doubt, the simpler the activity of the one, the more readily can it be inferred that the other would have reasonable knowledge thereof".[67]

5.99 Quantification of damages may be difficult in some cases. While financial or patrimonial loss may be relatively easy to work out where there is a loss of profits, some breaches may lead to other losses which are not as easy to calculate. For example, if a builder performs a contract to build a house but does not do it properly, then remedial work may be needed to put it right. In this sort of case, the measure of damages will be based either on the cost of putting it right or on the difference in value between the house as it should be if built properly and the actual valuation.[68] In contracts for entertainment or enjoyment such as holiday contracts, there may be no financial loss as a result of the breach of contract but the innocent party has suffered disappointment or inconvenience. In limited circumstances, the courts will award damages for this non-patrimonial loss.[69]

Action for payment

5.100 If the breach is a failure to pay a bill or invoice due under the contract, the innocent party can raise a court action to recover payment of this debt.

Action for specific implement

5.101 If the breach is a failure to do something other than pay money, then the innocent party can raise a court action for specific implement which is a court order compelling the party in breach to carry out his obligations under the contract. It is not available for payment of money nor for contracts which have a strong personal element such as employment or partnership contracts. The court will also consider whether compliance is likely to be very difficult and may refuse to grant it if that is the case. Breach of an order for specific implement is contempt of court and can carry a prison sentence of up to six months under the Law Reform (Miscellaneous Provisions) (Scotland) Act 1940.

Action for interdict

5.102 In this case, the innocent party is seeking a court order to prevent or stop the party in breach from doing something.

Rescission

5.103 If – and only if – the breach is material, then the innocent party can terminate the contract by rescission. This remedy is non-court based and allows the innocent party to walk away from the contract without penalty. He can still claim damages in court from the party in breach if there are any losses. However, the case of *Wade* v *Waldon*[70] shows that this remedy comes with a risk. If the breach is not in fact material, then the innocent

---

[67] Lord Jauncey of Tullichettle at 810F.
[68] However, the court will consider proportionality in making this decision: *McLaren Murdoch & Hamilton Ltd* v *Abercromby Motor Group Ltd* 2002 GWD 38–1242.
[69] *Diesen* v *Samson* 1971 SLT (Sh Ct) 49; *Farley* v *Skinner* [2002] 2 AC 732.
[70] 1909 SC 571.

party cannot rescind the contract and, by doing so, he becomes the party in breach and is open to action being taken against him.

Retention

This non-court based remedy allows the innocent party to retain payment or withhold performance under the contract until the breach is remedied.   **5.104**

Lien

An innocent party can retain property of the party in breach which he has in his **5.105** possession until the breach is remedied. This is a non-court based remedy and will be particularly useful for businesses which repair goods which can be retained until the repair bill is paid.

 In deciding which remedy to seek, the innocent party needs to identify the breach and **5.106** then choose the appropriate remedy.

TERMINATION OF CONTRACT AND OBLIGATIONS

A contract (or the obligations under it) will terminate in certain circumstances: **5.107**

ACCEPTILATION

The innocent party accepts the breach and treats the contract as terminated.   **5.108**

CONFUSION

The debtor and creditor under the same obligation become one and the same person.   **5.109**

COMPENSATION

If the parties owe each other money, then one debt can be used to cancel out or reduce **5.110** the other. Thus, if X owes Y £50 and Y owes X £20, then X can pay £30 to Y rather than pay the full £50 and try to recover the outstanding £20 from Y.

FRUSTRATION

There are certain situations in which the law recognises that a contract cannot be **5.111** performed and, in those narrow cases, frees the parties from further performance: the contract itself is not terminated but the need to perform it is. This can happen if there is supervening impossibility, supervening illegality or a supervening change in circumstances between the date the contract is made and the date of performance.

Supervening impossibility

Supervening impossibility can occur if the subject-matter of the contract is destroyed **5.112** (*rei interitus*). This may be actual or constructive destruction. Actual destruction occurred in *Taylor* v *Caldwell*[71] in which a music hall which had been hired for a particular date burned down before then. The court held that this frustrated the contract. Constructive destruction is demonstrated in *Mackeson* v *Boyd*,[72] in which a large house was to be let out under a contract. Unfortunately, war broke out and it was requisitioned for use by the authorities and so not available for use by the tenants.

Supervening illegality

5.113 The law may be changed during the period between the date the contract is made and the due date for performance which makes it illegal. This would happen if war was declared and the contracting parties belonged to enemy states, as in the case of *Fraser & Co Ltd* v *Denny, Mott & Dickson Ltd*.[73]

Supervening change in circumstances

5.114 A contract may still be frustrated even if it is not impossible or illegal to perform but events take a turn which means that the nature of the contract is changed and it becomes something different from that contemplated by the parties when they made the contract. However, that would not extend to something simply becoming less profitable than hoped for. The application of this type of frustration is demonstrated in the case of *Krell* v *Henry*:[74] Henry hired a flat in Pall Mall from Krell for two days. It was not stated in the contract that the purpose of the hire was to view the Coronation procession of Edward VII, but the letting was for the two days for which the Coronation was scheduled. The Coronation was postponed because of the King's illness, and Henry tried to cancel his contract with Krell who refused and sued him for the rent. The court held that the contract was for licence to use rooms for a particular purpose (implied condition since it was not express in the contract), and since the Coronation was postponed, the contract was frustrated. This decision was based on the court's findings that the whole point of the contract and the reason that it had been entered into by both of the parties was for the purpose of watching the Coronation. However, this case has been treated with reserve in later cases and so this type of frustration is very narrow.

5.115 What if the parties have already carried out some of their obligations before the contract is frustrated and monies have been paid over in anticipation of the contract being performed? If that has happened then the law of unjustified enrichment may be used to "settle up" between the parties.[75]

NOVATION

5.116 One contract will be terminated if the parties to it decide to replace it with a new agreement.

---

[71] (1863) 122 ER 309.
[72] 1942 SC 56.
[73] 1944 SC (HL) 35.
[74] [1903] 2 KB 740.
[75] *Cantiere San Rocco* v *Clyde Shipbuilding Co* 1923 SC (HL) 105.

PRESCRIPTION (PRESCRIPTION AND LIMITATION (SCOTLAND) ACT 1973)

What happens if a long period of time passes after the contract is concluded without any action being taken to perform or enforce it? Does it last forever? The answer is "no" – the Prescription and Limitation (Scotland) Act 1973 places a time limit on how long certain obligations can last if no action is taken on them for a specified period of time. The relevant time period for contracts (unless specifically excluded under the Act) is called the short negative prescription and lasts for 5 years. The effect of prescription means that if a contract is not subject to a "relevant claim" or "relevant acknowledgement" within that five-year period, the obligations under it are extinguished. **5.117**

A relevant claim would include one party trying to enforce the contract and a relevant acknowledgement would include one party actually performing his obligations or writing to the other party making it clear that the obligations were still "live". **5.118**

The excepted contracts are: **5.119**

    (i)   contracts contained or evidenced in a probative writ (except guarantees or those which contain an obligation to pay a periodical sum of money such as rent);

    (ii)   partnership and agency contracts;

    (iii)   contracts relating to land (except those requiring a periodical sum of money);

    (iv)   imprescriptible obligations (this includes real rights of ownership in land and the right to challenge a contract on the grounds of invalidity *ex facie* or forgery).

ESSENTIAL FACTS

INTRODUCTION

5.120

- A contract is a voluntary obligation arising out of an agreement between two parties which creates legal obligations between them.
- A promise is a gratuitous unilateral obligation (not requiring the promisee's consent) which can only be enforced by the promisee against the promisor.

FORMATION

- A contract is formed when an offer is met with an acceptance.
- An offer must be capable of acceptance, it must be communicated in clear terms and it must include the intention to be legally bound. Offers do not include: invitations to treat, requests for quotations, tenders and willingness to negotiate.
- Offers lapse if not accepted on time (time limit/reasonable period of time) or if met with a counter-offer. Offers can be revoked at any time before acceptance, unless a time period has been set for acceptance
- An acceptance cannot be revoked/cancelled as it concludes the contract. The postal rule applies to contracts made by post: a contract is concluded as soon as the acceptance is posted. Once concluded, it cannot be

cancelled unless the parties agree or it is a regulated contract such as certain consumer credit contracts.
- Written contracts are subject to the Contract (Scotland) Act 1997 which presumes that the written contract contains all contractual terms.
- The rules of incorporation apply to all contracts: contractual terms must be incorporated into the contract when the contract is made and not afterwards.

PROBLEMS WITH CONTRACTS

- A contract which appears to have been formed by offer and acceptance may have have a flaw which renders it void, voidable or unenforceable.
- Void: so fundamentally flawed that it does not amount to a contract at all. Voidable: less flawed but can be challenged by one of the parties and set aside by a court. An unenforceable contract such as an illegal contract is neither void nor voidable but will not be enforced by the courts.
- The main problems which can affect contracts are as follows:

(1) Lack of consensus
- The parties must have consensus (agreement). Lack of consensus may be caused by error if it goes right to the heart of the contract (NB: that is not an *automatic* consequence of essential error).
- Uninduced error: the general rule is that an uninduced unilateral error will not affect the contract. Induced error includes innocent misrepresentation, fraudulent misrepresentation and negligent misrepresentation.
- Bilateral error: an error made by both parties will render the contract void if essential.

(2) Lack of consent
- The parties must intend to create legal obligations. This is not usually found in social, domestic and trivial arrangements such as gaming contracts. See also illegal contracts.

(3) Lack of capacity
- Both parties must have the capacity or legal ability to enter into the contract.
- The capacity of certain groups of persons is restricted in law as follows:
  - *Children and young persons*: capacity is governed by the Age of Legal Capacity (Scotland) Act 1991. Generally, children under 16 have no contractual capacity and young persons aged 16 and over have full capacity. Exceptions: (1) under 16s can enter into contracts of a type normal for their age on reasonable terms; and (2) young persons can apply to the court to have any "prejudicial transaction" made at the ages of 16 or 17 set aside.
  - Insane adults have no capacity at common law.
  - Intoxicated persons: a person has to be very drunk or high on drugs to lose capacity.

- Registered companies have capacity to contract. This will only be limited if its constitution limits what the directors of the company can do and the third party with whom they are dealing is in bad faith.
- Partnerships: firms have capacity.
- Unincorporated bodies: no capacity.

(4) Lack of formality
- Contracts which must be in writing to be valid are listed in the Requirements of Writing (Scotland) Act 1995. These are contracts relating to creation, transfer, variation or extinction of an interest in land (eg buying a house). Promises (except if given in the course of business) must also be in writing.
- A lack of formality can be cured if the circumstances of ss 1(3) and (4) apply.
- If writing is required then it must be written (not electronic) and subscribed under s 2 of the 1995 Act. A contract can be made probative (self-proving) by attestation (witnessing) under s 3 of the 1995 Act or by being endorsed with a court certificate under s 4 of the 1995 Act.
- Notarial execution is permitted under s 9 of the 1995 Act.

(5) Illegality
- A contract formed for an illegal purpose is unenforceable. A contract may also be unenforceable if it is to be performed in an illegal way.
- Contracts illegal at common law include those contrary to public policy (eg criminal/ sexual morality/ interfering with justice/restrictive covenants).
- Restrictive covenants are found in employment contracts, sale and purchase of business contracts and solus agreements and are unenforceable unless they protect legitimate business interests of the party seeking to enforce the covenant, are reasonable (court will consider geographical limits, time limits, trade secrets etc) and in the public interest.

(6) Restrictions on freedom to contract
- These include common law on exclusion clauses, Unfair Contract Terms Act 1977 and Unfair Terms in Consumer Contracts Regulations 1999.
- Common law and exclusion clauses: courts not keen to enforce attempts to contract to exclude obligations or restrict liability. Such clauses are construed *contra proferens* (against the party seeking to rely on it).
- Unfair Contract Terms Act 1977 (UCTA): applies to many (but not all) contracts. It does five things: (a) it renders clauses which limit/exclude liability for death or personal injury arising out of breach of duty void; (b) it allows clauses which limit/exclude liability for other losses arising out of breach of duty if they are fair and reasonable; (c) it allows clauses in standard form or consumer contracts which limit/exclude liability for breach of contract if they are fair and reasonable; (d) it allows indemnity clauses in consumer contracts if fair and reasonable; and (e) it prohibits sellers of goods from excluding certain implied terms found in the Sale of Goods Act 1979 in contracts with consumers and only allows such exclusions in other contracts if fair and reasonable.

- Unfair Terms in Consumer Contracts Regulations 1999: these apply to certain consumer contracts (if consumer a natural person). Terms deemed unfair (those which are too pro-business and anti-consumer) are not enforceable against the consumer.

(7) Other prejudicial circumstances
- Facility and circumvention (voidable): taking advantage of vulnerable person may render contract voidable.
- Undue influence (voidable): similar but different – position of trust is abused.
- Force and fear: effect depends on level of and nature of methods used. Physical force = void through lack of consensus. Economic pressure = OK unless unlawful means used (eg blackmail).

BREACH OF CONTRACT

- A breach of contract is a failure to perform the contract in whole or in part. This allows the innocent party to take certain action against the party in breach.
- There are three main types of breach: repudiation/anticipatory breach; late (or non-) performance; and defective performance.
- Remedies fall into the following categories: contractual remedies (interest clauses and liquidate damages clauses); damages (raise court action for monetary compensation); action for payment (raise court action to obtain order to get outstanding bill paid); action for specific implement (raise court action to obtain court order telling party in breach to fulfil the contract); action for interdict (raise court action to obtain court order telling party in breach to stop doing something); rescission (self-help remedy – innocent party's right to terminate the contract); retention (self-help remedy – withhold performance until breach remedied); and lien (self-help remedy – keep goods belonging to party in breach until breach remedied). There are for remedies available under sale of goods contracts.
- Damages: most widely available remedy. Must show that the breach has caused the damages claimed for (causation) and that the loss is not too remote (general and special damages).

TERMINATION OF CONTRACT AND OBLIGATIONS

- Contracts can be terminated by acceptilation, confusion, compensation, novation and prescription. The parties may also be freed from their obligations if the contract is frustrated.
- Frustration happens when there is supervening impossibility: destruction of the subject-matter; supervening illegality; or a supervening change in the circumstances.
- Prescription is regulated by the Prescription and Limitation (Scotland) Act 1973.

ESSENTIAL CASES

INTRODUCTION

Morton's Trustees v *Aged Christian Friend Society of Scotland* (1899): gratuitous contract;

Littlejohn v *Hadwen* (1882): promise in business (keeping an offer open);

Stone v *MacDonald* (1979): promise in business (option granted over land in favour of another).

FORMATION

Thornton v *Shoe Lane Parking Ltd* (1971): offer and acceptance by action (slot machine);

Fisher v *Bell* (1961): flick-knife case – shop window display is invitation to treat;

Pharmaceutical Society of GB v *Boots* (1953): medicines case – display did not amount to offer;

Carlill v *Carbolic Smoke Ball Co* (1893): an advert by a company was an offer. The customer accepted by action;

Jaeger Bros Ltd v *J & A McMorland* (1902): a detailed quotation can amount to offer;

Harvey v *Facey* (1893): expressing willingness to negotiate is not an offer;

Littlejohn v *Hadwen* (1882): offer cannot be revoked during period specified for acceptance;

Wylie & Lochhead v *McElroy & Sons* (1873): offer lapses if not accepted within a reasonable period of time;

Wolf & Wolf v *Forfar Potato Co Ltd* (1984): counter-offer causes original offer to lapse;

Dunlop, Wilson & Co. v *Higgins and Son* (1848): established postal rule;

Mason v *Benhar* (1882): not a firm decision but indicates that Scots courts would treat acceptance lost in the post as not concluding the contract;

Jacobsen, Sons & Co v *Underwood & Son Ltd* (1894): postal rule – incorrectly addressed letter still concluded contract;

Countess of Dunmore v *Alexander* (1830): controversial postal rule case;

Williamson v *North of Scotland and Orkney Steam Navigation Co* (1916): tiny print can prevent incorporation of terms;

Parker v *South Eastern Railway Co* (1877): "see back" printed on front of ticket incorporated those terms into the contract;

Taylor v *Glasgow Corporation* (1952): receipt for baths could not contain contractual terms;

Olley v *Marlborough Court Ltd* (1949): post-contractual notice in bedroom case.

PROBLEMS WITH CONTRACTS

(1) Lack of consensus

Mathieson Gee (Ayrshire) Ltd v *Quigley* (1952): parties agreed to different things. No consensus so no contract;

Stewart v *Kennedy* (1890): an essential error, provided it is not induced by the other party, does not invalidate a written onerous contract;

Hunter v *Bradford Property Trust* (1970): errors in gratuitous contracts are more likely to adversely affect the contract;

Boyd & Forrest v *Glasgow & South Western Railway Co* (1912, 1915): a genuine mistake in figures = innocent misrepresentation;

Raffles v *Wichelhaus* (1864): each party had a different ship in mind when forming contract to transport cargo – contract void through lack of consensus;

Morrison v *Robertson* (1908): error about the identity of the other party: contract void. Contrast with *McLeod* v *Kerr* (1965);

Macleod v *Kerr* (1965): the error was not essential here because the seller of the car entered into contract with a purchaser – it didn't matter to him who the purchaser was. Contract was only voidable;

Wilson v *Marquis of Breadalbane* (1859): error as to price not always essential.

(2) Lack of consent

Stobo Ltd v *Morrisons (Gowns) Ltd* (1949): pre-contractual negotiations in business;

Dawson International plc v *Coats Paton plc* (1988): breach of pre-contractual agreement;

Balfour v *Balfour* (1919): domestic arrangement did not imply consent to be legally bound;

Kelly v *Murphy* (1940) and *Ferguson* v *Littlewoods Pools Ltd*) (1997): gaming contracts are sponsiones ludicrae;

Robertson v *Anderson* (2003): an agreement to share bingo winnings was enforceable.

(3) Lack of capacity, (4) Lack of formality and (5) Illegality

Barr v *Crawford* (1983): a contract of bribery in exchange for liquor licence renewal was illegal and unenforceable;

Dowling & Rutter v *Abacus Frozen Foods Ltd (No 2)* (2002): supply of labour contract performed illegally because it breached immigration legislation. However, court allowed it to be enforced (lack of knowledge a factor);

Bridge v *Deacons* (1984): criteria for enforceability of restrictive covenants;

Bluebell Apparel Ltd v *Dickinson* (1978): restrictive covenant case – wide ban on working for rival jeans company upheld to protect trade secrets;

Stewart v *Stewart* (1899): restrictive covenant – 20-mile restriction around Elgin was enforceable;

Dallas, McMillan & Sinclair v *Simpson* (1989): restrictive covenant – 20-mile radius around Glasgow Cross not enforceable;

Mulvein v *Murray* (1908): severable clauses can be saved if some reasonable but others not – court will delete unreasonable parts;

Nordenfelt v *Maxim Nordenfelt Guns and Ammunition Co Ltd* (1894): the ultimate restraint – 25 years, worldwide but still enforceable in the circumstances;
Dumbarton Steamboat Co Ltd v *Macfarlane* (1899): the purchaser of a business operating on the west coast of Scotland only could not impose a UK-wide ban on its seller;
Esso Petroleum Co Ltd v *Harper's Garages (Stourport) Ltd* (1968): 21-year solus agreement too long.

(6) Restrictions on freedom to contract and (7) Other prejudicial circumstances

MacGilvary v *Gilmartin* (1986): facility and circumvention case – contract entered into by widowed mother with daughter was set aside;
Gray v *Binny* (1879): undue influence case – mother influenced son to make a bad bargain over his inheritance;
Honeyman's Executors v *Sharp* (1978): undue influence case involving professional adviser;
Earl of Orkney v *Vinfra* (1606): force and fear case – sign contract or be stabbed: void;
Allen v *Flood* (1898): economic pressure not force and fear unless unlawful.

BREACH OF CONTRACT

Dingwall v *Burnett* (1912): liquidate damages clauses will only be enforced if they are a fair assessment of likely losses;
Graham & Co v *United Turkey Red Co* (1922): a party cannot seek a remedy for breach of contract by the other party if he is also in breach of the contract;
Wade v *Waldon* (1909): note rescission only available if breach material;
White & Carter (Councils) Ltd v *McGregor* (1962): in a case of anticipatory breach, the innocent party is not obliged to accept it and can therefore go on with his part of the contract;
Hadley v *Baxendale* (1854): established two-part test for remoteness of damages: loss naturally arising as a consequence of breach and loss for special circumstances if party in breach knew about them when contract made;
Victoria Laundry (Windsor) Ltd v *Newman Industries* (1949): loss naturally arising includes things known about in the ordinary course of things but special circumstances must actually be known and not implied;
Balfour Beatty Construction (Scotland) Ltd v *Scottish Power plc* (1994): "ordinary course of things" did not include detailed knowledge of concrete pouring procedures;
McLaren Murdoch & Hamilton Ltd v *Abercromby Motor Group Ltd* (2002): courts will look at proportionality in assessing pursuer's claim for damages in defective performance of building contracts;
Diesen v *Samson* (1971): wedding photos ruined – damages awarded for non-patrimonial loss (in this case, disappointment);
Farley v *Skinner* (2002): country house valued correctly but client had asked for "peaceful" retreat and it was ruined by flight path – damages could be

awarded for non-patrimonial loss (in this case, loss of amenity) although no actual financial loss.

TERMINATION OF CONTRACT AND OBLIGATIONS

Taylor v *Caldwell* (1863): music hall case. Contract for hire of hall frustrated when it was burned down;

Mackeson v *Boyd* (1942): tenancy frustrated when country house requisitioned in the war (constructive destruction of subject-matter);

Fraser & Co Ltd v *Denny, Mott & Dickson* (1944): supervening illegality caused by declaration of war;

Krell v *Henry* (1903): Coronation case – purpose of contract thwarted when Coronation postponed.

6 DISPUTE RESOLUTION

We face disputes every day: at home, at work, even in the street. Most of the time, these **6.1** disputes are amicably resolved. Usually this resolution occurs following a negotiation process. Sometimes, more formal dispute resolution methods require to be used.

In this chapter, we examine some of the main ways in which disputes can be resolved **6.2** in Scotland.

RESOLVING DISPUTES IN THE PUBLIC COURTS

Earlier in this book, the court structure of Scotland was explained. Essentially, for civil **6.3** cases, a case can be resolved by an action or application in the sheriff court, the Court of Session or before one of the specialist statutory tribunals.

One important feature of the specialist tribunals is that cases of a certain nature **6.4** (for example immigration, employment and social security) *must* be resolved in the relevant tribunal. Otherwise, there is a *right* of access to the general public courts (sheriff court and Court of Session) except where the parties both agree to adopt a different method of resolution (such as arbitration or mediation – see below on these).

COURT AND TRIBUNAL PROCEDURE

Each of the statutory tribunals has its own procedural rules, setting out what the **6.5** obligations of the parties are as well as those of the tribunal members themselves.

In the sheriff court and the Court of Session, there are different procedural rules that **6.6** apply to different types of cases. For instance, in the sheriff court, there are different rules that apply to small claims, summary causes and ordinary causes.[1] In the Court of Session, there are specialist procedures for a personal injury claim and a commercial claim.[2]

Although these procedures vary with each type of case, some common features exist. **6.7** These will now be examined.

---

[1] For an examination of these different forms of procedure, see paras **2.7–2.13**. The most recent form of the rules can be found on the Scottish Courts website at http://www.scotcourts.gov.uk under "Rules and Legislation". A detailed commentary on the sheriff court rules applicable in civil cases can be found in C Hennessy, *Civil Procedure and Practice* (2nd edn, 2005), Chapters 9–12.

[2] See paras **2.14–2.19** for a discussion of the Court of Session. Again, the rules can be found on the Scottish Courts website: see above. See also C Hennessy, *Civil Procedure and Practice* (2nd edn, 2005), Chapters 5–8.

Basic timetable

6.8   All of these procedures (whether tribunal or public court) involve a basic timetable for the conduct of the case. This will usually begin with a request by the party seeking a remedy submitting a document to the court or tribunal. This document will usually be in a special written form (usually known as an initial writ, a summons or an application) containing certain specific information. That written request is normally served on (sent to or personally handed to) the other party to the dispute. That party will be in a position to reply in writing to the request for a remedy by lodging a document in the court or tribunal, known as either "defences" or "answers". There will then usually be some form of procedural hearing where evidence will not be heard, but where a decision is taken as to whether the case is to proceed further and if so how. The culmination of the procedure will usually be a final hearing at which evidence from witnesses and arguments on the law is heard. A decision is either announced at that hearing or is issued later, with reasons.

6.9   This timetable varies, and in some cases is more complex, but this outline applies to most tribunal and court proceedings.

Pleadings[3]

6.10   As stated above, the arguments of the parties involved in a litigation (action taken through a public court or tribunal) will be exchanged in writing near the beginning of the case. The collective name for these documents is "pleadings". The purpose of requiring the parties to commit their arguments to writing is so that all parties can have "fair notice" of the case their opponent is making. This is so that when the final hearing of the case takes place, both parties will be fully aware of what evidence is likely to be led and so will be able to make sure that the relevant witnesses are available to give evidence for their case. It also allows the parties (or more commonly their lawyers) to prepare to make arguments on any relevant legal point. The idea of fair notice is to avoid any surprises when the final hearing takes place.

6.11   Once the basic pleadings (request for a remedy and the response) are exchanged, the parties can usually expand or change their case, as more details emerge, or in response to points raised by the opponent in his written argument.

6.12   The framing of detailed and accurate pleadings is essential since, if a party wishes to lead evidence from a witness or make a particular argument in law, and neither is provided for in the pleadings, the court might refuse to allow the evidence or argument to be presented. Where that evidence or argument is crucial or important to the success of that party's case, the inept pleadings can be disastrous, and even lead to the loss of the case for that party.

6.13   Pleadings are normally written by lawyers acting for the parties. However, in less formal proceedings (for example small claim actions) a party litigant[4] might prepare his own pleadings.

---

[3] For a full examination of this subject in Scotland, see J S MacKenzie, *Written Pleadings* (2003). See also C Hennessy, *Civil Procedure and Practice* (2nd edn, 2005), Chapter 3.

[4] This is the name given to a party in an action who is not represented, and who represents himself.

EXPENSES

This is the single most practical consideration in any public court or tribunal case. It is **6.14** particularly important in public court cases.[5]

In public court cases, there is a rule that "expenses follow success". This means that **6.15** where a party is successful in an action, that party will be able to claim legal expenses from the other (unsuccessful) party to the action. Generally, the longer a case goes on before a negotiated settlement or decision by the court takes place, the higher the expenses sum due to the winner will be. Unfortunately, it is almost always impossible to predict with certainty what the result of the case will be. This means that if the parties do not negotiate a settlement of the case, and allow the court to decide who wins, the result can be very painful. This is particularly so where (as is usually the case) a sum of money is at stake: the losing party will have to pay the money due plus his opponent's legal expenses.[6] Given this uncertainty, and depending on the amount of money at stake between the parties, the potential expenses liability for the loser will often become a major issue. It should also be noted that the loser will have to pay his own legal fees as well as those of the winner.

Take the following example: **6.16**

A is suing B for £50,000 and the likely costs of his lawyer will be £30,000, if the case is his financial loss litigated to a final hearing. The likely costs of his opponent will be £60,000. If A loses, his financial loss will total £140,000 (£50,000 in the lost sum being sought, £60,000 in his opponent's costs and £30,000 to his own lawyers). If he wins, he will gain £50,000 plus his legal costs will be met. B is in a similar quandary. If he loses, he pays £40,000; if he wins, his costs are paid and he retains his £50,000.

In this way, it will be seen that the expenses issue dominates the economics of the case. In such a situation, a negotiated settlement where both parties compromise may well be an attractive way to avoid the risk of having to lose a much more significant sum in the event of losing the case.

Given that expenses (both between parties and between each party and his lawyer) **6.17** continue to rise as the action continues, pressure to settle the case by negotiation increases as time passes.

Where there is a chance of an appeal if the case is taken to a final hearing before the **6.18** initial court or tribunal, the stakes are raised even further. This is because the expenses for the whole process (including the appeal) go to the final winner of the case. These expenses will be significant.

THE ROLE OF NEGOTIATION IN COURT ACTIONS

In many cases (although not all[7]) there will be an initial period of negotiation between **6.19** the parties in dispute before a formal legal action begins. However, once an action is raised, whether in the public courts or a tribunal, the negotiation process does not end. Indeed, given that the vast majority of civil cases settle out of court, there may well be

---

[5] In tribunal cases, sometimes there is no power to award expenses or that power might be available only in exceptional circumstances.

[6] Not necessarily all of a lawyer's expenses to his client will be met by that client obtaining an award of expenses from the other party – often there will be a shortfall, but this is a complication that will be ignored for the purposes of the present discussion.

[7] In some cases, an emergency court order might be sought, for example in an interdict case. Here, there will be no time for negotiation and any negotiation will take place after the action has begun.

much negotiation still to be done. This is where the negotiation skills of the lawyer or the individual party can be a major influencing factor on the outcome of any dispute.

ARBITRATION

WHAT IS ARBITRATION?

6.20   It is, in essence, a procedure for the resolution of disputes between contracting parties.
6.21   One of the best definitions is given by Professor D M Walker:

> "The adjudication of a dispute or controversy on fact or law or both outside the ordinary civil courts, by one or more persons to whom the parties who are at issue refer the matter for a decision."[8]

6.22   Sometimes arbitration is categorised as a form of dispute resolution. However, it is better dealt with on its own – it possesses a more "judicial" character than some other dispute resolution methods.

THE NATURE OF ARBITRATION

6.23   There follows an examination of some of the main features of arbitration. During that examination, some of the advantages (and disadvantages) of arbitration over public court proceedings will emerge.

Source

6.24   An arbitration will not occur unless the parties agree.[9] This agreement will usually be recorded in a clause of a contract between the parties, known as an "arbitration clause". This clause will normally cover all disputes arising out of the contract. A typical arbitration clause might look like this:

> "Any dispute or difference arising out of or in connection with this contract shall be determined by the appointment of a single arbitrator to be agreed between the parties, or failing agreement within fourteen days, after either party has given to the other a written request to concur in the appointment of an arbitrator, by an arbitrator to be appointed by the President or a Vice President of the Chartered Institute of Arbitrators."[10]

6.25   The agreement will normally provide for arbitration in the event of any dispute arising out of the terms of the contract (as with the clause above). Alternatively, only certain

---

[8] D M Walker, *Principles of Scottish Private Law* (3rd edn, 1982), vol I, p 60.
[9] There are some forms of statutory arbitration, but these are very obscure and will not be dealt with here. These include, for example, agricultural arbitrations under the Agricultural Holdings (Scotland) Act 1991 and employment dispute arbitrations under the Trade Union and Labour Relations (Consolidation) Act 1992, s 212A.
[10] This is a sample clause suggested for use by the main arbitral body in the UK, the Chartered Institute of Arbitrators. For more on this Institute, see its website at www.arbitrators.org.

clauses of the contract or types of dispute arising out of the contract might be referred to arbitration. In such cases, for disputes arising outwith the remit of the arbitration clause, these will fall to be dealt with through the public court system.

It is possible to agree orally or in writing to refer a particular dispute to arbitration   **6.26** after it has arisen. This is called an *"ad hoc* arbitration". Normally, however, the contract will make provision for arbitration in advance.

In Scotland, an oral arbitration agreement is binding. It is always wise, however, to   **6.27** commit that agreement to writing, since it will then be easier to prove that an agreement of this nature has been reached.

Binding nature

If the contract (or oral agreement) provides for arbitration, the decision of the arbitrator   **6.28** (the third-party neutral who conducts the arbitration)[11] is final and enforceable against the parties, as if it were a court decree (order).[12] Arbitration differs from other forms of dispute resolution such as mediation, since, in the latter case, the mediator tries to persuade the parties to agree; he cannot force a decision on the parties which they must abide by. The decision of the arbitrator will be recorded in an "arbitral award" which is just another name for a "decree", which is the word used for a court order.

Judicial nature

An arbitrator cannot act as he likes. He must act fairly towards the parties. Subject to   **6.29** that basic requirement, arbitrators have more freedom than judges in the public courts, particularly as regards procedure (see below). Where the arbitrator does not abide by the basic rules of fairness, however, his decision can be challenged by the losing party through the courts. Such a challenge is not a popular move, since the whole point of arbitration is to avoid litigation in the public courts. As noted below, any appeal against a Scottish arbitral award must be to the Court of Session.

Sources and content of arbitration rules

It is one thing to agree to arbitrate – another to determine how the arbitration is to take   **6.30** place. The rules for the conduct of an arbitration can come from a number of sources, but by far the most common source is the rules of an arbitral body. There are dozens of sets of arbitration rules that exist to cover all kinds of arbitrations. These rules are often produced by arbitral organisations[13] that also offer access to a list of approved arbitrators and possibly also venues in which the arbitration can take place.

Arbitral rules tend to cover similar ground to that covered by court and tribunal rules   **6.31** such as timetable for the case, pleadings and how evidence is to be presented.

---

[11] Sometimes in Scotland the term "arbiter" is used. This is an old Scots name and although it is still sometimes used today, the more common term is the more globally applicable "arbitrator".

[12] Generally, the same enforcement measures are available as with a court decree.

[13] Some of the main examples include the Chartered Institute of Arbitrators (CiArb) (see www.arbitrators.org), the London Court of International Arbitration (LCIA) (see www.lcia-arbitration.com), and the International Chamber of Commerce (ICC) (see www.iccwbo.org).

6.32 Sometimes oral evidence is not required (if the argument is one of law only and the facts are agreed – for example interpretation of a contractual term) and such an arbitration is called a "documents only" arbitration.

Freedom of choice

6.33 One of the major advantages of arbitration is the fact that the parties can chose their own judge – or allow an arbitral body to do so. The parties do not, then, have to accept the judge who happens to be in court on that particular day. That judge might have little or no expertise of what might be a complex subject area. Where the parties choose a particular person, there can be an element of trust in that person's decision on both sides.

6.34 Choice can also be exercised in the area of procedure. The parties can set their own timetable for lodging documents and for a hearing. Alternatively, they can leave that to the arbitrator, or to a chosen set of arbitration rules. The parties are not stuck with the court procedures and timetables, which tend to be inflexible.

6.35 Also, the parties can agree the expenses to be awarded by the arbitrator, and are not required to pay costs according to the fixed scale in place for court actions (see further on expenses, below).

Expense

6.36 The question of whether arbitration is cheaper than a court action is not easy to answer. It will depend on the particular case. The following are influencing factors:

(1) No lawyer is needed for an arbitration. Generally, one is required in a court action. This could be a saving but it means that someone will have to prepare the case – presumably someone in the firm involved in the dispute – and this might be more expensive than simply hiring a lawyer.

(2) Delay is minimised in arbitration; the case is on its own procedural track. It is not locked into the rigid and long court timetable – delay can add to cost, particularly where a large sum of money is outstanding. For instance, if the parties want the arbitrator to hear the case and make a decision within, say, two months, this might well be possible. Such speed will not be possible in the public court system, where the equivalent minimum period will be more like 8 months, and often much longer. However, if a case is complex, as much time may be taken in an arbitration as in a court action.

(3) In arbitration, the costs of the venue, the arbitrator and all other ancillary costs have to be met by the parties – in a court action, the state meets these costs. Any saving in resolving the dispute more quickly may be lost on these extra administration expenses. The costs can spiral even further if a central administration is being used to run the arbitration, such as the International Chamber of Commerce (ICC).[14]

---

[14] The costs of such an arbitration can be very high. See the details on the ICC's website at http://www.iccwbo.org.

Overall, in most cases (but not all) arbitration will be cheaper. However, sometimes **6.37** arbitration is criticised as being overly complex and legalistic, especially where the parties are represented by lawyers, so that it can be as costly and lengthy as court proceedings.

Privacy

Any public court proceedings are held, of course, in public. This means that members of **6.38** the public can come along and watch, and that includes the Press. In addition, all court papers are accessible to members of the public, again including the Press.

Some companies value their public image and reputation sufficiently to wish to **6.39** protect against an adverse image and they enter an arbitration clause in all (or at least most) contracts for all disputes. Another privacy consideration might be the desire to prevent market-sensitive information falling into the wrong hands, such as those of competitors. Where the desire for privacy is strong, the company may overlook any disadvantages of arbitration, in order to ensure secrecy.

The arbitrator

Arbitrations are commonly conducted by only one arbitrator. Sometimes three are **6.40** appointed, but this is less common, for costs reasons.

Any adult can be appointed as an arbitrator – there are no minimum qualifications. **6.41** However, in practice the arbitrator will be a professional person of some significant experience. Some professionals will specialise in arbitrations, so that they will do only arbitrations and no other work. Other arbitrators will conduct arbitrations as a secondary activity to their main occupation. Arbitrators are not normally lawyers, but will usually be professionals with expertise in the subject-matter of a contract, such as a surveyor, engineer or accountant. The arbitrator who is not a lawyer will often be assisted on matters of law by his clerk, who will usually be legally qualified.

ARBITRATION LAW IN SCOTLAND

The law of arbitration in Scotland is not codified and is to be found scattered in different **6.42** places. Much of the law is case law, although there are some important statutory provisions on the appointment of arbitrators.[15] In England and Wales, the law of arbitration has been codified and can be found in the Arbitration Act 1996.[16] Unlike the position in Scotland,[17] this Act applies in England and Wales to domestic as well as international arbitrations. There is presently a Bill with the Scottish Executive which is

---

[15] These provisions are to be found in the Arbitration (Scotland) Act 1894, ss 1–4 and 6. For a full and contemporary discussion of the law in this area, see RLC Hunter, *The Law of Arbitration in Scotland* (2nd edn, 2002).

[16] See, for a detailed commentary on the provisions of the 1996 Act, B Harris, R Planterose and J Tecks, *The Arbitration Act 1996: A Commentary* (3rd edn, 2003).

[17] International arbitrations occour where there is more than one jurisdiction involved in the dispute, for example Scotland and England. In Scotland, there is a separate regime governing international commercial arbitration procedure: it is covered by an international treaty called the UNCITRAL Model Law on International Commercial Arbitrations 1985. There is not space in this chapter to examine this Treaty and its application in Scotland.

seeking to codify the law of arbitration in Scotland.[18] It is unclear when (and if) the Bill will become law.

6.43   Many of the cases on arbitration are decided around disputes about whether the arbitrator was in same way biased in his conduct of the arbitration toward one of the parties, or about whether the arbitration clause is valid. In cases where there is an argument about whether the arbitration clause is valid, this sometimes has to be sorted out by the courts. This happens where one of the parties wishes to try to avoid arbitration (having originally agreed to it) and instead raises a court action to resolve the dispute. Where this happens, the court has to decide whether it has jurisdiction to decide on the dispute or whether the case should go to arbitration. If the decision by the court is that the arbitration clause is valid, it will send the case to arbitration. Where the decision is that the clause is invalid, the court will simply decide the case itself.

Appeal from the decision of an arbitral tribunal

6.44   The grounds of appeal from an arbitrator's decision are limited. This is one of the advantages of arbitration over court proceedings. One major difference between the two is that an arbitrator's decision cannot be appealed against on the ground that the arbitrator has made a mistake in applying the law. On court proceedings, this is one of the main grounds of appeal. Most parties who choose arbitration do so in order to limit the prospect of an appeal, since appeals lead to delay and extra expense.

6.45   Having said that, since arbitration is a judicial process, certain minimum basic grounds of appeal exist, to prevent unfairness:

- *breach of rules of fairness*, for example treating parties during the hearing unequally or showing bias toward one party;
- *close connection with one of the arbitral parties to the arbitration*, for example a former business connection;
- *pecuniary or other personal interest on the part of the arbitrator* in the outcome of the case, perhaps where there is a financial interest in one of the parties, for example where one of the parties is a customer of the company for which the arbitrator is working;
- *corruption* by the arbitrator;
- *bribery* of the arbitrator;
- *falsehood* – deceit by the arbitrator or the parties during the arbitration;
- *failure by the arbitrator to deal properly with the reference* ("reference" is the word used to refer to all issues validly referred to the arbitrator) – this would occour where the arbitrator does not deal with the whole reference or where he exceeded the terms of the reference and would also cover the situation of an award which is void from uncertainty, ie written in a way in which it is too vague to understand or enforce;
- *misconduct* – this is difficult to separate from a mistake in law or fact. The rule is that where the arbitrator has made an error in applying the law, for example if

---

[18] The Bill is the Arbitration (Scotland) Bill and can be accessed at the website of the Scottish Council for International Arbitration (SCIA) at http://www.scia.co.uk/arbbillconsult.htm.
[19] The phrase "arbitral tribunal" is used to describe the arbitrator(s) who preside over the arbitration.

he has misinterpreted it, his decision (although not correct in law) will not be able to be successfully appealed. If such a decision were made by a judge in court, the losing party *could* appeal. But where an arbitrator is in ignorance of or *disregards* the law, the courts, if asked by the losing party, may be willing to cancel the arbitrator's decision on appeal;[20]

- *fraud* – again by the arbitrator or by either party.

Any appeal would be to the Court of Session. As can be seen, the grounds of challenge **6.46** are extreme, highlighting the fact that an arbitrator's decision will usually, in practice, be final.

THE USE OF ARBITRATION

Arbitration is used in a number of situations. The arbitration of consumer disputes is on **6.47** the rise, although this is still relatively uncommon.[21] The use of arbitration to resolve sports law disagreements is also available.[22] However, by far the most common use of arbitration is for the resolution of disputes arising from commercial contracts. Often these contracts will be of high value. Particular industries favour arbitration as a method of dispute resolution over others. It is commonly used in, for instance, the construction and oil and gas industries.

ALTERNATIVE DISPUTE RESOLUTION

Alternative Dispute Resolution (ADR) is a generic name for a number of different **6.48** techniques used to resolve disputes. There are many definitions of ADR. The following definition is useful:

> *A means of settlement of a dispute, which is not litigation or arbitration.*

Some people include arbitration as a form of ADR. Others believe that it is too close to **6.49** litigation (in other words, resolution by the public courts) to classify it as a form of ADR. Arbitration is probably somewhere in between the two extremes – it is binding but does not involve the public court system. It is probably best not considered as a form of ADR and so is dealt with on its own, above.

ADR comes in many forms. There are probably around 10–20 main forms of ADR **6.50** which are recognised, some of them being variants of others.

ADR is used in a wide variety of settings. It is most commonly used in the form of **6.51** mediation in family disputes. It is also, however, used in civil and commercial matters, criminal cases, neighbour disputes, consumer disputes, employment disputes, to name a few. In fact, where there is any kind of dispute, ADR in one of its forms will be available.

---

[20] *Mitchell-Gill* v *Buchan* 1921 SC 390 at 395.
[21] See the wide range of consumer dispute resolution services offered under the umbrella of the Chartered Institute of Arbitrators on its website at http://www.drs-ciarb.com/Consumer/Services.asp.
[22] The main sporting arbitral body is the Court of Arbitration for Sport, based in Lausanne, Switzerland – see the organisation's website at www.tas-cas.org.

FORMS OF ADR

6.52 In this part we will examine some of the main types of ADR available to resolve a wide range of disputes.

Negotiation

6.53 This is the most basic and frequently used ADR method. It is particularly prevalent in commercial disputes. This is perhaps partly because a "personal" element to the dispute will often not be present. In other words, businessmen try to do business and lengthy disputes only take up time and money. Another reason might be the relationship between the parties. If they do business regularly, they will not wish to jeopardise future deals that may be worth more than the one at hand.

6.54 Where such considerations do not apply, negotiation is less likely to work. It is still, however, easily the most successful and important ADR method.

6.55 Brown and Marriot make the following general observations on negotiation:

> "Everyone learns to negotiate from the earliest age. As time passes, our negotiation becomes more refined. We learn to use it as the way to get what we need or want. Usually, we must give up something in order to get something else in return. By adulthood, we will probably have negotiated many different kinds of agreements, personal and financial, and we will have developed our own individual styles for trying to persuade others to give us what we want, which is what negotiation involves. We may bargain with ease or be uncomfortable with haggling; we may explicitly or implicitly adopt a pleading manner or a browbeating style: we may hector, cajole or threaten; we may avoid or withdraw from situations which involve confronting others in resolving differences; or we may use the threat of withdrawal as a strategy. These and many other ways of negotiating will to some extent become part of our individual personalities, although obviously learned negotiation skills will enhance and augment natural inclinations."[23]

6.56 Much has been written on the subject of negotiation, particularly in the US. Although negotiation techniques cannot in any comprehensive way be discussed here, there are some very useful and user-friendly texts available.[24] There are many other guides to negotiation skills and, of course, there are courses and classes available to improve negotiation skills.[25]

General negotiating techniques

6.57 Broadly speaking, there are two main theories of negotiation: the problem-solving approach and the competitive theory.

6.58 The *problem-solving approach* involves the negotiator trying to resolve the dispute by suggesting resolutions that can be to the advantage of both parties. In other words, the

---

[23] H Brown and A Marriott, *ADR Principles and Practice* (2nd edn, 1999), p 103.
[24] R Fisher and W Ury, *Getting to Yes: Negotiating Agreement Without Giving In,* (2nd edn, 1991); R Fisher and S Brown, *Getting Together: Building a Relationship that Gets to Yes* (1989); W Ury, *Getting Past No: Negotiating With Difficult People* (1991).
[25] There is, for example, a very well-known Program on Negotiation offered by Harvard Law School in the US. For more details see the web pages at http://www.pon.harvard.edu/main/home/index.php3.

negotiator adopting this approach concentrates not on the negotiating party's own position, but on seeking a mutually beneficial outcome by focusing on both parties' interests.

By contrast, the *competitive theory* involves a tough, powerful and competitive **6.59** negotiation. According to this theory, the aim is to obtain the best outcome for the individual negotiator and the "common good" is irrelevant. In fact, in this theory, gestures of empathy or attempts to reach a mutually beneficial solution are seen as signs of weakness – each side is out to gain as much as possible and lose as little as possible.

These approaches are not the only ones. Also, there are degrees of approach in **6.60** between. In fact, during the course of a negotiation or series of negotiations the approach adopted by a party may alter, perhaps several times. In addition, one party to the negotiation may use one approach, and the other a different approach.

The question of which approach to use will vary according to a number of factors, for **6.61** example the relative bargaining position of the parties, the value of the dispute and whether the parties are regularly contracting with each other.

Preparation for a negotiation

Often a negotiation is entered into with little or no preparation. This is a mistake. A **6.62** negotiation can produce (and is designed to produce) the end result of the dispute. Normally, much preparation goes into being ready for a tribunal, court or arbitral hearing. There seems no reason, therefore, to ignore preparation of a negotiation.

Each negotiation will involve a greater or lesser degree of preparation depending **6.63** mainly on the complexity and value of the dispute. However, in any negotiation, there are three basic essential areas of preparation:

(1) *Consideration of the "bottom line"*. Whether the negotiation is about money or not, the negotiator should decide the point beyond which he will not go. This point should not be breached in the negotiation – in other words, it is important in every case to stick to the pre-determined "bottom line". It might be possible to come back later with a new "bottom line", but this should be recalculated not on the spur of the moment during the discussions, but away from the heat of negotiation. Otherwise, the negotiator might, against his better judgement, be talked into offering more/accepting less than he is later comfortable with.

(2) *Planning of the negotiating style*. Each negotiator should decide in advance how he will conduct the negotiation – will he be bullish or conciliatory? As stated above, he may wish to alter his approach during the negotiation, but he should at least have an idea as to his starting point. Where the style is not planned, the negotiator may start sending out the wrong signals and this might jeopardise the success of the negotiation. For example, one party might adopt a style that is too strong and robust. Alternatively, his position might be weakened by behaving in a conciliatory way.

(3) *Knowing what the best and worst alternatives are before entering the negotiation process*. In other words, in order to know whether to accept what is on the table, each party needs to be aware of what might happen if the negotiation process breaks down. Authors Fisher and Ury have developed the famous

BATNA theory (Best Alternative to a Negotiated Agreement),[26] which basically refers to the best case alternative scenario to a negotiated agreement. Elsewhere, there has been talk of the importance of WATNA (Worst Alternative to a Negotiated Agreement).[27] This represents the worst-case scenario if the negotiation fails. The idea is that the party negotiating should be able to try to find a solution somewhere in between these two extremes, preferably toward the upper end. If a party does not know where these two extremes lie for his case, there is a possibility that he will accept a negotiated settlement below the WATNA level.

Mediation

The nature of mediation

6.64   Brown and Marriot define mediation as follows:

> "a facilitative process in which disputing parties engage the assistance of an impartial third party, the mediator, who helps them to try to arrive at an agreed resolution of their dispute. The mediator has no authority to make any decisions that are binding on them, but uses certain procedures, techniques and skills to help them to negotiate an agreed resolution of their dispute without adjudication."[28]

6.65   Mediation is used in many different kinds of disputes. The form and procedure of the mediation will depend on the type of dispute, the mediator's views on how to proceed, the parties' views and on the terms of any set of rules or guidelines that apply (sometimes by agreement between the parties).

6.66   Mediation (as will be seen from the above definition) has the following basic and universal features:

- *impartial mediator*: this is obvious;
- *facilitator not negotiator*: the mediator is not there to negotiate a solution as such – his role is to propose certain possible resolutions and by doing so to encourage the parties to negotiate the dispute to a conclusion;
- *purely consensual*: the parties cannot be *forced* to mediate (but see court-annexed mediation and contractual mediation below) and they can withdraw from the mediation process at any time;
- *the aim is resolution*: a very different strategy is employed from the litigation or arbitration processes as the mediation process tries to bring the parties together, not keep them apart (although courts and arbitrators will encourage settlement either informally or formally: see below). This will usually involve the pursuit by the mediator of a problem- solving as opposed to a competitive

---

[26] R Fisher and W Ury, *Getting to Yes: Negotiating Agreement Without Giving In* (2nd edn, 1992).

[27] J Haynes and G Haynes, *Mediating Divorce* (1989). A very good summary of these theories can be found at H Brown and A Marriott, *ADR Principles and Practice* (2nd edn, 1999), p 105.

[28] H Brown and A Marriott, *ADR Principles and Practice* (2nd edn, 1999), p 127. For more detailed examinations of the mediation process, see S Roberts and M Palmer, *Dispute Processes: ADR and the Primary Forms of Decision Making* (2005), Chapter 6; A Bevan, *Alternative Dispute Resolution* (1992), Chapters 2–6 and J W Cooley, *Mediation Advocacy* (2nd edn, 2002).

approach. This will, in an ideal mediation, prevent the "winner takes all" mentality of litigation and arbitration – both parties will at least be partly successful;

- *mediators do not give advice*: often, if a number of alternative settlement proposals are discussed, the parties will want to take legal advice, at least on the terms of any written agreement which may be prepared and signed following the mediation. The mediator must not give advice, either legal or on the best course of action for either party to follow, he must simply present alternatives;
- *confidentiality*: the mediator is normally, either explicitly or by implication, bound not to reveal the contents of any discussions which take place during mediation, either to those outside the mediation or (in the case of private discussions with the parties individually – see below) to the other party. This allows the parties to discuss the dispute freely, without fear of the terms of their discussions being used against them in future, for example during a future court case or arbitration, where mediation fails;
- *personal presence of the parties*: this can be important; in many other dispute resolution methods such as litigation or arbitration, the parties themselves might never meet. Often the lawyers will meet to discuss the case. Sometimes when the parties meet, as they will during mediation, this can be valuable in bringing them together – there is not the same sense of detachment that exists when lawyers are meeting and simply discussing the case on their clients' behalf.

The progress of a mediation

When a dispute arises, the parties normally try to sort it out themselves first (negotiation). When that does not prove possible, the parties (particularly commercial ones) will usually seek legal advice. Their lawyers will normally try to sort the matter out (negotiation again). If this fails, the parties might go straight to adjudication of some kind.[29] Alternatively, the lawyer may propose mediation (or any other form of ADR). Sometimes the parties have already agreed in their contract to try mediation of any disputes before going further. If this is the case, the parties will need to attempt mediation before commencing an arbitration or litigation. **6.67**

If mediation is chosen by both parties (or forced by one as a result of a contractual obligation), a separate mediation contract will usually entered into. This contract will contain terms as to costs of the mediator, the conduct of the mediation, the rights and duties of the parties and the mediator, confidentiality and procedural rules such as a timetable for the process including when the parties should lodge documentation with the mediator. **6.68**

Once the contract is agreed, there will be some arrangements made for venue, timing etc. The parties will attend in person or send a representative from the organisation or attend with a lawyer. **6.69**

---

[29] The word "adjudication" is used in this sense as a generic term encompassing all formal dispute resolution methods, such as arbitration and court actions. The word is sometimes also used to refer to a special kind of dispute resolution applicable only in construction cases and regulated under the Housing Grants, Construction and Regeneration Act 1996.

6.70   In particular in commercial disputes, the mediator will want in advance a written submission by each party setting out the facts, the terms of the dispute and the arguments in favour of his position. All other relevant documentation, including contracts expert reports and relevant correspondence will be sought by the mediator.

6.71   The mediation itself can take a number of forms. Usually, the mediator will meet with the parties together to introduce himself and to explain the procedure and his duties. The contract will normally be discussed. Each party may then be asked to outline their position. The mediator may then meet parties separately (and in confidence – see above on confidentiality) to discuss their attitude and the limits of their positions. There may then be a further joint meeting to discuss progress.

6.72   If an agreement is reached during the mediation, normally the terms of the agreement will be recorded in writing (with the help of lawyers, if present) and signed before the parties depart. An agreement might not be reached there and then but a number of proposals may have been discussed and the parties may agree to resume negotiations, failing which to return to mediation.

6.73   The above is a very basic description of how a mediation session *might* proceed. Any particular stage might be missed out or expanded. Mediation may occur over a number of sessions over weeks or even months.

Use of mediation in the UK

6.74   In Scotland, traditionally mediation is a dispute resolution method seen as most applicable in family disputes. It is true that family disputes are the most commonly mediated disputes in the UK. However, mediation has taken hold in other areas. In criminal cases, there is a Scottish mediation scheme.[30] Mediation is also used in commercial cases.[31] This use is less prominent in Scotland than in England. However, due to the increase in use of mediation in England and Wales, it is likely that this method of resolution will become more popular in Scotland in future. Although there are training courses available for mediators,[32] there is no government system of accreditation of mediators in the UK, so not all mediators will have been trained to the same level.

6.75   A number of mediation bodies have sprung up over the years.[33] These bodies will usually provide access to a list of accredited (approved) mediators as well as a set of mediation rules and perhaps appropriate mediation venues.

---

[30] This is operated by SACRO, a charity providing mediation for a number of types of community dispute including criminal cases – see its website at: www.sacro.org.uk.

[31] The main mediation body for commercial cases is the Centre for Effective Dispute Resolution (CEDR) which can offer access to a list of commercial mediators as well as other dispute resolution services for commercial cases. See its website at:www.cedr.co.uk. See also the Academy of Experts at www.academy-experts.org.

[32] Training of mediators is often carried out through mediation bodies. Such training schemes are most prominent in relation to family mediators: see, for example, the schemes approved by the umbrella body, the UK College of Family Mediators, on its website at: http://www.ukcfm.co.uk/default.html.

[33] See notes 31 and 32, above, for some UK examples of these. In Scotland, there is the umbrella body of the Scottish Mediation Network – see its website for a comprehensive list of Scottish mediation services: www.scottishmediation.org.uk/index.asp.

Costs of mediation

Of course, mediation is normally not provided free of charge. The mediator will usually   **6.76**
be an experienced lawyer and will charge a significant hourly rate. Normally the costs of
mediation are shared equally between the parties. One of the disadvantages of mediation is that there is no guarantee of a resolution to the dispute. This could lead to the
parties paying significant sums in both mediator's and usually legal fees and finding
themselves no further forward. This means that unless the parties can go on to negotiate
a solution (unlikely in the face of a failed mediation) they will have to resort to a more
formal process, such as arbitration or mediation.

Agreement to mediate

The parties might agree in the contract between them to mediate before adopting a more   **6.77**
formal dispute resolution method. Alternatively, the parties may agree, once the dispute
has arisen, to mediate even in the face of a clause in the contract providing for some
other form of dispute resolution (this is called an *"ad hoc* mediation"). Style mediation
clauses are available.[34]

In such clauses, a "back-up" form of dispute resolution will be agreed; this will   **6.78**
happen in all mediation agreements (whether *ad hoc* or not) since mediation does not
involve a final binding decision being made on the dispute by the mediator.

Court-annexed ADR

In many courts, tribunals and arbitrations around the world, the decision-maker will   **6.79**
informally seek to encourage the parties to settle the case. This is not court-annexed
ADR, but is rather a practice that is adopted to a greater or lesser extent according to
individual taste. It is not compulsory: some decision-makers will simply refuse to get
involved in settlement encouragement and will simply decide the case placed before
them. This verbal encouragement to settle takes place most notably on the day of the
final hearing when the parties themselves will be present. This method can be
particularly effective since the parties will not want to upset a judge or arbitrator
who believes that the case should resolve itself by insisting that it goes ahead in front of
that judge or arbitrator. The judge or arbitrator must, however, be careful when
expressing his views informally that he does not show bias.

Sometimes a court has certain formal powers to encourage the parties to negotiate or   **6.80**
even to refer the case to mediation. In Scotland, for example, the courts can refer a family
law case to mediation (but not any other type of case).[35] However, the parties cannot be
forced to make a real effort to allow mediation to work – they may only be forced to
attend mediation sessions.

In England, the importance of ADR is more pronounced. There are specific court   **6.81**
practice rules dealing with the duty on the court to encourage settlement by ADR
methods, and even delay the progress of the case (with or without the parties consent)

---

[34] See, for example, the clause suggested by the Chartered Institute of Arbitrators on its website
at: www.drs-ciarb.com/Resources/ArbMed.asp.
[35] See r 33.22 of the Sheriff Court Ordinary Cause Rules (Act of Sederunt (Sheriff Court Ordinary
Cause Rules)) 1993 (SI 1993/1956).

for this purpose.[36] These rules apply to all civil cases in England and Wales, not just family cases.

6.82　These more formal powers are known generally as examples of "court-annexed ADR".

ADR by contract

6.83　Some contracts (particularly commercial contracts) oblige the parties to resolve disputes by, say, mediation before commencing a litigation or proceeding to arbitration. This is an enforceable contractual term, like any other, at least in theory. In practice a party can go through the motions of the process (for example, mediation) with no real intention of making it work.

6.84　However, there is no need to agree any ADR process in the contract between the parties. Such a process can be entered into, like arbitration, on an *ad hoc* basis, for example after a dispute has arisen. It is even possible to agree to switch to a different process from that agreed earlier (either in the contract or since). So, for example, the parties may agree in the contract to arbitrate on any disputes arising under the contract; later, they may abandon that agreement and try mediation instead.

6.85　Where no method of dispute resolution is agreed, and where the parties do not agree a method of resolution alternative to the public courts or the relevant statutory tribunal (such as arbitration or mediation), the parties always have a right of recourse to the public courts or the relevant tribunal.

---

[36] See rr 26.4 and 1.4 of the Civil Procedure Rules 1998.

ESSENTIAL FACTS

In this chapter, we examined the main forms of dispute resolution: **6.86**

THE PUBLIC COURTS

- Court of Session, sheriff court and statutory tribunals.
- Procedure: basic timetable and pleadings.
- The role of expenses as a common economic determining factor.
- The continuing role of negotiation during the court process.

ARBITRATION

- Alternative to litigation.
- Judicial process, but no use of judge.
- Freedom of choice on arbitrator and rules of procedure.
- Cost implications – can be more or less expensive than litigation.
- Time implications – can agree a shorter timetable than court.
- The arbitrator – professional, neutral decision-maker, not usually a lawyer.
- Sources of arbitration rules – arbitral institutions.
- Restricted appeal against an arbitral award.
- Variety of uses of arbitration.

ADR

- Negotiation – problem-solving and competitive techniques; the importance of preparation.
- Mediation – third-party impartial decision-maker in consensual, not forced process, by agreement of the parties with a litigation or arbitration "back-up" in case of failure
- Court-annexed ADR – order by courts to resort to ADR; distinct from informal encouragement by court to settle.
- ADR by contract – can be by agreement in contract or by an *ad hoc* agreement.

7 EMPLOYMENT LAW

CONTRACT AND STATUTE

Employment law is primarily concerned with the law which regulates the relations **7.1** between employers and employees. As will be explored in the first section, there are more employment relationships than employer – employee, and employment law is also concerned with these. At the centre of the employment relationship is the contract of employment, so that an understanding of the principles of contract law is essential. The contractual basis has also been supplemented and in some cases supplanted by statutory rights. Statutory employment rights have increased dramatically since the mid-1960s, in areas concerned with employment security, discrimination, maternity rights, industrial action and a wide range of individual rights. Part of this expansion has been caused by obligations arising out of the UK's membership of the European Union. An understanding of EU law and the relationship between it and national law is also necessary for an understanding of employment law. This chapter will examine the contractual relationship in some depth, and then outline a selection of statutory rights.

EU AND NATIONAL LAW[1]

The doctrine of "subsidiarity" places the responsibility on the Member State to **7.2** implement legislation to give effect to EU Directives. In principle, once this has been done, it is the national legislation which is the source of law in the Member State. Thus, the Working Time Regulations 1998 were introduced in order to implement the Working Time Directive 93/104. Anyone who wishes to establish what their rights are in relation to working time should look in the first instance to the 1998 Regulations.

However, the doctrine of "supremacy of EU law", gives the underlying EU Directive **7.3** a continuing relevance. National law must be interpreted so as to comply with the EU law so far as is possible, even if this may not be the most obvious reading of the words in the national law. In addition, certain parts EC law may be of direct effect so that they can be relied on directly in the national court or tribunal. It has been established that Art 141 of the Treaty of Rome, the equal pay article, has "horizontal" direct effect, so that those employed by private as well as state employers may rely on it. In those cases where a (part of a) Directive is of direct effect it will be "vertical" only and thus only those who are employed by state employers may rely on it.

---

[1] See paras **3.7** and **3.36–3.38**

EUROPEAN CONVENTION ON HUMAN RIGHTS (ECHR)

7.4   Under the Human Rights Act 1998, courts and tribunals have had to interpret the law in such a way as to be consistent with the "convention rights" made enforceable by the Act.[2] This means that, although only employees of public authorities may raise an action against their employer under the Act,[3] indirectly the Act affects the way all employment law is interpreted, both common law and statutory. The ECHR rights are civil, not social, rights and do not apply explicitly to the workplace. However, a number of rights are relevant to employment. For example, Art 8, which provides for the right to respect for private and family life, has been found to be relevant in cases of workplace surveillance.[4] However, like many of the ECHR rights, Art 8 is qualified and interference with it may be justified in certain circumstances so long as it is proportionate and in pursuit of a relevant interest, such as the prevention of crime. In *McGowan* v *Scottish Water*[5] covert surveillance of the home of an employee who was suspected of falsifying his time sheets was found to be proportionate in the circumstances.

EMPLOYMENT TRIBUNALS

7.5   Employment tribunals (called industrial tribunals until 1998[6]) (ETs) were first established in 1964. Their primary function is to hear cases brought by individuals to enforce their employment rights under various statutes, principally the Employment Rights Act 1996 (ERA 1996) and the anti-discrimination statutes. The constitution and conduct of employment tribunals is governed by the Employment Tribunals Act 1996 (ETA 1996).

7.6   A standard tribunal hearing is heard by three people drawn from three panels, a legal panel appointed by the Lord President whose members act as chairs, and two other panels drawn up by the Secretary of State, one in consultation with organisations of employers, and the other in consultation with organisations of employees.[7] With the consent of both parties, a hearing may be heard by a chairman and one other, and in certain specific cases or where both parties agree in writing, or where the case is not longer contested, by a chairman alone.[8]

Statutory grievance procedure

7.7   An employee who wishes to raise an action against an employer must have complied with the statutory procedure established by the Employment Act 2002[9] which requires the employee to have given the employer a written statement of the complaint. The employer should arrange a meeting, in which the employee should co-operate. Failure to state a grievance will mean that the employee will lose the right to raise an action, and

---

[2] Section 3
[3] Section 6
[4] *Halford* v *UK* (1997) 24 EHRR 532.
[5] [2005] IRLR 167.
[6] Employment Rights (Dispute Resolution) Act 1998, s 1.
[7] Employment Tribunals (Constitution and Rules of Procedure) Regulations 2004, reg 8.
[8] ETA 1996, s 4(3).
[9] Section 32 and Sch 2: does not apply in the case of unfair dismissal except for constructive dismissal.

failure to co-operate fully may lead to reduction of any compensation. This applies to the types of cases referred to in the Act.

EMPLOYMENT APPEAL TRIBUNAL

It is possible to appeal against a decision of an ET to the Employment Appeals Tribunal **7.8** (EAT). From there, in Scotland an appeal can go to the Inner House of the Court of Session (its English equivalent being the Court of Appeal) and from there to the House of Lords. A reference could be made to the European Court of Justice for a ruling on a point of EC law if relevant at any stage. Like the ETs, the EAT sits with three members: one, the chair, being a Court of Session judge and the other two people with special knowledge or experience of industrial relations as either employers' representatives or workers' representatives.[10] Appeal to the EAT is on a point of law only, and it is not competent to appeal against a finding of fact by a tribunal.

THE EMPLOYMENT RELATIONSHIP

WHO IS AN EMPLOYEE?

An employee is someone employed under a contract employment. Its legal name is a **7.9** contract of service. This is a concept adopted without further definition in employment statutes.[11] Not everyone who is in employment is an employee. A person may be "employed" on a more casual basis, or may be employed through an agency or may be working for themselves. Some of these individuals, and their employers, may consider that they are "casual workers" or "agency workers" or "self-employed"; others may feel that they are in fact employees. While the terminology used by the parties to a contract is a strong indication of what their intentions were, it will not override other factors if the overall terms of the contract show otherwise.[12] It is important to identify under what sort of contract a person is employed. Some statutory rights apply only to employees. Employees are taxed under Schedule E, employers being obliged to deduct tax at source, while self-employed workers[13] are taxed under Schedule D and are responsible for their own payment of tax[14]. Employers are responsible for paying national insurance contributions for employees (in addition to paying the employee's own contributions at source), while self-employed workers are responsible for paying their own contributions.[15] An employer's common law vicarious liability is for employees only.[16] An employer owes specific common law and statutory health and safety duties to employees which are more extensive than those owed to others.

So far as the common law is concerned (and taxation and social security statutes), **7.10** there are only two ways of categorising contracts to carry out work: either as contracts

---

[10] ETA 1996, s 22.
[11] ERA 1996, s 230(1) and (2).
[12] *Dacas* v *Brook Street Bureau (UK) Ltd* [2003] IRLR 190.
[13] For tax and national insurance purposes, anyone who not an employee is a "self-employed worker".
[14] Income Tax (Earnings and Pensions) Act 2003, Pt 11.
[15] Social Security Contributions and Benefits Act 1992, ss 1 and 2.
[16] See paras **4.59–4.65.**

of service or as contracts for services. The parties to these contracts are respectively the employer and employee (formerly "master" and "servant"), and employer and independent contractor. This broadly is a distinction between an employee and a self-employed person. Common law and the taxation statutes do not make any finer distinction than that. Employment protection statutes, however, do make finer distinctions. While some rights only apply to those employed under a contract of employment/service, other rights apply to those who are classified as "workers". ERA 1996 contains 12 Parts which create a range of substantive rights, 11 of which apply only to employees. Only Part 2, relating to unauthorised deductions from wages, applies to workers more broadly. Other rights, such as the right to the national minimum wage, to working time protection and equal pay, also extend to workers as more broadly defined. There is a further even broader category, those who are "in employment", who receive protection under the anti-discrimination legislation.

Workers and those in employment

7.11   The statutory definition of a "worker" includes an employee and also someone who contracts to perform work personally so long as the contract does not make the other party a professional client[17] or a client or customer of his or her business.[18] The element of personal service is crucial to the definition of an employee, and this is not what distinguishes a worker and an employee. Employees are dependent on their employers economically, and in a subordinate position legally. The object of creating an "intermediate" category between employees and the self-employed is to recognise that there are workers in a position of dependency, who though not perhaps in the same position of subordination as employees are not sufficiently independent not to require protection. In *Byrne Brothers (Formwork) Ltd* v *Baird*[19] the EAT found that the applicants, who were self-employed labour-only sub-contractors in the construction industry, were exactly the kind of worker for whom this intermediate status was created: workers who, although nominally free to move from employer to employer, in fact work for lengthy periods for one employer, supplying no more than their own labour. In some cases such labour-only subcontractors would be employees, even although their contract may on the face of it state otherwise, if the contract as a whole is in fact one of employment.[20]

7.12   The anti-discrimination statutes place duties on employers not to discriminate against those who are "in employment".[21] This is a similar but broader concept to that of worker. It includes the employee, and again anyone who contracts to perform personal service, but without the qualification that the other party must not be a professional client or customer.

7.13   The Employment Relations Act 1999[22] gives the Secretary of State power to amend

---

[17] Trade Union and Labour Relations (Consolidation) Act 1992 (TULRCA 1992), s 296.
[18] ERA 1996, s 230(3).
[19] [2002] IRLR 96.
[20] *Ferguson* v *John Dawson & Partners (Contractors) Ltd* [1976] 3 All ER 817.
[21] Equal Pay Act 1970, s 1(6); Sex Discrimination Act 1975, s 82; Race Relations Act 1976, s 78; Disability Discrimination Act 1995, s 68; Employment Equality (Religion or Belief) Regulations 2003 (SI 2003/1660), reg 2; Employment Equality (Sexual Orientation) Regulations 2003 (SI 2003/1661), reg 2; Employment Equality (Age) Regulations 2006 (SI 2006/1031), reg 2
[22] Section 23.

ERA 1996 and TULR(C)A (1992) to extend rights to workers in particular categories, but this power has not been used yet.

While there are good reasons for ensuring that employees, as dependent and **7.14** subordinate workers, have protection, it is perhaps more questionable whether the full range of rights should be restricted. The form of employment contract may not be at the discretion of the worker, who may be more or less dependent and subordinate in fact even although formally not employed under a contract of employment. Where an employment relationship is in practice one in which the worker is of employee status, the courts and tribunals are able to find that it is so in law as well, but the distinction between a contract of employment and a worker's contract can be narrow, and the difference in dependency and subordination between a worker and employee scarcely enough to justify withholding job protection rights.

HOW TO IDENTIFY A CONTRACT OF EMPLOYMENT

At common law a contract of service is distinguished from a contract for services. While **7.15** the concept of employee at common law is the same concept as is used in the employment statutes, the concepts of "worker" and "in employment" are not directly equivalent to the contract for services: both will be employed under forms of contracts for services, but this is not part of their statutory definition. The difference between a contract of service and a contract for services was expressed in *Stagecraft Ltd v Minister of National Insurance*[23] as follows:

> "In the contract of service the person hired agrees to place his services under the direction and control of the hirer. In the contract for services the person hired agrees to perform a specific service for the hirer, the manner of the performance being left to the discretion of the person hired." [24]

In this case a comedian, contracted to appear for a season in "resident variety" in theatres in Britain, was held to be employed under a contract of service. The most important factor taken account of in determining the question was the degree of control exercised over the employee by the employer. The importance of control is such that the approach to determining the question of whether a contract was one of service was at one stage based entirely on control and known as the "control test." In *Stagecraft Ltd* this was expressed as follows: "A servant is a person subject to the command of his master as to the manner in which he shall do his work." [25] There is no longer a "control" test for determining who is an employee, but control is still an important criterion in the modern approach.

The modern approach

The most influential formulation of the modern approach is in *Ready Mixed Concrete (SE)* **7.16** *Ltd v Minister of Pensions and National Insurance*[26] in which the decision of the Minister

---

[23] 1952 SC 288.
[24] At 302.
[25] at 301, quoting Bramwell LJ in *Yewens v Noakes* [1880] 6 QBD 530 at 532.
[26] [1968] 2 QB 497.

that a lorry driver was employed under a contract of service was overturned on appeal. Three conditions were identified as necessary for a contract of service: agreement by the employee, in consideration for a wage, to provide his own work and skill to perform service for the employer; agreement by the employee to be subject to a sufficient degree of control by the employer; and the other terms of the contract being consistent with its being a contract of service.[27] This definition is often referred to as the "multiple" or "multi-factor" test. As a definition it leaves a lot of room for interpretation, not least the third condition where there is no prescribed list of factors which are consistent and inconsistent, but a matter of common sense in each case. A different emphasis can be seen in the contemporaneous case of *Market Investigations Ltd v Minister of Social Security*,[28] in which the Minister's decision that a market research interviewer was employed under a contract of service was upheld. It identified a fundamental difference between an employed person and someone who was self-employed through the key question "Is the person who has engaged himself to perform these services performing them as a person in business on his own account?".[29] Although this was in the context of confirming the move away from the single "control" test, control was still an important, but not the sole, factor. Additional factors were: whether the disputed service provider provides their own equipment; whether he or she hires out their own helpers; what degree of financial risk he or she takes; what degree of financial responsibility he or she has; and the extent to which he or she can profit from sound management in performing the task.[30] This approach concentrates on issues relating to dependency, and is sometimes described as the "entrepreneurial", "small businessman" or "economic reality" test. The question to be asked was phrased in down-to-earth terms by the EAT in *Withers v Flackwell Heath Football Supporters' Club*[31] as; "Are you your own boss?" In that case the EAT felt that the claimant, a bar steward, would certainly have answered "No", and that he was an employee.

7.17   The generality of the "multiple" test is such that different parts of it may be given more emphasis in one case rather than another, both as a matter of law and in relation to the particular contract. In some cases control has been very prominent; in others less so. This may depend on why the existence of the contract is being asserted or challenged. The "entrepreneurial" test arose in the context of tax and national insurance; the issue of control has been particularly influential in relation to vicarious liability; while in unfair dismissal and other employment protection cases the concept of mutuality of obligation, which will be discussed below, has been prominent. This may be inevitable, and is certainly confusing. It would seem that a unitary approach to the question is what is aspired to in the courts[32] but not what happens in practice.

An "irreducible minimum"?

7.18   Although the "economic reality" approach seems closer to identifying the essence of a contract of employment, it is the "multiple" test which has been the more influential,

---

[27] At 515.
[28] [1969] 2 QB 173.
[29] At 184.
[30] At 185.
[31] [1981] IRLR 307.
[32] *Lee v Chung* [1990] IRLR 236; *Lane v Shire Roofing Co (Oxford) Ltd* [1995] IRLR 493.

particularly in the context of employment protection rights. Although it is a multi-factor test, there has been a tendency to focus particularly on two aspects: control and "mutuality of obligation". In *Montgomery v Johnson Underwood Ltd*[33] these two concepts were described as the "irreducible minimum" of a contract of service, while in *Carmichael v National Power plc*[34] Lord Irving in the House of Lords restricted it to "that irreducible minimum of mutual obligation".[35] This implies that the balancing of consistent and inconsistent factors and taking account of all the factors in the "multiple" test is conditional on the contract first meeting the requirement of mutuality (or possibly mutuality and control).

Mutuality of obligation

In this context mutuality of obligation means that the employer is obliged to offer work, **7.19** and the employee obliged to perform work under the terms of the contract. This can be particularly problematic in the case of casual workers and agency workers. For casual workers the problem is that a contract whose terms are that work will be offered "as and when required" and will be accepted "if suitable" does not provide the necessary mutuality. For agency workers there is a different problem: agency workers have a contract with an employment agency, which has a contract with an end-user with whom the worker is placed. The worker has a contract with the agency (who will usually be responsible for paying remuneration) but is under the control of the end-user. Thus there is no mutuality between worker and end-user.

There is a line of decisions which have found mutuality established by implication. In **7.20** the case of casual workers the Court of Appeal in *Nethermere (St Neots) v Taverna and Gardiner*[36] considered the position of part-time homeworkers sewing pockets in to trousers where there was no obligation to provide or do the work. It found that, through a course of dealing over a number of years, implied mutuality of obligation had grown up. In the case of agency workers the Court of Appeal in *Dacas v Brook Street Bureau*[37] considered the case of a cleaner who had been working for four years with a local authority through the employment agency. The Tribunal had found that she had no contract with the end-user and her contract with the agency was not one of service. The EAT found that her contract with the agency was one of service since it paid her wages. The Court of Appeal, however, found that the question should not have been decided without considering whether there was an implied contract of service with the end-user as employer. Since Ms Dacas had not appealed against the finding that the local authority was not her employer, this did not become a live issue. There is no consistent approach here, and the implied contract analysis has been doubted in the Court of Session.[38]

Personal service

The contract is a personal one and the power to delegate is in general fatal to its being **7.21** one of service. It is also part of the statutory definitions of a worker's contract, and of the

---

[33] [2001] IRLR 269.
[34] [1999] ICR 1226.
[35] At 1230.
[36] [1984] ICR 612.
[37] [2004] ICR 1437.
[38] *Toms v Royal Mail Group plc* [2006] CSOH 32 per Lord Glennie at para 22.

concept of "in employment". McKenna J did say that "a limited or occasional power of delegation" might not be fatal[39] but it would have to be very limited, almost certainly restricted to a replacement approved by the employer. In *MacFarlane* v *Glasgow City Council*[40] a Tribunal had found that a gym instructor who, if she was unable to take a class, was entitled to send along a replacement from a register of instructors maintained by the council, and paid by the council, was not an employee because of the power to delegate. The EAT found that it had taken too absolute an approach to this and remitted it back for reconsideration, applying the correct test.

Control

7.22   Control is still an important, although not the sole, element. The definition of "control" adopted in *Ready Mixed Concrete* is: "It includes the power of deciding the thing to be done, the way in which it shall be done, the means to be employed in doing it, the time when and the place where it shall be done."[41] This can extend to the skilled worker whose employer is not capable of actually controlling the work. "It is the right of control not its exercise."[42]

SPECIAL GROUPS OF WORKERS

7.23   There are a number of employment relationships which are not governed by a contract of service. Some of them are treated for the most part in the same way as contracts of service. Civil servants, police officers and other Crown employees are not employed under contracts of service, but are given the benefit of most statutory employment rights.[43] Company directors are not employees by virtue of being directors (they are agents of the company), but may be employed under a contract of service as well as being a director. A director's employment contract is often referred to as a "service agreement".

Contract of apprenticeship

7.24   A contract of apprenticeship is not a contract of service: under such a contract the employer contracts to instruct the apprentice in a particular trade or skill and the apprentice contracts to learn. As a fixed- term contract it cannot be terminated on the giving of notice. Statutory definitions of employment in general include the contract of apprenticeship[44] along with the contract of service. While apprentices have additional protections by virtue of their status this is not the case for those working under training contracts which are not apprenticeships.[45] The status of someone working under a "modern apprenticeship" is not entirely clear but where there is a tripartite arrangement for training involving a training body and an

---

[39] *Ready Mixed Concrete (South Eastern) Ltd* v *Minister of Pensions and National Insurance* [1968] 2 QB 497 at 515.
[40] [2001] IRLR 7.
[41] At 515.
[42] ibid.
[43] See, for example, ERA 1996, ss 191–201.
[44] ERA 1996, s 230(2) and (3).
[45] *Wiltshire Police Authority* v *Wynn* [1981] QB 95.

employer, it is not a contract of apprenticeship, but is likely to be a contract of service if it meets the "multiple" test.[46]

Ministers of religion

Secular appointments by religious bodies are in the same category as any other **7.25** employment. However the traditional approach of the courts towards ministerial appointments has been to regard them as being on a spiritual rather than a commercial basis. Since there is no intention to be legally bound, a minister of religion could not be an employee (nor even a worker). The position was recently reviewed by the House of Lords in *Percy* v *Church of Scotland Board of National Mission*.[47] An associate minister of the Church of Scotland raised an unfair dismissal and a sex discrimination action when she was counselled to resign as a minister following an internal inquiry. Both actions were dismissed by the ET and the appeal was pursued only in relation to the sex discrimination action, which required proof that she was "in employment", not that she was an employee. The House of Lords found that she was in employment. There was a personal obligation to execute work: the contract between her and the Mission gave her the right to be paid and it the duty to enforce her performance of the duties of an associate minister.[48] The statutory rights related to civil, not spiritual, matters. Although this decision relates to an associate minister, there is no reason why its terms should not apply to all ministers of religion. The House did not consider whether she was employed under a contract of service because it did not have to, but equally there seems no reason, once it has been agreed that the contract is not a spiritual one entirely, and is intended to be legally binding, why it would not also meet the terms of the "multiple" test.

THE CONTRACT OF EMPLOYMENT

The contract of employment is governed by the general law of contract. While the **7.26** formal common law position that a contract is a voluntary agreement entered into by two consenting (and equal) parties may not reflect the realities of economic power, it does reflect the legal status. The formation of a contract of employment is subject to the same principles as any other contract. There is no requirement for writing, so that an employment contract may be formed in writing, verbally or by actions.

The contract of employment is made up of a number of sources. It is an ongoing **7.27** contract which may therefore be varied throughout its life. The principal sources are: express terms (written or verbal); implied terms (general principles); incorporated terms; implied terms (common law duties). Although there is no requirement for the contract to be in writing, there is a statutory requirement for there to be a written record of the terms of employment.

---

[46] *Flett* v *Matheson* [2005] IRLR 412
[47] 2006 SLT 11.
[48] At 28 per Baroness Hale.

DUTY TO PROVIDE WRITTEN STATEMENT OF EMPLOYMENT PARTICULARS

7.28 Employees who have 1 month's service and work at least 8 hours a week are entitled to receive, within 2 months of starting employment, a written statement of employment particulars. The statement must specify:[49]

- name of employer and employee;
- date when employment began;
- date when continuous employment began, if different;
- scale or rate of pay or method of calculating it;
- intervals when paid;
- terms and conditions of hours of work;
- terms and conditions of holidays and holiday pay;
- job title or brief description of work;
- place of work, or if various, indication of that and employer's address.

7.29 This information must all be given in one note. The following information must also be given but not necessarily in the same note:

- terms and conditions relating to sickness, including sickness pay;
- terms and conditions relating to pensions and pension schemes; [This information could be given by referring to a reasonably accessibly document.]
- the notice the employee is entitled to receive and obliged to give; [This information can be given by referring to statute or a collective agreement.]
- if the job is not permanent, the period for which it is expected to continue or the date when it is expected to end;
- any collective agreement directly affecting terms and conditions;
- if the employee is required to work outside the UK for over a month, information about work outside the UK.

If there are no particulars about any of the matters in this list, the statement must say so.

7.30 The employee must also be given a note about discipline and grievance rules and procedures, including the name of the person to whom an appeal against discipline can be made, or with whom a grievance can be lodged.[50]

7.31 If the employer has given the employee a written contract of employment covering all the required particulars, this document will count as fulfilling this obligation.[51] Any changes in any of the particulars must be notified to the employee within 1 month of the change.[52]

Legal status of the written statement

7.32 The written statement is not of itself contractual. It is a unilateral document drawn up by one party only: the employer. Though this is likely to reflect the contractual terms, it

---

[49] Sections 1 and 2.
[50] Section 3.
[51] Sections 7A and 7B.
[52] Section 4.

may not. A contract, on the other hand, is bilateral: it is the product of the agreement of employer and employee. If there is a conflict between the contractual agreement and the written statement, it is the contract which will prevail. In *Robertson* v *British Gas Corporation*[53] where employees relied on a contractual letter which gave a right to a bonus, and the employer relied on a written statement which stated it was a qualified right, the contractual terms prevailed.

IMPLIED TERMS

Express terms take precedence over all other terms. An implied term may supplement an ambiguous or partial provision, or fill a gap in a contract, but cannot contradict an express term. In *Tayside Regional Council* v *McIntosh*[54] an employee who had been dismissed from his job as a garage mechanic when he was disqualified from driving, claimed that his dismissal was unfair since there had been no term in his contract requiring that he possess a clean driving licence. This had been mentioned in the advertisement for the job, the application form and at interview, but not in the contractual letter. The EAT held that, while an implied term could not have contradicted an express term, it could supplement or clarify: in this case it was, it said, an essential term because of the nature of the work the employee had to do.   **7.33**

Tests for implied terms

The most influential test is the "business efficacy" test. Where it is necessary to imply a term into a contract to make it workable, such a term should be implied. This is essentially what happened in *Tayside Regional Council* v *McIntosh*. As a mechanic, it would be necessary for the employee to move or test drive the vehicle and thus a valid licence would be required. The contract, it could be argued, would be unworkable without it.   **7.34**

Another approach has been to imply into a contract a term which is so "obvious" that is must be assumed that the parties would have agreed to it if they had thought about it. This is sometimes called the "officious bystander" or "oh, of course" test – if a bystander had suggested to the parties that they include a certain term in the contract, they would both have said "oh, of course", that it was obvious it should be included.[55] What this approach emphasises is that the implied term must be something which both parties agree (or would have agreed) should be obligatory.   **7.35**

There is a possible conflict between these two approaches. Something which may be necessary, or reasonably necessary, to make the contract work, may not be so obvious that the parties must have agreed to it when made. It is more likely to be the employer's interests which would be allied with that of the business, so that a "business efficacy" test of some sort is more likely to help the employer's interpretation. In *Aparau* v *Iceland Frozen Foods*[56] there had been no express mobility contract in the employee's contract of employment. When the employer was taken over, employees were asked to agree to a new written statement which stated that employees could be transferred to any store   **7.36**

---

[53] [1983] IRLR 302.
[54] [1982] IRLR 272.
[55] *Lake* v *Essex County Council* [1979] ICR 577
[56] [1996] IRLR 119.

owned by the company. Mrs Aparau did not and, on transfer a year later to another branch, she resigned. Her resignation would only allow her to raise an unfair dismissal claim if it was a constructive dismissal, that is a legitimate response to a material breach of contract by her employer. While the ET had found that she had agreed to the new term by working on for 12 months without objecting, and, using the "oh, of course" test, that a mobility clause was implied in the original contract, the EAT did not agree: it held that because this was a change without immediate practical effect, working on did not imply that she had accepted the change. Nor did it agree that a mobility clause was implied in the original contract. It did not feel it was essential to make the contract work: a place of work is essential; a mobility clause makes life easier for management, but it is not always reasonably necessary.

Terms implied by custom and practice

7.37 It is possible, but not common, for a term to be implied by custom and practice. Such a custom would have to be "reasonable, certain and notorious".[57] It is important that implied contractual effect is shown. An implied agreement is not the same thing as an exercise of an employer's discretion, such as a one-off, or even two-off, enhanced redundancy pay.[58] Equally, agreement by employees on one occasion or a limited number of occasions, is not the same as agreeing to contractual change, such as reduction in hours for work shortage.[59] The important thing is to establish that the custom has been followed without exception for a substantial period, that the custom has been drawn to the attention of employees, and that it is possible to infer an intention to be bound contractually.

INCORPORATED TERMS

7.38 Incorporation of terms into a contract occurs when the parties agree to make an outside source into a term of the contract. The most common source of incorporated terms is the collective agreement. A collective agreement is an agreement between an employer and a trade union or trade unions, or a group of employers and trade unions. A collective agreement is not a legally binding contract in itself between the employer and the union.[60] However, although the collective agreement itself creates no legal rights, its terms, or certain of them, may become part of an individual contract of employment through the process of incorporation, and thus enforceable by the employer or employee as between each other.

7.39 The terms of a collective agreement can be incorporated into the individual contract expressly (by being referred to in the individual contract as a source of terms), or by being implied by custom (as discussed in the previous section). Not all terms of a collective agreement may be suitable for incorporation. Some agreements may relate to dispute resolution between employer and union, or general policy aims, such as how to deal with redundancies and these may not be incorporated if they are considered too general.[61]

---

[57] *Devonald v Rosser & Sons Ltd* [1906] 2 KB 728; *Sagar v H Ridehalgh & Son Ltd* [1931] 1 Ch 310.
[58] *Quinn v Calder Industrial Materials Ltd* [1996] IRLR 126.
[59] *International Packaging Corporation (UK) Ltd v Balfour* [2003] IRLR 11.
[60] TULRCA 1992, s 179, but note exception.
[61] *British Leyland (UK) Ltd v McQuilken* [1978] IRLR 245.

IMPLIED DUTIES: TERMS IMPLIED BY COMMON LAW

Both employer and employee have duties implied into the contract by the common law. **7.40**
These duties were developed in the 19th century and reflect the subordination inherent
in the relationship of employer and employee. There have also been more recent
developments expanding the employer's duties. The duties can be seen as underpinning
the essential nature of the contract whereby the employee agrees to provide work for the
employer in return for a wage (the "wage/work bargain").

The implied duties of the employee

Duty to be willing to give personal service

The contract is one of *delectus personae*. As it is personal, performance cannot be **7.41**
delegated to another.[62] Because the contract is personal it is not possible for either
employer or employee to be compelled to adhere to the contract: an employee cannot be
forced to remain in employment, and an employer cannot be forced to retain an
employee.[63] This is so even where an employee has been successful in winning
an unfair dismissal action.

Duty to obey lawful and reasonable orders

The employer's prerogative is to give orders to the employee which the employee must **7.42**
obey. However these orders must be within the scope of the contract, and must be
lawful and reasonable. An employee need not obey an order to do something which is
unlawful, nor something which is unreasonable. These two concepts came into conflict
in *Buckoke v Greater London Council*[64] with (in that case) reasonableness taking precedence. An instruction to firefighters to cross red lights when driving to an emergency,
while driving carefully in doing so, was found to be reasonable, and although, at that
time, technically unlawful, one which the employee should have obeyed.

Duty of loyalty

This duty is also referred to as the duty to give faithful service, or the duty of fidelity and **7.43**
comprises a number of headings. There is a fiduciary (good faith) relationship between
employer and employee, with the employee owing the employer a fiduciary duty. The
employee must put the employer's interests before his or her own in connection with the
employment, and must act in the employer's interests.

Duty of honesty. A contract of employment is not a contract *uberrimae fidei* (of the **7.44**
utmost good faith), so that there is no duty to disclose material facts. The employee's
duty is to be honest, but not necessarily to disclose prejudicial information if it is not
asked for.[65] There may be special circumstances where it is necessary to disclose such

---

[62] *Ready Mixed Concrete (SE) Ltd* v *Minister of Pensions and National Insurance* [1968] 2 QB 497.
[63] TULRCA 1992, s 236.
[64] [1971] 2 All ER 254.
[65] *Bell* v *Lever Bros* [1932] AC 161.

information: it may be part of the employee's contractual duty (express or implied, perhaps as a supervisor) to report others' wrongdoing, which might also involve their own.[66]

7.45   **Duty not to make a secret profit**. An employee should not make any personal gain from his or her employment, without the knowledge and consent of the employer. This includes not just taking a bribe but gaining any advantage or payment from the employment.[67]

7.46   **Duty to act in the employer's interests**. This aspect of the duty of loyalty as a duty to cooperate with or not to disrupt the employer's business emerged in the case of *Secretary of State for Employment* v *ASLEF (No 2)*.[68] A "work to contract" by train drivers, whereby they obeyed the employer's rule book to the letter, was held to be in breach of contract since it was done with the intention of disrupting the employer's business.

7.47   **Duty not to use confidential information**. Employers may protect themselves by an express term in the contract from confidential information being disclosed during and after employment.[69] Even without an express term, the implied duty gives protection.

7.48   *Duty not to work for rivals*. An employee may work for whoever he wishes in his own time. However in the case of a potential conflict between the interests of the employer and a secondary employer, there would be a breach of duty if there was danger that confidential information might be revealed.[70]

7.49   *Duty not to benefit personally*. An employee should not take advantage of his or her position in order to benefit their own interests for the present or the future, such as canvassing customers for a future business.[71]

7.50   *Duty not to disclose confidential information*. There is a difference in the implied duty between what an employee may not disclose while still an employee and what may not be disclosed after employment ends. The common law duty does have an impact after employment, but in a limited way. In *Faccenda Chicken* v *Fowler*[72] three categories of confidential information were distinguished: easily accessible information (which it would not be breach of contract to disclose); information which was told in confidence or which it was obvious was confidential but was part of the skill or memory of the employee (which it would be breach of contract to disclose during employment but not afterwards); and "trade secrets", information so confidential that it should never be divulged even after employment ended. Thus, using information in the second category, gained while an employee (such as the names of customers), would not be a breach of the implied term, but recording the information while an employee for use afterwards would be.

---

[66] *Sybron Corporation* v *Rochem Ltd* [1983] IRLR 253.
[67] *Boston Deep Sea Fishing Co* v *Ansell* (1888) 39 Ch D 339.
[68] [1972] ICR 19.
[69] See para **5.64**.
[70] *Hivac Ltd* v *Park Royal Scientific Instruments Ltd* [1946] 1 Ch 169.
[71] *Adamson* v *B & L Cleaning Services Ltd* [1995] IRLR 193.
[72] [1986] IRLR 69.

An employee might seek to justify or defend disclosing confidential information by **7.51** relying on a common law "public interest" defence,[73] or on the "whistleblower's" protection from dismissal or detriment introduced by the Public Interest Disclosure Act 1998.[74] It does not give a blanket protection: the disclosure must be a "qualifying disclosure" and it must be made to one of the specified categories of persons. Any court or tribunal considering this issue would also have to take account of Art 10 of the ECHR ("Freedom of Expression") which is a qualified right.

Inventions. At common law an invention which is connected with the employee's employ- **7.52** ment is the employer's as the employee must work in the best interests of the employer. However, this position has been ameliorated by the Patents Act 1977[75] so that the employer only has ownership where the invention was made in the course of the employee's duties; or was made in the course of specifically assigned duties from which the invention might reasonably be expected to result; or was made in the course of the employee's duties, and the employee's responsibility gives him or her a duty to further the employer's interests.

Duty to show reasonable skill and care

If an employee does not exercise reasonable care and skill, he or she may be required to **7.53** indemnify the employer for loss caused by the breach.[76]

The implied duties of the employer

Duty to pay wages

If the employer pays wages, the primary duty is fulfilled: there is no duty to provide work. **7.54** As a judge said over 60 years ago: "Provided I pay my cook her wages regularly, she cannot complain if I choose to take any or all of my meals out."[77] Thus, an employer who suspends an employee on full pay will not be in breach of contract, though suspension without pay will be a breach unless there is an express contractual term permitting it.

There are limited circumstances in which an employee can demand work as well as **7.55** wages: where the failure to provide the work as well as wages could lead to a loss of reputation or publicity, usually applying in the case of actors;[78] where the wages are dependent on work, as in the case of piecework or commission; and possibly where skills need to be kept up to date by practical application.[79]

Duty to indemnify

The employer has a duty to indemnify or reimburse an employee for losses or expenses **7.56** incurred in the course of employment.

---

[73] *Initial Services Ltd v Putterill* [1968] 1 QB 396.
[74] Inserted ss 43A–H, 47B and 103A into ERA 1996.
[75] Sections 39–45.
[76] *Lister v Romford Ice and Cold Storage Co Ltd* [1957] AC 555.
[77] *Collier v Sunday Referee Publishing Co Ltd* [1940] 4 All ER 234 at 236.
[78] *Herbert Clayton & Jack Waller Ltd v Oliver* [1930] AC 209.
[79] *Langston v AEUW (No 2)* [1974] ICR 510.

Duty to take reasonable care for the employee's safety

7.57   At common law an employer has a duty to take reasonable care for an employee's safety and to protect him or her from foreseeable risks. It is both contractual and delictual.[80]

"Mutual duty of trust and confidence"

7.58   This is a duty which has developed relatively recently. It is often viewed as the employer's counterpart to the employee's duty of loyalty. It has had the effect of placing a greater requirement for fair and reasonable treatment of the employee on the employer. It was acknowledged by the House of Lords in *Malik* v *Bank of Credit and Commerce International*.[81] The duty was stated to be that the employer "shall not without reasonable and proper cause, conduct itself in a manner calculated to or likely to destroy or seriously damage the relationship of confidence and trust between employer and employee".[82] In *Malik*, the employer's breach had consisted in conducting the bank's business in a fraudulent manner, which, the employees concerned alleged, had caused them to become unemployable even though they had not been involved in the corrupt practices.

7.59   The employer does not have to have intended to damage the relationship with the employee: the question is to be answered objectively, looking at whether the behaviour was likely to have that effect. The sort of behaviour caught by this duty is varied. It extends to bullying and harassment,[83] failing to take a complaint seriously,[84] and insulting an employee.[85]

TERMINATION AND ENFORCEMENT OF THE CONTRACT OF EMPLOYMENT

TERMINATION BY NOTICE

7.60   Termination by the employer is dismissal; termination by the employee is resignation. At common law either may terminate a contract of employment by giving notice. What would commonly be considered to be a "permanent" employee, a term used in the Fixed Term Employees (Prevention of Less Favourable Treatment) Regulations 2002 in contrast to a fixed term employee, has at common law a "periodic" contract. Such a contract is automatically renewed, by the principle of tacit relocation, unless one of the parties gives notice to terminate it. The length of notice may be provided in the contract, but must be no less than the statutory minimum: from the employer, 1 week for every year of employment to a maximum of 12 weeks' notice; from the employee, 1 week.[86]

---

[80] See Chapters 4 and 5.
[81] [1997] ICR 606.
[82] At 621, quoting *Woods* v *WM Car Services Ltd* [1981] ICR 666 at 670.
[83] *Horkulak* v *Cantor Fitzgerald International* [2003] IRLR 756.
[84] *Bracebridge Engineering Ltd* v *Darby* [1990] IRLR 3.
[85] *Isle of Wight Tourist Board* v *Coombes* [1976] IRLR 413.
[86] ERA 1996, s 86.

Wrongful dismissal

Dismissal without notice is called *summary* dismissal, and is justified only when the employee **7.61** is in material breach of contract. An employee who is unjustifiably dismissed may raise a common law action for wrongful dismissal. The measure of damages for wrongful dismissal will be calculated in the usual way for breach of contract, and will be sufficient to restore the employee to the position he or she would have been in but for the wrongful dismissal. Since the employer would have been entitled to dismiss with notice, compensation is often restricted to the amount due for notice. Unlike wrongful dismissal, the statutory remedy of unfair dismissal is available when the employer dismisses with notice and when the employer fails to renew a fixed-term contract, and damages are not restricted to the notice period.

OTHER FORMS OF TERMINATION

At common law a contract for a fixed period or a fixed task ends when the period or task **7.62** comes to an end. This is not the case so far as statutory employment protection rights are concerned: failure to renew a fixed-term contract is a dismissal so far as the law of unfair dismissal and redundancy pay is concerned.[87] Employer and employee may agree to end the contract: this is neither a resignation nor a dismissal. The contract of employment may be frustrated under the doctrine of impossibility of performance, but the courts are reluctant to apply this doctrine to periodic employment contracts.[88] Death of either party, the dissolution of a partnership or the winding up of a company will also terminate the contract, but if a business is acquired as a going concern the Transfer of Undertakings (Protection of Employment) Regulations 2006 (TUPE) will operate to transfer the contracts of existing employees to the new employer,[89] though an employee cannot be forced to transfer if he or she does not wish to.[90]

BREACH OF CONTRACT

Where one party materially breaches or repudiates the contract, the other is entitled to **7.63** terminate the contract without notice. It is the action of the innocent party in accepting the breach which terminates the contract, not the breach itself. Thus, where an employee materially breaches a contract of employment and the employer says that the contract is at an end because of the breach, this is a dismissal since it is the action of the employer which has ended the contract, not the breach.[91]

REMEDIES FOR BREACH OF CONTRACT

Specific implement/interdict

An action of specific implement cannot be used to compel either employee or employer **7.64** to continue with a contract of employment. This common law rule is reinforced by

---

[87] ERA 1996, ss 95 and 136.
[88] *Williams* v *Watson Luxury Coaches* [1990] IRLR 164.
[89] reg 4. For transfers before 6 April 2006 TUPE Regulations 1981 will apply.
[90] reg 4(7).
[91] *London Transport Executive* v *Clarke* [1981] ICR 355.

statute.[92] There are, however, some circumstances in which it may be possible to obtain an interdict. An employer may be able to obtain an interdict to prohibit an employee working for another in breach of an express or implied contractual term, but this would only be granted if the employer is prepared to carry on with the contract, and the order is necessary to protect the employer's legitimate interests.[93] An employee might be able to obtain an interdict to postpone a contractually improper dismissal, but this would only be granted if the employee still retained the confidence of the employer and would only postpone the dismissal until contractual procedures had been gone through.[94]

Withholding wages

7.65 If an employee refuses to carry out a significant part of their employment duties, this is a repudiation of contract, which would entitle the employer to terminate it. If the employer does not terminate it, he or she is not obliged to accept partial performance and pay for it. If the employer decides not to pay wages, he or she must have told the employee that partial performance will not be accepted.[95]

Unlawful deductions from wages

7.66 Where an employer fails to pay what is contractually due, there is a statutory procedure for raising an action for unlawful deductions in an ET.[96] This procedure is appropriate both where the employer has consciously made a deduction from wages, and also where the employer is simply in breach of contract in failure to pay or in the amount paid. In the former case a deduction is only lawful where it is required or authorised by statute or the contract of employment, or the worker has given prior agreement in writing to such a deduction.[97]

STATUTORY EMPLOYMENT RIGHTS

7.67 This section looks in outline at three statutory employment rights. The national minimum wage and working time legislation lay a base line for minimum pay and maximum hours. Both apply to workers as well as employees. The right not to be unfairly dismissed is an important right giving some protection of job security. It only applies to employees. There are many other rights, principally in ERA 1996 but also in individual legislation which are beyond the scope of a chapter.

NATIONAL MINIMUM WAGE

7.68 There had been minimum wage legislation since the beginning of the 20th century, but this applied only to specific low pay sectors of the economy through Wages Councils,

---

[92] TULRCA 1992, s 236.
[93] *GFI Group Inc* v *Eaglestone* [1994] IRLR 119.
[94] *Hughes* v *London Borough of Brent* [1988] IRLR 55.
[95] *Wiluszynski* v *London Borough of Tower Hamlets* [1989] IRLR 259.
[96] ERA 1996, Pt 2.
[97] Section 13.

which were abolished in 1993. The National Minimum Wage Act 1998 (NMWA 1998) introduced a national minimum wage (NMW) applying to all sectors, supplemented by the National Minimum Wage Regulations 1999 (NMWR 1999).

Qualification

Although it is a national standard, not every working person is entitled to the NMW. To qualify, the individual must be over compulsory school age, must be working in the UK and must be a "worker".[98] In addition to those employed under a worker's contract, the Act also applies to agency workers, homeworkers and Crown employees even if they are not otherwise workers.[99] However, there are a number of categories of workers who do not benefit. Certain classes of people have been excluded by the Regulations, including apprentices (for the first year), workers on certain government training schemes, students on work placement for less than a year and workers on schemes for homeless people or those on income support who are provided with shelter in return for work.[100] Further exclusions include voluntary workers for charities and voluntary organisations, prisoners, members of the armed forces and people living as part of a family.[101]   **7.69**

Rate of NMW

The rate is determined by the Secretary of State upon a recommendation by the Low Pay Commission, and is set as an hourly rate. The rates are as follows: **7.70**

- for those aged 22 and over (£5.35);
- for those aged between 18 and 22 (£4.45);
- for those aged 16 and 17 (but not apprentices) (£3.30).

Calculation of the rate

The NMWR 1999 provide the method for calculating whether NMW has been paid. A worker's hourly rate is calculated by dividing the total remuneration (TR) paid to the worker during the pay reference period (PRP) by the number of hours or work during that period (NHW): that is (TR in PRP) / NHW must be no less than NMW.   **7.71**

Total remuneration. This is determined by adding together all money payment paid by the employer to the worker in and relating to the PRP in question. Certain payment is deducted from the total, including overtime or shift premium, tips or gratuities not paid through the payroll and payment of expenses due to a third party.   **7.72**

Pay reference period. The pay reference period is 1 month, or, if pay is paid by reference to a period of less than a month, that period.   **7.73**

---

[98] NMWA 1998, ss 1 and 54.
[99] NMWA 1998, ss 34–36.
[100] NMWR 1999, reg 2.
[101] NMWA 1998, ss 37–44 and 45; NMWR 1999, reg 2.

7.74   **Number of hours of work**. How the hours of work are determined depends on the category of work, whether it is time work, salaried hours work, output work or measured hours work. The NMWR explain how the hours are to be calculated for each category or work.

Enforcement

7.75   The NMW is enforceable as a contractual right by the individual worker. The Inland Revenue has enforcement powers which enable it to serve notice on employers who do not comply, getting progressively more serious with failure to comply, with the sanction of criminal proceedings if the failure is wilful.[102]

WORKING HOURS

7.76   The Working Time Regulations 1998 (WTR 1998) were introduced in order to comply with the EC Working Time Directive 93/104. This Directive was passed as a health and safety measure, and the WTR are viewed both as a health and safety measure and as "family friendly" measure. The EC Directive was amended in 2000 to include a number of excluded workers, including junior doctors, within its scope, and the WTR were subsequently amended to comply. Following the scope for derogation in the Directive, many of the provisions of the WTR can be varied so long as the employer obtains a "relevant agreement": in some cases a collective agreement or workforce agreement, in others individual agreement. The WTR apply to workers, not just employees. Contracting out of the obligations under the WTR, other than expressly allowed, is void.[103] For each provision of the WTR there are exclusions or variations.

Working time

7.77   Working time is defined as any period during which a worker is working at his or her employer's disposal and carrying out his or her activities or duties, and not during a rest period when not working. This includes time when he or she is receiving relevant training related to work.[104] On-call time, where a worker is on call and during the on-call period is required to be present at a place determined by the employer counts as working time, even if the worker is permitted to sleep.[105]

Maximum weekly working time

7.78   The maximum weekly hours is 48 hours in each 7 days, including overtime.[106] This is calculated as an average over a reference period. The basic reference period is 17 weeks; special classes of worker (such as seasonal workers) have a 26-week reference period; and a reference period of up to 52 weeks could be agreed by a collective or workforce

---

[102] NMWA 1998, ss 17–22; and 31–32.
[103] NMWR 1999, reg 35.
[104] NMWR 1999, reg 2.
[105] *Sindicato de Medicos de Asistencia Publica (SIMAP)* v *Conselleria de Sanidad y Consumo de la Generalidad Valenciana* [2000] IRLR 845.
[106] NMWR 1999, regs 4–5.

agreement. For young workers, that is those over compulsory school age but under 18, the maximum working time is 8 hours a day and 40 hours a week, aggregating hours worked for more than one employer.[107] It is the employer's responsibility to see that each worker complies with the limit.

Individual opt-out

Unlike most other EU countries, the UK has included a provision whereby the employer **7.79** can obtain a worker's agreement in writing so that the 48-hour limit does not apply. The reference period may be varied by collective or workforce agreement, but the complete opt-out from the limit requires the individual worker's written agreement. The EU has been attempting to restrict the use of this opt-out, but, in spite of the health and safety arguments, the UK Government has continued to argue for the retention of this flexibility.

Rest

Adult workers are entitled to at least 11 hours' consecutive rest in each 24-hour period; **7.80** young workers to 12 hours. Adult workers are entitled to an uninterrupted weekly rest period of at least 24 hours in each 7-day period; young workers to 48 hours. An adult worker is entitled to a minimum of 20 minutes' break where more than 6 hours a day is worked; young workers to a minimum of 30 minutes for over 4.5 hours. For monotonous or other work patterns that might put health and safety at risk, rest breaks must be "adequate".[108]

Night working

A night worker is someone who normally works at least 3 hours at night, night being 11 **7.81** pm to 6 am unless agreed otherwise by a collective or workforce agreement (but the period must include midnight to 5 am). A night worker's normal hours of work cannot exceed an average of 8 hours for each 24 hours, calculated either according to the 17-week reference period, or for workers involved in special hazards or heavy mental or physical strain their actual working hours cannot exceed 8 in any 24-hour period.[109] Workers cannot be required to work at night without having had the opportunity to undergo a free health assessment, and should have regular assessments. There is a right to be transferred to day work if certified by a doctor that it is necessary.

An employer should ensure that young workers do not work during the "restricted **7.82** period", that is 10 pm to 6 am (or 11 pm to 7 am, according to contract).

Holidays

The WTR 1998 provide for a minimum of 4 weeks' paid annual leave. When they were **7.83** first introduced there was a 13-week qualification period for entitlement but this was held to be contrary to the Directive.[110]

---

[107] NMWR 1999, reg 5A.
[108] NMWR 1999, regs 8; 10–12.
[109] NMWR 1999, regs 6–8.
[110] *R v Secretary of State for Trade and Industry, ex p BECTU* [2001] ICR 1152.

7.84   A question to which the Scottish and English courts gave different answers was whether "rolled up" holiday pay was permissible. This is where a worker is not paid when he or she takes their holiday, but the pay for hours worked includes an element for holiday pay. The Scottish answer was that this was impermissible;[111] the English that it was permissible.[112] The ECJ has given its ruling on the question in a number of cases referred from the English Court of Appeal.[113] The answer may be described as impermissible, with qualifications. Formally it is contrary to the Directive since it may militate against workers taking holidays if they do not get paid at the time they are due to take them. However, if the situation is transparent, that is the precise proportion paid as holiday pay is made clear when it is actually paid, it may be permissible.

Enforcement

7.85   The individual worker may enforce the rest period and holiday provisions at an ET.[114] The working time and night work provisions are enforced by the Health and Safety Executive using a range of administrative and criminal sanctions.[115]

UNFAIR DISMISSAL

7.86   ERA 1996 provides a right not to be unfairly dismissed.[116] The statutory right of unfair dismissal should not be confused with the common law action of wrongful dismissal.[117]

Qualifying for the right not to be unfairly dismissed

7.87   Only employees have the right not to be unfairly dismissed. The employee must have been in employment with the dismissing employer for a continuous period of a year, working back from the date of dismissal.[118] Whether or not there is an unbroken period of qualifying service is calculated according to the statutory rules.[119] Continuity is presumed and it is up to the employer to prove that there has been a break. In cases of automatically unfair dismissal there is no qualifying period.

Dismissal

7.88   An action for unfair dismissal can only be raised if an employee has been dismissed. "Dismissal" is given an extended meaning in ERA 1996, both for unfair dismissal and for the right to redundancy pay. Dismissal can occur in three ways:

---

[111] *MPB Structure Ltd* v *Munro* [2003] IRLR 350.
[112] *Marshalls Clay Products* v *Caulfield* [2004] IRLR 564.
[113] *Robinson-Steele* v *RD Retail Services Ltd* (C–131/04) 2006 (ECJ).
[114] WTR 1998, reg 30.
[115] WTR 1998, regs 28–29.
[116] ERA 1996, s 94.
[117] See para **7.61**.
[118] ERA 1996, s 108.
[119] ERA 1996, ss 210–219.

(1)   termination of the contract by the employer, with or without notice;

(2)   expiry of a fixed-term contract without renewal;

(3)   termination of the contract by the employee with or without notice where the employer's conduct would have entitled the employee to resign without giving notice.[120]

If there is a dispute as to whether the employee has been dismissed, the burden of proof lies with the employee to show that he or she was dismissed.

Termination by the employer

Tribunals have been careful to look at the reality of the situation as well as the form of words to see if the reality is that the termination was at the instance of the employer. If an employer gives an employee an ultimatum to resign or be dismissed, that will be an employer termination;[121] similarly, if an employee is pressurised to agree to resign, that will also be an employer termination.   **7.89**

Non-renewal of a fixed-term contract

A fixed-term contract includes both a common law fixed-term contract (which cannot be terminated by notice before the end of the fixed term), and also a contract with a fixed termination date which can also be terminated by notice before that date, the latter being more common.[122]   **7.90**

Resignation justified by employer's conduct (constructive dismissal)

The courts have adopted a common law analysis of this provision of ERA 1996.[123] At common law, and therefore under this provision, only a material breach of contract by the employer can entitle the employee to resign without notice. The breach by the employer may be of any term in the contract, express or implied. It can include a breach of the mutual duty of trust and confidence: indeed, it is in the context of the concept of constructive dismissal that this duty developed.   **7.91**

The employee must resign in order to qualify as having been dismissed in this way, and should do so without delay. There may, however, be a series of actions by the employer, leading up to a "final straw" which precipitates the actual resignation. In *Lewis* v *Motorwold Garages Ltd*[124] an employee who was demoted continued to work, but resigned some time later after continued criticism and threats. While the ET and EAT had held that he had affirmed the contract by working on after demotion and the subsequent actions by the employer were not material, the Court of Appeal found that he could rely on the original demotion and subsequent actions cumulatively as a breach of the mutual duty of trust and confidence.   **7.92**

---

[120] ERA 1996, s 95.
[121] *Robertson* v *Securicor Transport Ltd* [1972] IRLR 70.
[122] *Dixon* v *BBC* [1979] IRLR 114.
[123] *Western Excavating (ECC) Ltd* v *Sharp* [1979] IRLR 27.
[124] [1985] IRLR 465.

Reason for the dismissal

7.93 In a "standard" unfair dismissal claim the employer must show what the reason or principal reason for the dismissal was.[125] In the case of automatically unfair dismissals the burden of proof will rest with the employee.

Automatically unfair dismissals

7.94 These are dismissals for specific inadmissible reasons. They differ from standard unfair dismissals in that there is no requirement for a period of continuous employment, and once the inadmissible reason has been established the dismissal is automatically unfair without any further proof of fairness or unfairness. Among the inadmissible reasons are pregnancy and maternity;[126] trade union membership and activity;[127] official industrial action;[128] health and safety;[129] spent convictions;[130] asserting a statutory right;[131] and making a protected disclosure.[132]

Reason in standard unfair dismissals

7.95 The employer must establish that the reason falls within one of the potentially fair reasons specified in the Act.[133] These are: capability or qualifications; conduct; retirement;[134] redundancy; contravention of a statutory duty; and some other substantial reason justifying dismissal. Capability is assessed by reference to skill, aptitude, health or any other physical or mental quality.

7.96   It is the reason which the employer actually relied on when dismissing the employee which is relevant, not any reason either discovered after dismissal or elevated in importance after dismissal.[135]

Fairness

7.97 Once the reason has been proved by the employer the ET will consider whether the dismissal for that reason was fair. This will be decided according to the terms of s 98(4) of ERA 1996. Whether a dismissal is fair or unfair is to be judged in the light of the reason shown by the employer, and depends on whether in the circumstances the employer acted reasonably or unreasonably in treating it as a sufficient reason for dismissing the employee. The subsection requires account to be taken of the size and administrative resources of the employer's undertaking, and for the question to be determined by an ET in accordance with equity and the substantial merits of the case.

---

[125] ERA 1996, s 98(1).
[126] ERA 1996, s 99; Maternity and Parental Leave etc. Regulations 1999 (SI 1999/3312), reg 20.
[127] TULRCA 1992, s 152.
[128] TULRCA 1992, s 238A.
[129] ERA 1996, ss 100.
[130] Rehabilitation of Offenders Act 1974.
[131] ERA 1996, s 104.
[132] ERA 1996, s 103A.
[133] ERA 1996, s 98(1) and (2).
[134] From 1 October 2006.
[135] *W Devis & Sons Ltd* v *Atkins* [1977] IRLR 314.

Section 98(4) does not place a burden of proof on either employer or employee. While   **7.98**
the burden is on the employee to prove there has been a dismissal, if disputed, and to
prove one of the automatically unfair grounds, if that is what is alleged, and the burden
is on the employer in a standard unfair dismissal to prove that it was for a potentially
fair reason, there is no burden of proof in relation to fairness in a standard unfair
dismissal.

Size and administrative resources of the employer

Small employers must behave fairly no less than large employers. Nevertheless the size   **7.99**
and administrative resources could determine the kind of procedures which an employer is able to adopt. The ACAS Code of Practice[136] suggests that it might not be
practicable for small establishment to adopt all its detailed provisions, and suggests
that some provisions[137] could be adapted for small businesses. For example, smaller
employers may not be able to adopt the same standards of independence at all stages of
a disciplinary hearing.

Equity and the substantial merits of the case

Each case must be determined on its own merits. A component of fairness is equitable,   **7.100**
or consistent, treatment of employees. Nevertheless, each case depends on its own facts
and it may be that it is appropriate to treat different employees differently for the same
(mis)conduct where their personal situation or record is different.[138]

Reasonableness

The Tribunal has to decide whether a reasonable employer would have taken the   **7.101**
decision to dismiss in the circumstances. It must not decide what they would have done
had they been the employer, but must decide if the employer's decision was within the
"band of reasonable responses" of a reasonable employer.[139] This presumes that there is
a spectrum of reasonable responses, with a harsh but reasonable decision at one end and
a lenient but reasonable decision at the other. The band of reasonable responses test has
been criticised for following rather than setting standards, and for in effect placing the
burden of proof on the employee by making the question one of whether no reasonable
employer would have decided to dismiss. The EAT decided not to follow it in *Haddon* v
Van Den Bergh Foods Ltd,[140], but the Court of Appeal rapidly overruled this and
reaffirmed the test in *HSBC Bank plc* v *Madden*.[141]

Reasonableness relates to whether there was sufficient reason to dismiss, and also   **7.102**
whether the employer adopted a reasonable procedure in making the decision.

---

[136] ACAS (Advisory, Conciliation and Arbitration Service) Code of Practice on Disciplinary and
Grievance Procedures (Revised 2004), para 7.
[137] Paras 9 and 38–41.
[138] *Securicor Ltd* v *Smith* [1989] IRLR 356.
[139] *British Leyland* v *Swift* [1981] IRLR 91.
[140] [1999] IRLR 672.
[141] [2000] IRLR 827.

Statutory procedures

7.103 **Retirement dismissals**. An employee may be fairly dismissed because of retirement, so long as the retiral age is 65 or over, or lower so long as the employer can justify it as a proportionate means of achieving a legitimate aim and thus not age discrimination.[142] The employer must also comply with the provisions of ss 98ZA–ZF of ERA 1996, and the procedures in the Employment Equality (Age) Regulations 2006 (EEAR 2006)[143] which give a right to be considered for working past retirement age.

7.104 **Statutory discipline and dismissal procedures**. All employers, regardless of size, must comply with the statutory procedures introduced by the Employment Act 2002.[144] These apply to most dismissals, but there are exceptions, including constructive dismissals and collective redundancy dismissals.[145] These are minimum procedural standards: failure to follow or complete them, where this is the fault of the employer, will make a dismissal automatically unfair,[146] and increase the amount of compensation due to the employee. There are two minimum procedures: the standard and the modified procedures.

7.105 *Standard procedure*. This is a three stage procedure. Before dismissing the employee, the employer must give a written statement of the circumstances which have led to his or her considering dismissal. There must be a meeting between the employer and employee before the decision to dismiss is taken. There must be a right to appeal against the decision.

7.106 *Modified procedure*. This is a two-stage procedure. It requires the employer to give a written statement of the alleged misconduct which led to the dismissal. There must be a right of appeal. The general rule is that the standard procedure applies. The modified procedure applies where the employer dismisses the employee without notice immediately on discovering the misconduct. The employer must have been entitled to dismiss without notice for this misconduct, and it must have been reasonable to dismiss without further enquiry.[147]

"No difference" rule

7.107 Before the introduction of the statutory discipline and dismissal procedures the House of Lords had held that it was an error of law for a Tribunal to decide, in cases where a dismissal was procedurally unfair, that the dismissal was fair because it would have made no difference if a proper procedure had been used.[148]

7.108   The position now is that failure to follow the statutory procedures will make a dismissal automatically unfair even if it would have made no difference. If an employer

---

[142] Employment Equality (Age) Regulations 2006 (SI 2006/1031) (EEAR 2006), reg 3 (from 1 October 2006).
[143] Sch 6; ERA 1996, s 98ZG.
[144] Implemented by the Employment Act 2002 (Dispute Resolution) Regulations 2004 (SI 2004/752) (EADRR 2004).
[145] EADRR 2004, reg 4.
[146] ERA 1996, s 98A.
[147] EADRR 2004, reg 3.
[148] *Polkey* v *A E Dayton Services Ltd* [1987] IRLR 503.

has complied with the statutory procedure, a failure in another aspect of procedure will not make a dismissal unfair, if the employer can show that he or she would have decide to dismiss the employee anyway even if a proper procedure had been followed.[149] The burden of proof is on the employer to show that it would have made no difference.

Conduct dismissals

The ACAS Code of Practice deals primarily with this form of dismissal. Much of the case law is concerned with broader issues of procedure. The employer's own disciplinary procedure should be followed, and if it gives clear warning of the sort of conduct which will merit dismissal, a dismissal for that reason is more likely to be found to be reasonable.[150] However a Tribunal can still consider whether a dismissal is reasonable even where it is in terms of the contract.[151]

7.109

The Burchell test

The decision of the EAT in *British Home Stores* v *Burchell*[152] has been very influential, and although it was challenged at the same time as the band of reasonable responses test it was also reaffirmed by the Court of Appeal.[153] In *Burchell* an employer's decision to dismiss an employee for suspected dishonesty, when there had been insufficient evidence for a prosecution and where it was now accepted that she was innocent, was held to have been reasonable. The employer had met a threefold test: there was a genuine belief in the employee's guilt; the employer had reasonable grounds for this belief; and the employer had carried out a reasonable investigation as the basis of these grounds. This may not be fair to the innocent employee, but it focuses on the reasonableness of the employer's behaviour as s 98(4) requires.

7.110

Good practice

The importance of investigation, hearing the employee and a system of appeal has been emphasised both in the ACAS Code of Practice and in many cases. The EAT have given helpful guidelines in some cases as to what makes good practice. General guidelines about conducting hearings are given in *Clark* v *Civil Aviation Authority*.[154] Guidelines as to the acceptable use of anonymous informants are given in *Linfood Cash and Carry Ltd* v *Thomson and Bell*.[155]

7.111

Capability dismissals

Although these are not misconduct dismissals so that a disciplinary approach is not appropriate, the *Burchell* test of genuine belief (in lack of capability), reasonable

7.112

[149] ERA 1996, s 98A.
[150] *Beedell* v *West Ferry Printers Ltd* [2000] IRLR 650.
[151] *Scottish Midland Co-operative Society Ltd* v *Oliphant* [1991] IRLR 261.
[152] [1980] ICR 303.
[153] *HSBC Bank plc* v *Madden* [2001] 1 All ER 550.
[154] [1991] IRLR 412.
[155] [1989] IRLR 235.

grounds and reasonable investigation has been approved for capability dismissals.[156] A reasonable employer will consider whether assistance or training would be appropriate.

7.113   Ill health may be a reason for a capability dismissal, and such a dismissal may be fair, so long as the employer has followed a proper procedure (in addition to the statutory discipline and dismissal procedure), taking account of the nature of the illness, the length of absence, the need to get the job done, the possibility of transfer, medical advice and the views of the employee.[157] An employee who suffers from ill health may also be a disabled person and thus have the protection of the Disability Discrimination Act 1995. Unfair dismissal and disability discrimination are to be dealt with as separate issues, although a discriminatory dismissal is likely to be unfair.[158]

Redundancy dismissals

7.114   Selection of an employee for redundancy for an inadmissible reason will make the dismissal automatically unfair.[159] In other cases the question is whether or not the employer acted reasonably. The Tribunal will not in general examine the economic reasons for the redundancy. The relevant issues are whether the employee was fairly selected by objective selection criteria, fairly applied; whether the employee (and any trade union) was adequately consulted and warned; and whether the possibility of alternative work was properly investigated.[160]

7.115   Fair consultation means consultation when the proposal is still at a formative stage, giving adequate information and adequate time to respond. The statutory discipline and dismissal procedure does not apply in the case of collective redundances. However, there are also statutory procedures in the case of collective redundancies requiring the employer to consult with trade union or employee representatives.[161]

Contravention of statute dismissals

7.116   If the employee's continued employment in his or her job would be contrary to legislation (such as if a driver was disqualified from driving), the dismissal is potentially fair. Relevant additional consideration could include the length of the likely illegality, the extent to which the employee is prevented from working and whether there is any alternative work.[162]

Dismissals for some other substantial reason

7.117   The full statutory wording is "some other substantial reason of a kind such as to justify the dismissal of an employee holding the position which that employee held".[163] Some other substantial reason may include any reason which a reasonable employer would

---

[156] *Taylor* v *Alidair Ltd* [1978] IRLR 82.
[157] *East Lindsey District Council* v *Daubney* [1977] IRLR 181.
[158] *Rothwell* v *Pelikan Hardcopy Scotland Ltd* [2006] IRLR 24.
[159] TULRCA 1992, ss 105 and 153.
[160] *Williams* v *Compair Maxam Ltd* [1982] ICR 156.
[161] TULRCA 1992, s 188.
[162] *Sutcliffe & Eaton Ltd* v *Pinney* [1977] IRLR 349.
[163] ERA 1996, s 98(1).

think necessary in the best interests of the business. A management style or personality which has led to a breakdown in relations may be such a reason.[164]

There have been a number of cases involving dismissal as a consequence of a business reorganisation. A Tribunal will consider whether the reorganisation was considered necessary for the business, whether the change relating to the employee was necessary to effect the reorganisation and whether there was adequate consultation in relation to the reorganisation and the consequences for the employee. A Tribunal will look for a balance between the effect on the employee and the needs of the employer's business.[165] However, fairness to the employee and the needs of the business may conflict and so long as the employer has behaved reasonably it will be the needs of the business which will usually prevail.   **7.118**

Remedies

Re-instatement or re-engagement[166]

This remedy is not awarded very often, since the relationship between ex-employer and ex-employee has usually completely broken down on both sides by the time of the ET hearing. The relevant considerations are the wish of the employee, whether it is practicable for the employer to re-instate or re-engage, and whether it would be just to make such an order. Re-instatement means that the employee must be treated as if never dismissed; re-engagement that the employee is to be re-employed in comparable employment. If the employer does not comply, additional compensation can be awarded.   **7.119**

Compensation[167]

Basic award. This is calculated according to the formula: $1\frac{1}{2}$ weeks' pay for every year the employee worked and was 41 or over; 1 week's pay for every year aged 22 or over; half a week's pay for every year under 22. The maximum number of years' employment to be taken into account is 20. There is a cap on the week's pay, fixed usually annually by ministerial order: at the time of writing it is £290. There is a minimum basic award where the dismissal is for a trade union reason, or for acting as certain types of worker representative (£4,000). The basic award can be reduced by any redundancy pay awarded, a just and equitable amount if the employee had unreasonably refused reinstatement and a just and equitable amount if the employee's conduct before dismissal warrants it.   **7.120**

Compensatory award. This is the amount which the tribunal thinks is "just and equitable in all the circumstances". It is to compensate for the loss suffered as a result of the dismissal. There is a cap on this award (£58,400), except where the dismissal is for a health and safety reason or for a protected disclosure. The employee must mitigate his or her loss. The compensatory award can be reduced or increased if there has been a failure to co-operate by employer or employee in the statutory discipline and dismissal procedure or grievance procedure. It may also be reduced by any redundancy pay   **7.121**

---

[164] *Perkin v St George's Healthcare NHS Trust* [2005] IRLR 934.
[165] *St John of God (Care Services) Ltd v Brooks* [1992] IRLR 546.
[166] ERA 1996, ss 112–117.
[167] ERA 1996, ss 118–127.

received, and by a just and equitable amount if the employee caused or contributed to his or her dismissal

7.122   A tribunal will take into account immediate loss of earnings, the financial loss caused by the dismissal, future loss of wages, loss of statutory rights, loss of pension rights and expenses.[168] The award compensates for financial loss, not distress, humiliation or damage to reputation.[169]

Interim relief

7.123   Where an employee has been dismissed for a trade union reason or one of a number of the automatically unfair reasons he or she may apply to a tribunal for an order of interim relief within 7 days.[170] The effect of such an order is (if the employer is willing) re-instatement or re-engagement until the tribunal hearing or (if the employer is not willing) payment of wages and benefits until the hearing.

DISCRIMINATION IN EMPLOYMENT

7.124   An important areas of employee protection is the protection against discrimination in employment. There are six prohibited grounds of discrimination. Many of the concepts of discrimination and equal treatment are the same across the different legislation, but there are also some important differences. It is beyond the scope of a chapter to deal with this issue in depth, but a summary of the sources of the law is included.

7.125   The prohibited grounds of discrimination are sex, race, disability, religion or belief, sexual orientation and age. Each has its own separate legislation and each is also subject to EC law. The underlying principle behind the legislation relating to sex, race, religion, sexual orientation and age is essentially the same: that of formal equality. The legislation is neutral in that it is designed to ensure equality of treatment between sexes, races etc and can be used by men, women, members of any racial group, followers of any religion or none, homosexual and heterosexual people, and young and old. With some important exceptions, it does not permit more favourable treatment of a member of a disadvantaged group since that would be to discriminate against a member of another group. This is not the case in relation to disability. The purpose of the legislation there is to provide protection for people with disabilities: the legislation does not apply to other people, and it to an extent requires positive action for people with disabilities.

7.126   The legislation is not restricted to employees. The equal pay legislation applies to workers, while all of the anti-discrimination legislation applies to those in employment.

SEX DISCRIMINATION AND EQUAL PAY

Equal pay

7.127   The Equal Pay Act 1970 (EPA 1970) was introduced before the UK joined the EU. It came into effect at the end of 1975. Although not introduced to comply with EU law, it has

---

[168] *Norton Tool Co Ltd* v *Tewson* [1973] 1 WLR 45.
[169] *Dunnachie* v *Kingston upon Hull City Council* [2004] IRLR 727.
[170] ERA 1996, ss 128–132; TULRCA 1992, ss 160–166.

been heavily influenced by it since, in order to comply with decisions of the European Court of Justice under Art 141 of the Treaty of Rome (equal pay) and the Equal Pay Directive 75/117.

The EPA 1970 only applies to gender inequality. As originally introduced, the main **7.128** entitlement was to equal pay for like work, that is work that is the same or broadly similar. As a result of enforcement action taken against the UK by the European Commission,[171] an additional entitlement to equal pay for work of equal value was introduced.[172] For an equal pay claim to succeed, a woman must identify an actual male comparator employed by her employer, and must establish that she does like work or work of equal value to him. It is then open to the employer to prove in defence that the difference in pay is due to a genuine material factor, which is not tainted by sex discrimination.

Sex discrimination

The Sex Discrimination Act 1975 (SDA 1975) places a duty on an employer not to **7.129** discriminate against people in his or her employment on grounds of sex. The Act has also been heavily influenced by decisions under EC law, in this case the Equal Treatment Directive 76/207. The 1975 Act prohibits discrimination on grounds of an employee's sex, applying equally to men and women. It also prohibits discrimination against transsexuals[173] and discrimination because of pregnancy or maternity.

There are four prohibited forms of discrimination which are also found in the **7.130** other legislation, though there are important differences in disability and age discrimination. These are direct discrimination; indirect discrimination; victimisation; and harassment.

Direct discrimination

Direct discrimination occurs where an employer treats someone in employment less **7.131** favourably on grounds of his or her sex than an employee of the opposite sex was or would have been treated. Unlike under EPA 1970, it is not necessary to have an actual comparator. Direct discrimination cannot be justified, but there are some jobs where sex might be a "genuine occupational qualification".

Indirect discrimination

This occurs where an employer applies a provision, criterion or practice which, **7.132** although it is neutral on the face of it, in fact places women at a disadvantage to men, and which disadvantages the person making the complaint. An example might be refusing to allow an employee to work part-time hours. It could be argued that a refusal to allow part-time work would disadvantage more women than men. Unlike direct discrimination, indirect discrimination can be justified so long as the application of the provision, criterion or practice is to further a legitimate aim and is proportionate.

---

[171] *Commission of the EC v UK* [1982] ECR 2601.
[172] Equal Pay (Amendment) Regulations 1983 (SI 1983/1794).
[173] Introduced to SDA 1975 by the Sex Discrimination (Gender Reassignment) Regulations 1999 (SI 1999/1102).

Victimisation

7.133 This is where the employer treats someone in employment less favourably because they have asserted their rights under the legislation, whether by raising an action, making an allegation, giving evidence in support of someone else, or doing something else which refers to the legislation. The ground of the less favourable treatment is not sex but raising the action.

Harassment

7.134 There are three types of unlawful harassment under SDA 1975. The first is common to all the grounds. It occurs where A engages in conduct which is unwanted by B and which has the purpose or effect of violating B's dignity or creating a hostile, degrading, humiliating or offensive environment for B.

7.135 There are two additional forms of harassment under SDA 1975 which relate specifically to sexual conduct, including less favourable treatment of someone who rejected (or submitted to) sexual advances.

RACE DISCRIMINATION

7.136 The UK has had race discrimination legislation for many years. An EU Directive prohibiting race discrimination was not passed until 2000.[174] The UK legislation is broader than required by this Directive since it prohibits discrimination on grounds of nationality which Directive 2000/43 does not. The Race Relations Act 1976 (RRA 1976) prohibits discrimination on grounds of race, colour, nationality, ethnic origins and national origins. "Nationality" means citizenship of a particular country. "National origins" may refer to a person's original nationality (where they have later adopted a different nationality) or might refer to a person's origins in an area which was formerly a state (such as Scotland, England or Wales). "Ethnic origins" relates to membership of a group with a long shared history and cultural traditions, and other relevant characteristics.[175] Gypsies have been held to be such a group.

7.137 The concepts of direct discrimination, indirect discrimination, victimisation and harassment in RRA 1976 are equivalent to those in SDA 1975. There are some jobs for which race might be a "genuine occupational requirement".

DISABILITY DISCRIMINATION

7.138 The Disability Discrimination Act 1995 (DDA 1995) pre-dated the EU Equal Treatment Directive 2000/78 which required member states to legislate to prohibit disability, religious, sexual orientation and age discrimination. It prohibits discrimination against people with disabilities. "Disability" is defined very closely in the Act: it arises where a person has a physical or mental impairment which has a substantial and long-term adverse effect on the person's ability to carry out normal day-to-day activities. Thus, in order to qualify as a disabled person, it must be established that there is a physical or

---

[174] Race Directive 2000/43.
[175] *Mandla* v *Dowell Lee* [1983] IRLR 209.

mental impairment, that the impairment affects the person's ability to carry out day-to-day activities (defined in the Act) adversely, that the adverse effect is substantial and long term (lasts or likely to last 12 months or more).

There are five prohibited forms of discrimination under DDA 1995. These are direct   **7.139**
discrimination; disability-related discrimination; breach of the duty to make reasonable
adjustments; victimisation; and harassment. The concepts of victimisation and harassment are equivalent to those in SDA 1975 and RRA 1976.

Direct discrimination

This occurs where a person is treated less favourably on grounds of their disability   **7.140**
than someone without that disability was or would have been treated. There is no
parallel provision for a person without a disability. Direct discrimination cannot be
justified.

Disability-related discrimination

This occurs where a person is treated less favourably than another was or would be   **7.141**
treated for a reason which relates to their disability. In this case the reason for the less
favourable treatment would not be the disability as such, but something which relates to
it, such as possible absences from work due to the impairment. This form of discrimination can be justified by the employer, so long as the reason for it is material and
substantial.

Breach of the duty to make reasonable adjustments

An employer must make adjustments where a disabled worker is placed at a dis-   **7.142**
advantage by any provision, criterion or practice applied, or by any physical feature of
the employer's premises. Examples of possible adjustments are given in DDA 1995, such
as making adjustments to the premises, transferring the worker to another vacant job,
altering hours and modifying equipment. The duty is to do what is reasonable, which
can take account of financial considerations.

RELIGIOUS DISCRIMINATION

The legislation prohibiting discrimination on this ground and the following two was   **7.143**
introduced to comply with Equal Treatment Directive 2000/78. The Employment
Equality (Religion or Belief) Regulations 2003 (EEROBR 2003) prohibit discrimination
in employment on grounds of religion, religious belief or "other similar philosophical
belief". This includes no religious belief.

The concepts of direct discrimination, indirect discrimination, victimisation and   **7.144**
harassment are equivalent to those in SDA 1975 and RRA 1976. There are some jobs
for which religion might be a genuine occupational requirement.

SEXUAL ORIENTATION DISCRIMINATION

Sexual orientation is not covered by SDA 1975 or EC Directive 76/207 (sex discrimina-   **7.145**
tion Equal Treatment Directive). To comply with EC Directive 2000/78 the Employment

Equality (Sexual Orientation) Regulations 2003 (EESOR 2003) were passed which prohibit discrimination on grounds of sexual orientation, whether this is an orientation towards people of the same sex, of the opposite sex, or both.

7.146 The concepts of direct discrimination, indirect discrimination, victimisation and harassment are equivalent to those in SDA 1975, RRA 1976 and EEROBR 2003. There are some jobs for which sexual orientation might be a genuine occupational requirement.

AGE DISCRIMINATION

7.147 Age discrimination is the last of the grounds covered by Directive 2000/78 to be legislated on in the UK. The Employment Equality (Age) Regulations 2006 prohibit discrimination on grounds of age. Because many distinctions were made in law on the basis of age there was longer consultation about this ground of discrimination, and there are more exceptions built into the legislation. In particular, age discrimination in NMWA 1998 is excluded, as is compulsory retirement either at 65 or over or an objectively justifiable earlier age, but with provisions for possible extensions of employment beyond normal retiral age.

7.148 The concepts of indirect discrimination, victimisation and harassment are equivalent to those in SDA 1975, RRA 1976, EEROBR 2003 and EESOR 2003. The concept of direct discrimination differs in that it is possible to justify direct discrimination on ground of age, using the same justification as for indirect discrimination. Thus it is made easier to discriminate on ground of age than the other grounds.

ESSENTIAL FACTS

7.149

- Employment law is concerned with the relationship between employer and employee. It comprises a common law basis of the contract of employment and a range of statutory provisions. It is heavily influenced by EC law.
- An employee is employed under a contract of employment. The legal form of this is a contract of service. The parties are employer and employee.
- People who contract to provide work or services but who are not employees are employed under contracts for services. The parties are employer and independent contractor.
- The test adopted by the courts for deciding whether a contract is of service or for services is the "multiple" test. This is a three-part test: a contract of service requires a duty to give personal service, the existence of a sufficient degree of control and the terms of the contract being consistent with service.
- The concept of mutuality of obligation has been influential: there must be mutual obligations to give and to carry out work underpinning the contract. This may be implied as well as express.

- There are intermediate categories under legislation that attract some protection, but not such extensive protection as that of employees. These are "workers", and those who are "in employment".
- A contract of employment is made up of many sources: express terms, implied terms, incorporated terms and implied duties.
- The most common incorporated terms are those incorporated into the contract of employment from a collective agreement agreed between employer and trade union.
- The implied duties are common law terms implied into every contract. An employee has the implied duties of personal service, to obey reasonable and lawful orders, to take reasonable care and of loyalty. An employer has the implied duties to pay wages, to take reasonable care of safety, to reimburse expenses and of trust and confidence.
- Wrongful dismissal is the common law remedy where an employee is unjustifiably dismissed without notice. Unfair dismissal is a statutory remedy. It may be used by someone who has been dismissed with or without notice, by someone whose fixed-term contract has not been renewed, and by someone who has resigned because of the employer's material breach of contract.
- The National Minimum Wage Act 1998 provides for the setting and calculation of the national minimum wage.
- The Working Time Regulations 1998 provide for maximum hours of work and minimum rest, break and holiday periods.
- Discrimination in employment is prohibited where it takes place on grounds of race, sex, religion, disability, age or sexual orientation.

ESSENTIAL CASES

- *Ready Mixed Concrete (SE) Ltd* v *Minister of Pensions and National Insurance* (1968): A lorry driver buying his lorry on hire purchase from the company was found to be employed under a contract for services, not a contract of service. The case is authority for the three-fold multiple test to determine whether there is a contract of service: personal service, control and consistent terms.   **7.150**
- *Market Investigations Ltd* v *Minister of Social Security* (1969): A market researcher was found to be employed under a contract of service, not a contract for services. This case identified the underlying element of being in business on one's own account in relation to the multiple test.
- *Carmichael* v *National Power plc* (1999): A casual worker was found not to be employed under a contract of service. This case found that mutuality of obligation was an "irreducible minimum" of a contract of service.

- *Percy* v *Church of Scotland Board of National Mission* (2006): An associate minister was found to be "in employment" for the purposes of the Sex Discrimination Act 1975. This provided statutory rights which were civil and not spiritual matters.
- *Robertson* v *British Gas Corporation* (1983): Employees were found to be entitled to a bonus provided for in the contract of employment. The statutory written statement of employment particulars is not contractual in itself and cannot override the contract.
- *Faccenda Chicken* v *Fowler* (1986): Employees who set up in competition with their former employer and canvassed its customers were not in breach of the implied duty of loyalty. This case clarified the circumstances in which the implied duty not to reveal confidential information continues after employment has ended.
- *Malik* v *Bank of Credit and Commerce International* (1997): Former employees of an employer which had traded fraudulently were entitled to raise an action for damages because their employment prospects had been damaged by the bank's breach of the implied mutual duty of trust and confidence. The House of Lords recognised and defined the duty.
- *Western Excavating (ECC) Ltd* v *Sharp* (1979): For the purposes of unfair dismissal law a resignation is treated as a dismissal ("constructive dismissal") only when the resignation is in response to a material breach of contract by the employer.
- *HSBC Bank plc* v *Madden* (2000): In an unfair dismissal action the employment tribunal decides the question of whether the employer has acted reasonably or unreasonably in dismissing the employee not by deciding whether in its view the employer acted reasonably, but by determining whether the employer's decision was within the "band of reasonable responses" of a reasonable employer.
- *British Home Stores* v *Burchell* (1980): In deciding to dismiss, an employer does not require proof of misconduct or incompetence to the standard which would satisfy a court. The employer must have a genuine belief in the guilt or lack of competence, must have reasonable grounds for this belief and must have established these reasonable grounds after a reasonable investigation.

8 COMPANY LAW

This chapter will provide a brief introduction to the laws of Scotland in relation to private companies limited by shares, corporate insolvency, partnerships and limited liability partnerships. This will be achieved by considering the current legislative framework governing each of these business vehicles, together with the development of common law.

8.1

PRIVATE COMPANIES LIMITED BY SHARES

Private companies limited by shares are by far the most common type of company and are primarily governed by the Companies Act 1985 (as amended) (CA 1985) and common law. However, it is important to be aware that other types of companies also exist, including companies limited by guarantee, public limited companies and companies with unlimited liability.

8.2

A private company limited by shares cannot exist without the appointment of officers and the existence of shareholders.[1] Despite this fact, a company is a separate legal entity distinct from its members. In reality this means that a company can enter into contracts, hold property in its own name, sue and be sued. This principle was first referred to in the case of *Salomon* v *A Salomon & Co Ltd*[2] and is known as the "veil of incorporation".

8.3

The "veil of incorporation" protects members of a company from liability; however, there are certain circumstances where the "veil" may be lifted, for example:

8.4

(1)   where a company is not a single-member company and continues to carry on its business, for more than 6 months, with less than two members;[3] or

(2)   where a company has gone into insolvent liquidation and its directors thereafter become involved with another company with a similar name.[4]

Where the "veil" is lifted, the limited liability which members ordinarily enjoy is removed and they may become personally liable for their acts and/or omissions. Usually this will result in a personal contribution to the company's assets by the members concerned, who may also face criminal prosecution.

8.5

---

[1] Also known as members.
[2] [1887] AC 22.
[3] CA 1985, s 24.
[4] Insolvency Act 1986, s. 216.

PRE-INCORPORATION

8.6   Before a company is incorporated, it has no legal status and therefore no capacity to enter into contracts. However, it is sometimes necessary, in anticipation of a company's incorporation, for transactions to be concluded and property purchased. This is often done by a promoter, who will usually become one of the first directors of a company. A promoter's relationship with a company cannot be described as one of agency, given that a company, pre-incorporation, is not a distinct legal entity. The relationship is fiduciary in nature, and as such promoters owe certain duties to a company including a duty to disclose any benefits they personally receive in connection with the promotion of a company.

PROMOTER'S LIABILITY

8.7   A promoter, while acting on a company's behalf, is personally liable in relation to all contracts entered into, unless express agreement is made to the contrary with a third party.[5] This means that where a third party relinquishes a promoter from personal liability they would be unable to sue the promoter, if the company did not subsequently comply with the terms of the contract.

UNENFORCEABLE CONTRACTS

8.8   Contracts made on a company's behalf cannot be enforced or relied upon by a company, once incorporated. Given this lack of enforceability, it is advisable that no business should be carried on prior to incorporation.

INCORPORATION OF A PRIVATE COMPANY LIMITED BY SHARES

8.9   To incorporate a company, Forms 10 and 12 must be delivered to the Registrar of Companies together with a memorandum of association ("memorandum"), articles of association ("articles") and an incorporation fee. If the documents are accepted by the Registrar, a certificate of incorporation will be issued. It is at this point that a company is seen as a separate legal entity and can contract in its own name. The content and purpose of each incorporation document will be considered in turn:

FORM 10

8.10   (i)   *Company name.* There are number of restrictions and requirements to consider when selecting a company name. The end of the name must include the word "Limited" or "Ltd", there cannot be a company with the same or similar name already incorporated,[6] and certain restrictions apply in relation to the use of particular words.[7]

---

[5] CA 1985, s 36C.
[6] Including limited liability partnerships.
[7] CA 1985, ss 26–34. Restrictions are also provided by the Business Names Act 1985, and under common law ("passing off").

(ii) *Registered office.* This is a company's official address. It is available to view at Companies House and will appear on all official documentation of a company, for example its annual return. It is a legal requirement for a company always to have a registered office in order that communications and notices may be received directly by it. It also indicates where the company books are held,[8] which is important since the register of members is open to inspection by a company's members and/or third parties.[9]

(iii) *Directors.* Are officers of a company. It is now possible for a company to be incorporated with one director, and there is no upper limit on the number directors, provided that no restrictions exist in a company's articles. A director's personal details must be disclosed together with any previous and/or current directorships.

(iv) *Company secretary.* Similarly, an officer of a company with ostensible authority to contract on a company's behalf. When a company is incorporated with only one director, the officer appointed as company secretary must be a different person. Where more than one director is appointed, any one of the directors may also hold the office of company secretary.

(v) *Subscribers.* Are the first shareholders of a company. They, or an agent on behalf of them, must sign and date the Form 10.

FORM 12

Form 12 is a statutory declaration which is ordinarily completed by a solicitor involved in the incorporation of a company. The completion and filing of this document are required by virtue of CA 1985, and the document simply verifies a company's compliance with the statutory provisions.   **8.11**

MEMORANDUM OF ASSOCIATION

The memorandum can be described as the external constitutional document of a company and each subscriber must sign the memorandum, which will detail the number of shares being issued to them.[10] A memorandum provides information and guidance in relation to how a company will deal with third parties and must include certain information such as the name of the company, location of its registered office, initial share capital, liability of members and the objects of the company.[11]   **8.12**

ARTICLES OF ASSOCIATION

Articles are sometimes described as the internal constitutional document of a company. They primarily govern the relationship between members of a company, and there are no statutory requirements relating to the type of information which should be included   **8.13**

---

[8] CA 1985, s 353.
[9] CA 1985, s 356 regulates the inspection of the register and index.
[10] Subscriber signatures should be witnessed by a third party.
[11] CA 1985, s 2.

in a company's articles. Typical articles will include details on the appointment and removal of officers of a company, and the process of convening meetings. It is not uncommon for companies simply to adopt as their articles Table A, in whole or in part. Table A is found in the Companies (Tables A to F) Regulations 1995[12] and is essentially a template of model articles. It remains possible, following incorporation, for a company's articles to be altered, provided that they do not attempt to circumvent the applicability of legislation.

MEMBERS' MEETINGS

8.14   Meetings of company members can be categorised as either general or class meetings, and are called in order to deal with the business of a company. General meetings can be further classified as either annual or extraordinary.

ANNUAL GENERAL MEETING ("AGM")

8.15   Every company is under an obligation to hold an AGM.[13] A company must convene an AGM within the first 18 months from the date of incorporation, and thereafter there cannot be more than 15 months between each subsequent AGM. If a company fails to convene the necessary AGM, the Secretary of State has the power to convene an AGM on behalf of a company. Often the primary reasons for holding an AGM are to allow a company's accounts to be laid before its members, for the members to appoint auditors[14] and for the payment of dividends to be approved.

Notice

8.16   In order to convene an AGM, 21 days' notice must be given, in writing, to company members,[15] although it is possible to convene an AGM on short notice, provided that there is unanimous consent by all members. It is possible, by members passing an elective resolution, to dispense with the necessity to convene an AGM each year.[16]

EXTRAORDINARY GENERAL MEETING ("EGM")

8.17   An EGM is any general meeting held by a company which is not an AGM, and is normally called to deal with business that cannot wait until the next AGM. An EGM is usually convened by the directors of a company when requisitioned by members who hold at least one-tenth of the paid-up share capital[17] of a company. The directors shall within 21 days from receipt[18] of a requisition proceed to convene

---

[12] SI 1985/805.
[13] CA 1985, s 366.
[14] CA 1985, s 384.
[15] CA 1985, s 369.
[16] CA 1985, s 366A.
[17] CA 1985, s 368(2). Shares must carry voting rights at a general meeting.
[18] CA 1985, s 368(4).

an EGM and this should be held within 28 days from the date of the notice convening the meeting.[19]

Notice

Notice of an EGM must be given to all the members, in writing, 14 days before the EGM, **8.18** or 21 days prior, if the intention is to pass a special resolution at the EGM. Similarly to an AGM, it is possible for an EGM to be called on short notice, provided that 95 per cent of the members concur.[20]

CLASS MEETINGS

This type of meeting is held by a particular class of shareholders, where decisions **8.19** affecting only that class of shares are being taken, for example varying their class rights.

Notice

The amount of notice required to be given is dependent on the type of meeting being **8.20** convened and the business to be dealt with. The notice must clearly state the location, time, general nature of the business,[21] and the type of general meeting being convened. Notice must be validly served on every member.[22]

RESOLUTIONS

A resolution records a decision made by the members (or particular class of members) of **8.21** a company. There are a variety of resolutions which may be passed by members in general meetings and in certain circumstances CA 1985 specifies the type of resolution to be passed.

Type of resolution	Voting requirements
Ordinary	Simple majority
Special	75% or more
Extraordinary	75% or more
Elective	100%

8.22

As an alternative to passing one of the above resolutions, CA 1985[23] provides that a written resolution may be passed in its place. A written resolution requires the consent of 100 per cent of a company's members entitled to vote on a specific matter. To be effective, each member must sign the resolution.[24]

The undernoted table provides a number of examples of the type of resolution to be **8.23** passed (and applicable notice periods) in particular circumstances:

---

[19] CA 1985, s 368(8).
[20] Can be reduced to a 90% majority by the passing of an elective resolution.
[21] Table A, art 38.
[22] CA 1985, s 370(2).
[23] CA 1985, s 381A(1).
[24] CA 1985, s 381A(2). All signatures do not have to be on the same document.

Issue	Type of resolution	Notice (days)
Change of company name[25]	Special	21
Alteration of articles[26]	Special	21
Removal of a director[27]	Ordinary	28 (special notice)
Revoking an elective resolution[28]	Ordinary	14
Varying class rights[29]	Extraordinary	21 or 14 (depending on type of meeting)
Creditors' voluntary liquidation[30]	Extraordinary	14
Dispensing with an AGM[31]	Elective	21

The articles of a company may provide additional requirements and/or restrictions and should be consulted before any resolution is proposed.

DIRECTORS

8.24   Directors are under a duty to comply both with the provisions of a company's constitutional documents and with current legislation. The obligations can on occasion be onerous, and may include how a director should manage a company, take major decisions or enter into substantial contracts.

8.25   Given the responsibilities placed on directors, it is perhaps unhelpful that who constitutes a director is not clearly defined.[32] Consequently, there are a variety of recognised types of directors, other than those formally appointed,[33] and they include:

    (i)   *de facto director* – not formally appointed to the board but professes to act as a director of a company;

    (ii)   *shadow director* – an individual who has not been formally appointed as a director but who, as a matter of fact, influences the decisions of a company;

    (iii)   *alternate director* – appointed by an existing director to perform all the functions of the appointer in their absence;

    (iv)   *nominee director* – members have a specific right to appoint, remove and/or replace one or more of these directors, eg in joint venture companies.

DIRECTORS' DUTIES

8.26   The relationship between a director and a company can be described as fiduciary in nature. There are a number of fiduciary duties under common law[34] which a director owes to a company and they include:

---

[25] CA 1985, s 28.

[26] CA 1985, s 9.

[27] CA 1985, s 303.

[28] CA 1985, s 379A(3).

[29] CA 1985, s 125.

[30] Insolvency Act 1986, s 84(1)(c).

[31] CA 1985, s 366A.

[32] CA 1985, s 741(1).

[33] CA 1985, s 288.

[34] Company Law Reform Bill transposes them into statute.

(i)   to act for the benefit of a company as a whole and not to fetter their discretion;

(ii)   to avoid conflicts between the personal interest of directors and the interests of a company; and

(iii)   to act honestly and in good faith when making decisions affecting a company.

A director also owes a duty of care, skill and diligence to a company. This is measured **8.27** objectively, with a comparison being made to another individual holding a similar directorship, and subjectively to the extent that consideration is given to what can be reasonably expected from a director with their level of experience, skill and knowledge.

Despite the wide scope of fiduciary duties established by common law, a number of **8.28** statutory duties are also imposed on directors including, a requirement to declare any interest in contracts,[35] and to obtain membership approval before any substantial property transactions can be made between a company and one or more of its directors.[36]

PERSONAL LIABILITY

Directors become personally liable for their actions and/or omissions in circumstances **8.29** where the "veil of incorporation" is lifted.[37] Personal liability of directors can occur in a variety of circumstances including where a director concludes a contract (on a company's behalf) without the requisite authority, or where a director falls foul of legislative provisions. Certain sections of the Insolvency Act 1986 (IA 1986), if breached, may result in a director becoming personally liable, and include:

Fraudulent trading[38]

It may be concluded that trading has been fraudulent if it appears that any business of a **8.30** company has been carried out with the intent to "defraud creditors of the company or creditors of any other person, or for any fraudulent purpose"[39] during the course of winding up a company. Where a court makes this finding, it may order that any person who knowingly was a party to this fraudulent behaviour is financially liable to contribute to a company's assets to such extent as the court deems appropriate.

Only a liquidator has the power to make an application to the court in relation to a **8.31** director's fraudulent trading. By way of illustration, a liquidator may pursue an application where advanced payment for goods is accepted by a company or a company gains credit, knowing that it will not be able to repay the money on the due date.

Wrongful trading[40]

In order for a director (or shadow director)[41] to incur personal liability, a company must **8.32** have gone into insolvent liquidation and at some point prior to winding up, a director

---

[35] CA 1985, s 317.
[36] CA 1985, s 320.
[37] For example, CA 1985; ss 221 and 222.
[38] IA 1986, s 213.
[39] IA 1986, s 213(1).
[40] IA 1986, s 214.
[41] Current or past.

"knew or ought to have concluded that there was no reasonable prospect that the company would avoid going into insolvent liquidation".[42] Provided that this test is met, the court may, on application by the liquidator, order that a director is liable to contribute to a company's assets. A director's defence, in this circumstance, is that he or she took every possible step to mitigate potential losses to a company's creditors.

REMUNERATION

8.33   Directors do not, as a matter of course, receive remuneration for their services, although it is not uncommon for a company's articles[43] to make provision for the method by which remuneration should be decided.

LOANS

8.34   The 1985 Act expressly prohibits companies from making loans or providing guarantees and/or security directly to directors, or for the benefit of directors.[44] If a prohibited arrangement is entered into it will be deemed voidable. A director who authorised or arranged the loan will be personally liable to a company for any direct or indirect gain made, and shall personally indemnify a company for any losses on damages incurred.[45]

CESSATION OF DIRECTORSHIP

Resignation

8.35   It is recognised that directors are free to resign at any time. However, the articles of a company should be consulted as they generally specify the method of resignation. If a director is an employee of a company, their contract of employment should be reviewed to ensure that resignation does not breach any terms of their contract of employment.

Retirement by rotation

8.36   The articles of a company often stipulate that a number of directors should retire at every AGM and be eligible for re-election.[46]

Removal

8.37   Irrespective of the articles of a company, it is possible for members to remove a director from office by passing an ordinary resolution.[47] This process can be cumbersome given that special notice is required to be given to a company, although the articles may provide for a simplified procedure.

---

[42] IA 1986, s 214(2)(b).
[43] Table A, art 82.
[44] CA 1985, s 330.
[45] CA 1985, s 342.
[46] Table A, arts 73–80.
[47] CA 1985, s 303.

MEMBERSHIP

A company requires a minimum of one person to be a member at any one time. Given **8.38** the contractual nature of membership, restrictions exist in relation to certain individuals becoming members of a company, for example individuals who lack legal capacity, who are of unsound mind or who have been declared bankrupt.

Provided that a person is not restricted from being a shareholder and they agree to **8.39** membership, there are several ways for a person to become a member of a company, including:

(i)   subscription to a company's memorandum;[48]
(ii) being allotted shares;
(iii) receiving a transfer of shares from an existing member; or
(iv) receiving a transmission of shares which occurs on the bankruptcy or death of a member and results in the transmission of their shares to a trustee or personal representative.

Membership exists only once a person's name and details have been recorded in a **8.40** company's register of members.[49] Ordinarily, once registered, a company would then issue a share certificate to a member detailing their shareholding.

LIABILITY

A member's liability will be detailed in the memorandum of the company.[50] Generally, **8.41** a member is liable to pay to a company the full nominal value (and any agreed share premium) on all the shares held and registered in their name. On a minimum of 14 days' notice directors can make calls to members of a company for payment of any outstanding sums on unpaid shares.[51]

RIGHTS

A company's articles provide a membership contract between a company and its **8.42** members.[52] Consequently, where resolutions are passed at general meetings, all members of a company are bound by the decision, whether or not they personally vote in favour of passing the said resolutions.

Foss v *Harbottle*[53]

The principle of majority rule was expounded in the case of *Foss* v *Harbottle*, which **8.43** involved minority shareholders attempting to bring a case, on behalf of the company, alleging that the majority shareholders sold to the company a piece of land at an over

---

[48] CA 1985, s 22.
[49] CA 1985, s 361.
[50] CA 1985, s 2(3).
[51] Table A, art 12.
[52] CA 1985, s 14.
[53] (1843) 2 Hare 461, Ch D.

inflated price. The court held, *inter alia*, that the company alone was the "proper plaintiff"[54] (a company is a distinct legal entity and can bring legal proceedings in its own name).

8.44   This decision has subsequently, in part, been viewed as unacceptable. *Foss* gives no consideration to the fact that it was the majority shareholders themselves who were responsible for the excessive price being paid by the company, yet it was their approval which was required into order pursue an action (which in the circumstances was unlikely). The courts now recognise a number of exceptions to the rules laid down in *Foss*, which include, the ratification of *ultra vires* acts by a company,[55] provided that the acts are not of an illegal nature, acts which do not adhere the procedures laid down by a company's articles, fraud on minority members when perpetrated by the majority shareholders, and violations of members' personal rights.[56]

Legislative protection

8.45   Notwithstanding the rules provided by *Foss*, minority shareholders enjoy an element of legislative protection in certain circumstances.

8.46   Minority members may make a s 459[57] petition to the court alleging unfair prejudice in relation to the past or present acts or omissions of a company, which affect the members as whole, or some group of them.[58] If satisfied, the court may order such relief it deems appropriate, for example requiring that the majority members or the company purchase the minority members' shares, at a fair value.[59]

8.47   Alternatively, minority members may petition the court for a company to be wound up, based on the "just and equitable" principle.[60] The courts will usually only consider this type of petition in circumstances where no other option is available.

CESSATION OF MEMBERSHIP

8.48   An individual's membership ceases when it is documented in a company's register of members. This can occur in a variety of circumstances, including on the transfer or transmission of shares.

SHARE CAPITAL

MAINTAINING SHARE CAPITAL

8.49   The issued share capital[61] of a company may be viewed as a fund available to creditors of a company. As a result, companies are prohibited from issuing shares at less than

---

[54] English terminology.
[55] CA 1985, s 35.
[56] *Pender* v *Lushington* (1877) 6 Ch D 70.
[57] CA 1985.
[58] CA 1985, s 459(1).
[59] CA 1985, s 461(2).
[60] IA 1986, s 122(1)(g).
[61] The capital of allotted shares.

their nominal value[62] and any premium paid on a share must be deposited into a separate share premium account, which is non-distributable. Certain legislative provisions are designed to protect a company's capital, including regulating its reduction[63] and the purchase of its own shares.[64]

ALTERING SHARE CAPITAL

The share capital of a company may be altered,[65] if the necessary authorisation is provided in its articles. A company may: **8.50**

    (i)   increase its authorised share capital by the creation of new shares;

    (ii) consolidate or sub-divide all or part of the existing share capital into shares with an increased or decreased nominal value;

    (iii) convert all or part of the paid-up shares into stock, or reconvert stock into shares; and

    (iv) cancel any authorised but unissued shares of a company (this does not result in a reduction of the share capital of the company).

When altering the share capital of a company it is necessary to pass a resolution[66] and file the necessary form with the Registrar of Companies within 1 month from the date of the resolution.[67]   **8.51**

ALLOTTING SHARES

In order for a company to allot shares,[68] directors must have the necessary authority;[69] this will be provided for in a company's articles or can be given at a general meeting by a company's members. Failure to have the necessary authority will result in a director facing criminal sanctions, but will not invalidate the allotment.   **8.52**

Statutory pre-emption rights exist in relation to the issue of new shares[70] in a company. This means that a company must first offer to the existing shareholders the new issue of shares, in proportion to their existing shareholding. This provision is designed to prevent the dilution of existing members' rights with the issue of new shares to third parties.   **8.53**

The offer of new shares to existing members must be made in writing and is open for acceptance for 21 days.[71] If the shares are not taken up by the current members or they waive their pre-emption rights, the new shares can be offered to third parties. Once the shares have been allotted a company's register of members should be updated and a share certificate issued in respect of the newly allotted shares.[72]   **8.54**

---

[62] CA 1985, s 100 (ie the par value).
[63] CA 1985, s 135. Requires both member and court approval for the reduction of share capital.
[64] CA 1985, s 162.
[65] CA 1985, s 121.
[66] CA 1985, s 121(4).
[67] CA 1985, s 122.
[68] A company cannot allot more shares than its authorised share capital.
[69] CA 1985, s 80.
[70] CA 1985, s 89.
[71] CA 1985, s 95. It is possible to disapply pre–emption rights.
[72] CA 1985, s 185(1)(a).

TRANSFERRING SHARES

8.55   The transfer of shares is generally undertaken voluntarily, but circumstances can arise where there is a compulsory transfer of shares, for example on insolvency, death or termination of employment.

8.56   Unlike with the allotment of shares, statutory pre-emption rights do not exist in relation to the transfer of shares, although it is not uncommon for a company's articles to contain pre-emption rights.[73]

8.57   On the transfer of shares a company must have delivered to it an instrument of transfer duly signed and stamped (ie a stock transfer form). Stamp duty is payable at half a per cent of the total consideration payable (rounded up to the nearest £5), although certain transfers are totally or partially exempt from this duty. Again, a share certificate will be issued to the transferee, and the register of members will be amended accordingly.[74]

CONSIDERING INCORPORATION

8.58   When contemplating incorporating a company limited by shares it is important to consider whether this type of limited company is the most appropriate business vehicle to meet your needs. While there is certainly not an exhaustive list, some advantages and disadvantages include:

ADVANTAGES

8.59   (i)   A company has a separate legal personality and can enter into contracts, hold property in its own name, sue and be sued.
        (ii)   Perpetual succession – there is no transfer of assets when a member joins or leaves a company.
        (iii)   Members have, in most circumstances, limited liability.
        (iv)   Can assist in raising finance.
        (v)   There is no maximum limit to the number of members in a company (limits may be laid down in its articles).
        (vi)   The 1985 Act, the common law and a company's constitutional documents provide a readily available source of guidance.

DISADVANTAGES

8.60   (i)   Certain expenses will be incurred in incorporating a company.
        (ii)   There are certain limitations on the name a company can choose.
        (iii)   Increased formality, which may include the holding of AGMs, passing of resolutions and completing annual returns and accounts.
        (iv)   A company is required to file certain information with the Registrar of Companies, thus putting information in the public domain.

---

[73] Table A, arts 23–28.
[74] The register of members will need to record both the new shareholding of the transferor and that of the transferee.

(v) Limited liability in certain circumstances may be illusory, for example directors may be required to provide personal guarantees.

COMPANY LAW REFORM

The Company Law Reform Bill ("the Bill") was laid before the House of Lords in November 2005. It represents the most extensive review of company law in the last two decades. The 1985 Act will no longer be the primary piece of legislation in this area and, as well as being amended, it will have to work in tandem with the forthcoming Bill. **8.61**

In addition to consolidating existing company law, the Bill will introduce new elements, for example the codification of directors' duties.[75] Unlike the 1985 Act, the Bill is written with its focus firmly on smaller companies. It provides, *inter alia*, a more streamlined approach towards incorporation, which includes more concise model articles, and removes the necessity for a company secretary. In addition, many of the administrative burdens companies currently face will no longer be "opt out" but rather "opt in", for example companies will only hold an AGM if they positively opt to do so. **8.62**

The Bill is currently expected to receive Royal Assent in 2006, with many of its provisions coming into force in 2007. The extent and implications will, in part, only become fully evident once company law is operating under this double legislative regime. **8.63**

CORPORATE INSOLVENCY

The main legislation governing insolvency in Scotland is the Insolvency Act 1986 (as amended) (IA 1986).[76] When a company is in financial difficulties the aim of corporate insolvency can be described as trying to maintain a balance between: **8.64**

(a) the protection of creditors;
(b) competing interests of different groups;
(c) directors' responsibilities; and
(d) promoting the rescue of the company concerned.

Often it is not always clear when a company is in fact insolvent. However, for numerous reasons, it can be important to determine the solvency or otherwise of a company, particularly given that a company must be insolvent in order to initiate formal insolvency proceedings. **8.65**

There are two alternative tests used in determining insolvency: **8.66**

(a) the "cash flow" test – a company is solvent if it is able to pay all its debts as they fall due, irrespective of the balance sheet; or
(b) the "balance sheet" test – a company may be able to pay its debts as they fall due, however, according to the balance sheet the company's liabilities exceed its assets.

---

[75] Currently provided under common law.
[76] The Enterprise Act 2002 has made significant amendments to IA 1986.

8.67 If a test shows a company to be insolvent, or technically solvent, but experiencing financial problems, there has been a distinct shift towards the aim of promoting company rescue. There are four key rescue mechanisms that can be implemented.

ADMINISTRATION

8.68 This commences with the appointment of an administrator who is responsible for either rescuing or realising and distributing the assets to secured or preferential creditors[77] of a company, while it is in moratorium[78]. Prior to the Enterprise Act 2002 (EA 2002) the only method in which an administrator could be appointed was through the courts. This is no longer the case and there is now an out-of-court procedure[79] which potentially provides a more cost-effective route for companies having financial problems.

Court procedure

8.69 This process is instigated by an application to the court for an administrator to be appointed, who must be a qualified insolvency practitioner, and this can be made by a company, its directors or creditors.[80] If an administration order is made by the court, the administrator must notify the company and the Registrar of Companies of their appointment, together with the company's creditors. The administrator will receive a detailed report of the company's financial position which will enable them to prepare a proposal to achieve the objective of administration.[81] An administrator's appointment will automatically cease after one year, unless extended by the court.

Out-of-court procedure

8.70 This procedure is available to a company, it directors or the holder of a qualifying floating charge.[82] In most cases, for the latter category this effectively replaces the right they previously had to appoint an administrative receiver.

8.71 Depending on which category of persons instigates this procedure, the process varies considerably, and culminates with certain prescribed documents being filed with the court. Once an administrator has been appointed, a moratorium on all legal proceedings will take effect.

ADMINISTRATIVE RECEIVERSHIP

8.72 While not strictly a rescue mechanism, this has been dramatically curtailed by the introduction of the 2002 Act. A security can now only be enforced by an administrative receiver in circumstances where a floating charge was created before 15 September 2003[83]

---

[77] IA 1986, Sch B1, para 3.

[78] The moratorium is on all legal proceedings including winding-up.

[79] EA 2002, s 250. The procedure is only open to the company, its directors (subject to certain restrictions) or holders of a "qualifying" floating charge.

[80] Includes holders of a qualifying floating charge.

[81] IA 1986, Sch B1, para 51. The administrator may convene a creditors' meeting to approve or amend the proposal.

[82] IA 1986, Sch B1, para 14.

[83] IA 1986, s 72A.

or the security falls within one of the exceptions detailed in ss 72B–72GA of IA 1986.[84] An alternative for a qualifying floating charge holder is to use the new out-of-court procedure, and put the company into administration.

In circumstances where it remains possible to appoint an administrative receiver, **8.73** their main duty is owed to the holder of the floating charge who appointed them and not to all creditors of a company. This essentially means that the administrative receiver should attempt to recover monies owed to the holder of the floating charge. Their powers derive from IA 1986 and the relevant security document on which their appointment was based.

Administrative receivership does not trigger a statutory moratorium, therefore **8.74** creditors can continue or indeed commence legal proceedings against a company for for example, liquidation. However, an administrative receiver's appointment will automatically crystallise the floating charge and result in the directors of a company being replaced by the administrative receiver, who will in essence take on their management role.

The administrative receiver will notify a company and its creditors of their appoint- **8.75** ment and a notice must be placed in the *Edinburgh Gazette* and local newspapers. The director(s) must then produce a statement detailing the company's affairs for the administrative receiver, who will in turn produce a report and distribute it to the company's creditors and the Registrar of Companies. The report will include an approximation of the sum to be distributed to each class of creditors.

The administrative receiver will have discharged their duties either when the holder **8.76** of the floating charge who appointed them has been fully repaid or when all the assets of the company have been realised and the proceeds distributed. A final account of payments made should be reported to the company and its creditors.

COMPANY VOLUNTARY ARRANGEMENT ("CVA")

This is where an agreement is reached between a company and its creditors in a bid to **8.77** avoid other forms of insolvency procedures, although it can be used along side administration. CVAs can be used in relation to both solvent and insolvent companies and are instigated by an individual making a proposal (usually the directors) to a company and its creditors. The proposal should identify an individual suitable to act as a "nominee".[85]

During the process there is no automatic moratorium, however, for small companies **8.78** there is the possibility of an optional moratorium before the implementation of a CVA. This option is not available for larger companies and is arguably a weakness of the CVA.

In circumstances where the appointed nominee is not a liquidator or administrator[86] **8.79** they must submit to the court a report, which includes their opinion of the proposed CVA and whether meetings of the company and its creditors should be convened to consider the proposal.[87] The nominee may then convene the meetings at the time recommended in the report unless otherwise directed by the court. Where the nominee

---

[84] Inserted by EA 2002, s 250.
[85] IA 1986, s 1(2).
[86] Insolvency Act 2000, s 4 amends IA 1986, s 388 to allow the recognition of others, in addition to qualified insolvency practitioners.
[87] IA 1986, s 2(2).

is a liquidator or administrator there is no requirement to produce a report to the court, they can simply proceed to convene meetings of the shareholders and creditors.[88]

8.80   It is for the members and creditors of a company at their respective meetings to decide whether to accept or amend the proposals[89] of the nominee. Once agreement is reached it will take effect as though the voluntary arrangement was made by the company at the creditors' meeting.[90] The nominee will then be known as a "supervisor"[91] and will effectively implement the arrangement. A CVA will generally be deemed successful if, while carrying on its business, the company is able to satisfy the debts and liabilities which it incurred before the implementation of the CVA process.

SCHEMES OF ARRANGEMENT

8.81   These are made between a company and its members and/or creditors (or a particular class of them), pursuant to s 425 of CA 1985. This type of arrangement is essentially a compromise, in order to assist a company in meeting its financial liabilities and avoid a winding-up procedure. This rescue mechanism is typically used by companies which are insolvent. In order to put in place a scheme of arrangement, and bind all members and/or creditors, at least 75per cent approval is required from those entitled to vote, together with court approval.

8.82   It is possible to use this option in conjunction with administration, which will allow a moratorium, giving the company space to consider and agree on a suitable arrangement.

LIQUIDATION

8.83   If implementing a rescue mechanism is not suitable or possible in the circumstances, an alternative may be to liquidate a company. A liquidator, who must be a qualified insolvency practitioner, is appointed, and their responsibility is for realising the value of the assets of a company and paying its liabilities in a prescribed order.

8.84   The winding-up of a company can be split into two categories:

Compulsory liquidation

8.85   This occurs when the court orders a company to be wound up and IA 1986 provides a number of grounds on which a petition may be based,[92] including circumstances where it would be deemed "just and equitable" or where a company is not able to pay its debts. Given that commencement of compulsory liquidation is deemed to occur from the date of presentation of the petition and not the date of the winding-up order, a provisional liquidator may be appointed during this interim period[93] and their duties may be limited by the court order which appointed them.

---

[88] IA 1986, s 3(2).
[89] IA 1986, s 4(1).
[90] IA 1986, s 5(2).
[91] IA 1986, s 7(2).
[92] IA 1986, s 122(1).
[93] IA 1986, s 135(3).
[94] IA 1986, s 138(2).
[95] IA 1986, s 138(4). In certain circumstances only a creditors' meeting will be convened.

In circumstances where a winding-up order is then made, an "interim liquidator"[94] is **8.86** appointed until separate meetings of the company's creditors and members is convened. These meetings provide an opportunity for the appointment of a "liquidator",[95] to replace the "interim liquidator",[96] and if necessary the appointment of a liquidation committee[97] to act along side the liquidator.

Voluntary liquidation

This is instigated by the members of a company, usually by the passing of a resolution[98] at **8.87** a general meeting. Voluntary liquidation will commence on the date the resolution is passed.[99] This affects a company in numerous ways, including cessation of directors' powers and assumption by the liquidator, prohibition on the commencement or indeed continuance of court action against a company (without court approval), and the transfer of shares and/or the disposition of property (without court approval) becomes void.

Two categories of voluntary liquidation exist: **8.88**

Members' voluntary liquidation ("MVL")

A pre-requisite to as MLV is that a company must be solvent. Consequently, the **8.89** majority of directors must make a statutory declaration stating that the company is solvent, and this must be filed with the registrar of companies.[100] It is then for the members of a company, at a general meeting, to appoint a liquidator.[101]

Creditors' voluntary liquidation ("CVL")

In circumstances where a company's directors are unable to make a statutory declara- **8.90** tion as to the solvency of a company, a voluntary winding-up can be achieved by the company's creditors. In order for this to occur, a company must convene a creditors' meeting within 14 days from the date of passing the resolution for voluntary winding up. Notice must be sent to all known creditors of the company at least 7 days prior to the date of the creditors' meeting and a notice must also be placed in the *Edinburgh Gazette* and two local newspapers. It is then for the company's directors to provide the creditors with a detailed account of the company's financial affairs.

Although separate meetings of creditors and members are held, the liquidator **8.91** nominated at the creditors' meeting will be appointed.[102] The creditors may additionally appoint a "liquidation committee" to act with the liquidator,[103] and if this occurs the company's members are entitled to appoint individuals to act on this committee.[104]

---

[96] IA 1986, s 138(5). The court can intervene if a liquidator is not appointed.
[97] IA 1986, s 142.
[98] IA 1986, s 84.
[99] IA 1986, s 86.
[100] IA 1986, s 89(3).
[101] The liquidator must notify the registrar of companies of his appointment, and place a notice in the *Edinburgh Gazette*.
[102] IA 1986, s 100. Failure by the creditors to nominate a liquidator may result in the person nominated by the members being appointed as liquidator.
[103] IA 1986, s 101(1).
[104] IA 1986, s 101(2).

The liquidator's duties

8.92   The role of a liquidator in a winding-up process is for the most part the same, irrespective of whether the liquidation is compulsory or voluntary (although court supervision can vary substantially depending on the type of winding-up procedure). Once appointed, the liquidator essentially stands in the position previously occupied by the directors of a company, and consequently has a duty to act in the best interests of a company. The liquidator must consider a company's assets and review any transactions involving the disposal of its assets/property in the previous 5 years,[105] and in certain circumstances seek an order for reduction. When the liquidator has realised the value of a company's assets they must be distributed in a prescribed order.

8.93   In concluding a liquidation, a liquidator will convene a final general meeting where they will give an account to the company's members and/or creditors[106] of the winding-up process and how the company's assets were disposed of. The liquidator will then send a copy of the account and a return (in the prescribed format) to the Registrar of Companies, and if necessary to the court.[107] A company will then be dissolved 3 months later.

AFTER INSOLVENCY

8.94   When a company has been wound up, its directors are able to be directors of other companies, provided that they are not subject to a disqualification order or have been declared personally bankrupt.[108]

PARTNERSHIPS

8.95   The Partnership Act 1890 (PA 1890) established the foundations of partnership law. Where no formal partnership agreement is entered into, disputes or misunderstandings between the partners will be resolved based on the provisions of PA 1890. From both a practical and a commercial point of view, it is always advisable to reduce any agreement to writing.

8.96   The formation of a partnership is not subject to the same stringent formalities as other business vehicles and can be created verbally or be inferred by the conduct of the parties. In order for a partnership to exist, the individuals must have come together in order to carry on a business[109] with a view to making a profit.

8.97   Partnerships in Scotland are seen as separate legal entities, distinct from their partners. A partnership can enter into contracts, hold property, sue and be sued.

---

[105] IA 1986, s 242.

[106] IA 1986, s 146 an s 94, depending on the type of winding-up procedure.

[107] Notice must be given to the court in relation to a compulsory winding-up and the court will then order a company's dissolution.

[108] It may be possible to obtain the court's approval if they are disqualified and/or bankrupt.

[109] PA 1890, s 45 defines "business" as including "every trade, occupation, or profession".

However, partners are agents and guarantors of the partnership and are consequently jointly and severally liable for the debts and obligations of the partnership.[110]

FORMATION

The minimum number of partners required to form a partnership is two and the maximum number is usually 20, although there are a number of exceptions to this rule, for example in relation to solicitors and accountants. Each person must have capacity to be a partner in a firm, and this would include being of sound mind and sufficient age. Furthermore, where a partnership has been formed with the intention of carrying on an illegal business, any partnership agreement will be deemed void. In circumstances where a partnership fails to comply with all the statutory restrictions, it will leave each of the partners open to unlimited personal liability in respect of debts incurred by a firm. **8.98**

Additional restrictions are provided by the Business Names Act 1985, where a firm uses a trading name instead of the surnames of the partners; and common law ensures that the firm does not use a name which is the same or similar to an existing firm's name (this is in order to prevent third-party confusion). Where a firm ignores this duty, it may result in an interdict being sought on the basis of "passing off". **8.99**

CONTRACTING WITH THIRD PARTIES

In the ordinary course of business it is unlikely that third parties will have any knowledge of the specific authority bestowed on an individual partner of a firm. Given that a partner can be described as an agent of the firm, partners can contractually bind the firm by any acts carried on in the ordinary course of the firm's business.[111] Furthermore, where a partner has authority bestowed upon him to act on behalf of the firm, and he does so in the firm's name, he is able to bind the partnership and his fellow partners in relation to third-party contracts.[112] **8.100**

A partner's authority[113] can be restricted by a firm. Where a third party is unaware of the restriction, they can rely on the implied authority of a partner, when the contract concerns the ordinary business of a firm.[114] In circumstances where a partner attempts contractually to bind a firm in a transaction outwith the scope of its normal business, the partnership will not be required to comply with the terms of the contract, unless the partner concerned had express authority to contract.[115] Where a third party knows or believes that a partner does not have express authority, there is no valid contract, and the partner concerned is personally liable. **8.101**

---

[110] PA 1890, s 9.
[111] PA 1890, s 5.
[112] PA 1890, s 6.
[113] For example, express restrictions in a partnership agreement.
[114] PA 1890, s 5.
[115] PA 1890, s 7.

RELATIONSHIPS AND DUTIES

8.102 The relationship between partners and a firm can be described as fiduciary in nature. Sections 28–30 of PA 1890 provide guidance on the type of duties owed by partners; these include a duty to provide accounts of the firm's business to any partner, to account to the partnership for any personal profits derived from any transactions concerning the firm, and a duty not to compete with the partnership's business.

8.103   The rights which partners enjoy can be agreed or indeed varied by the consent of all the partners.[116] In the absence of any agreement between the partners as to their contractual rights, s 24 of PA 1890 provides guidance that includes:

    (i)   an entitlement to an equal share of capital and profits of a firm;

    (ii) indemnification for any financial outlays or personal liabilities a partner incurs in the ordinary course of a firm's business; and

    (iii) a right to be both involved in management of the partnership's business, and to inspect the partnership books.

8.104 Generally, partnership agreements will regulate the process of incoming and outgoing partners, and how the firm's debts should be dealt with. Pursuant to s 17 of PA 1890, an incoming partner is usually not liable for pre-existing debts of a firm, and outgoing partners typically cease to have liability for any debts incurred following their departure. This can, of course, be varied by agreement.

DISSOLUTION

8.105 Partnerships may be dissolved for a variety of reasons. Circumstances may include:

    (i)   where a partnership was created for a fixed period of time or for a specific purpose, and the time has expired or the purpose has be achieved, the partnership naturally dissolves;[117]

    (ii) automatic dissolution on death, bankruptcy[118] or resignation of a partner, unless an agreement has been made to the contrary; or

    (iii) it would be unlawful for a partnership to continue in its business.[119]

8.106 The 1890 Act provides a number of grounds where the court may intervene[120] and dissolve a partnership. This includes where:

    (i)   a partner is found to be permanently of unsound mind;

    (ii) a partner is guilty of persistently breaching the terms of the partnership agreement; or

    (iii) the firm's business can only go forward by making a loss.

---

[116] PA 1890, s 19.

[117] PA 1890, s 32.

[118] PA 1890, s 33.

[119] PA 1890, s 34.

[120] PA 1890, s 35.

Following the dissolution of a partnership, the partners typically have continued **8.107** authority to wind up the firm's business.[121] This may include completing any business a firm contractually undertook before dissolution, since failure to do so may result in the partners being held professionally negligent. Once all a partnership's business has been concluded and the debts settled, any surplus assets are shared among the partners.[122]

CONSIDERING PARTNERSHIPS

As with incorporating a company, when considering setting up a partnership, there are **8.108** pros and cons. Again, there is no definitive list, and as a business vehicle its suitability will largely be dependent on a person's business needs.

ADVANTAGES

   (i)   No requirement to put documents into the public domain. **8.109**
  (ii)   Informal and flexible business vehicle.

DISADVANTAGES

   (i)   Generally, partners have no personal protection against the financial liabilities **8.110** of the partnership, therefore their personal assets may be at risk.
  (ii)   Dissolution is often inevitable on the death of a partner or where a dispute arises between partners, which results in a partner's resignation.

LIMITED LIABILITY PARTNERSHIPS

The Limited Liability Partnerships Act 2000 (LLPA 2000) introduced a new corporate **8.111** vehicle to the world of business; the limited liability partnership ("LLP"). An LLP can be described as a hybrid vehicle, between a limited company and a partnership.

SETTING UP AN LLP

As with to the incorporation of a company, an LLP does not come into existence until all **8.112** the necessary formalities of incorporation have been completed,[123] and a certificate of incorporation has been issued by the Registrar.

In order to incorporate an LLP, an incorporation document (LLP2) requires to be **8.113** completed, and sent to the Registrar with the requisite fee. Two or more individuals are required to be the initial members of an LLP and their names and addresses must be included on the incorporation document. A unique requirement of an LLP is the appointment of a minimum of two "designated members". Failure to adhere to this requirement results in all members being deemed to be "designated members".[124]

---

[121] PA 1890, s 38.
[122] PA 1890, s 39.
[123] LLPA 2000, s 2.
[124] LLPA 2000, s 2(2)(f).

8.114   The role that designated members undertake cannot be found in any one piece of legislation. Their duties are largely administrative and are not dissimilar from the duties carried out by officers of a company. IA 2000 provides guidance on the appointment and removal of designated members and the type of information that they must file with the Registrar.

8.115   In addition, the incorporation document requires a name to be chosen for an LLP that ends with the words "Limited Liability Partnership" or "LLP" and it must not be the same name as any existing UK company or LLP (this can easily be checked online at Companies House).[125] A registered office must also be selected, and one of the subscribers or a solicitor involved in the incorporation of an LLP must acknowledge that the LLP is being set up to "carry on a lawful business with a view to profit".[126]

8.116   A membership agreement is not a requirement in order to incorporate an LLP, although it is advisable for members to regulate their relationship in advance of any issues arising. If no membership agreement is executed, the Schedule to the Limited Liability Partnership Regulations 2001 (LLPR 2001) provides guidance on how members' relationships with each other should be regulated. LLPR 2001 are essentially default rules, however, they are not extensive and may not accurately reflect the intention of the members of an LLP, both in relation to its internal management and to its commercial objectives.

KEY FEATURES

8.117   An LLP is often described as a hybrid between a partnership and limited liability company, given its mix of corporate and partnership features. Some of these features are detailed below:

Company features

8.118   (i)   An LLP has a legal personality distinct from those of its members,[127] consequently it enjoys perpetual succession. In addition, there is no limit to its capacity,[128] therefore the doctrine of ultra vires does not apply.

   (ii)   The members of an LLP act as its agents and therefore, enjoy limited liability as do shareholders of a company.[129]

   (iii)   Members can bind an LLP, in a similar way to directors of a company, and as a result LLPs can own property, enter into contracts, sue and be sued. An LLP is also liable for its own debts, up to the value of the assets of a LLP, since members are not jointly liable.

   (iv)   In order to offer a degree of protection to third parties, an LLP is under a statutory requirement to file documents with the Registrar, for example accounts and annual returns.

   (v)   Where a third party is contracting with an LLP, they can assume that a member has authority to act on its behalf. However, if they know that the

---

[125] Additional restrictions are stated in the Schedule to LLPA 2000.
[126] LLPA 2000, s 2(1)(a).
[127] LLPA 2000, s 1(1).
[128] LLPA 2000, s 1(3).
[129] LLPA 2000, s 6.

member does not have such authority, or they know or believe that he is not a member of the LLP then the LLP is not contractually bound by that member's actions. The assumption of membership can continue until notice of cessation has been intimated to the third party directly or to the Registrar.[130]

(vi) CA 1985 and IA 1986 apply to LLPs[131] in a similar way to the way in which they apply to companies. Consequently, members of LLPs, like company directors, have to be fully aware of how the provisions relating to wrongful and fraudulent trading, insolvency and disqualification may be applicable.

Partnership features

(i)   An LLP does not have any directors, shareholders or share capital.   8.119

(ii)   Members' autonomy is similar to that enjoyed by partners. There is little regulation governing the internal management of an LLP, therefore members can chose how decisions should be made and profits shared, and how to regulate the appointment and retirement of members.

(iii) A membership agreement is similar to a partnership agreement, in that it is optional (given that default provisions are provided by LLPR 2001) and there is no requirement to place the document in the public domain, by filing it with the Registrar.

(iv)   Insolvency procedures for LLPs are very similar to those applicable to companies. However, the notable difference is that LLPs are subject to the "clawback" rule. This means that members have a very real personal interest in keeping abreast of the financial position of an LLP. In reality, if a member withdraws money from an LLP within the 2 years prior to an insolvent winding-up, and knew, or ought to have known, that given the withdrawal, an insolvent liquidation was unavoidable,[132] the amount can be clawed back from that individual member. In this way members' personal exposure is similar to that of partners.

(v)   LLPs enjoy similar tax transparency to partnerships. Generally, members will have the same income tax and corporation tax liabilities as partners and may enjoy similar benefits in relation to national insurance contributions.

CONSIDERING AN LLP

When considering incorporating an LLP, the positives and negatives associated with   8.120
this type of business vehicle should be weighted up. They include:

ADVANTAGES

(i)   Substantial protection of members' personal assets.   8.121

(ii)   Internal flexibility regarding management and structure.

(iii) Tax transparency and benefits.

---

[130] LLPA 2000, s 6(3).
[131] The Regulations apply the legislation to LLPs.
[132] IA 1986, s 214(2)(b).

DISADVANTAGES

8.122   (i)   Limited financial privacy, given the filing requirements.

(ii)   It is a relatively new entity, therefore limited case law exists, and this perhaps gives a perception of legal uncertainty, and in turn may dissuade third parties from contracting with LLPs.

ESSENTIAL FACTS

COMPANIES LIMITED BY SHARES

8.123   **Legislation**

- The Companies Act 1985 Act (as amended). The Company Law Reform Bill will ultimately result in two substantive Acts governing company law.

Incorporation

- Pre-incorporation contracts do not bind a company or third party.
- A company, once incorporated, is seen as a separate legal entity.
- Members enjoy limited liability, provided that the "veil of incorporation" is not lifted.

Members' meetings and resolutions

- Members can hold either general meetings (AGMs or EGMs) or class meetings.
- The notice period of meetings depends on the type of meeting and the nature of business intended to be dealt with.
- Resolutions are decisions taken by members of a company.

Directors

- A variety of types of directors are recognised, other than those formally appointed, for example de facto, shadow, nominee and alternate directors.
- Directors owe fiduciary duties to a company as well as statutory duties.
- Directors can become personally liable where the "veil of incorporation" is lifted, for example in cases of fraudulent or wrongful trading.

Members

- Membership only exists when a person's name is entered into a company's register of members.
- A member's liability is detailed in a company's memorandum.
- The key case in relation to minority protection is *Foss* v *Harbottle* (1843). Certain exceptions to the principles of this case are now accepted.

Share capital

- Maintenance of a company's share capital is important; consequently, statutory safeguards exist.
- To alter a company's share capital, a resolution must be passed and filed with the Registrar of Companies.
- Companies must have s 80 (CA 1985) authority to allot shares and statutory pre-emption rights exist (CA 1985, s 89).
- Share transfers are usually voluntary, and no statutory pre-emption rights exist.

CORPORATE INSOLVENCY

- Key legislation: Insolvency Act 1986 (as amended).
- Two tests exist to determine the insolvency of a company – the "cash flow" test and the "balance sheet" test.
- There are four key rescue mechanisms when a company is experiencing financial difficulties: administration; administrative receivership; company voluntary arrangements; and schemes of arrangement.
- If a company cannot be rescued, a common alternative is liquidation, and this can be categorised as either compulsory or voluntary liquidation. The latter can be classified further as either a members' voluntary liquidation or a creditors' voluntary liquidation.

PARTNERSHIPS

- Legislation: the Partnership Act 1890.
- A partnership can be created verbally, and a partnership agreement is optional. The minimum number of partners is two and the maximum number is usually 20.
- Partnerships are separate legal entities.
- The relationship between a firm and its partners is fiduciary in nature.
- Partners are agents of a firm and can bind a partnership, and are jointly and severally liable.
- Failure to comply with statutory requirements can open partners to unlimited personal liability.

LIMITED LIABILITY PARTNERSHIPS (LLP)

- Legislation: the Limited Liability Partnerships Act 2000 (as amended)
- An LLP can be described as a hybrid between a limited company and a partnership.
- An LLP is incorporated by sending an incorporation document to the Registrar, with the requisite fee.
- An LLP has a legal personality distinct from those of its members; therefore, it can hold property in its own name and enter into contracts.
- Members are agents of an LLP and therefore enjoy substantial limited liability.
- A membership agreement is optional, and default rules are provided in LLPR 2001.

ESSENTIAL CASES

8.124

Foss v *Harbottle* (1843): Refers to the principle of majority rule. In circumstances where an alleged wrong has been done to a company, minority shareholders cannot being an action on behalf of the company. A company is a distinct legal entity and therefore the "proper plaintiff". It is now judicially accepted that there are certain exceptions to this principle.

Salomon v *A Salomon Co Ltd* (1887): Refers to the principle known as the "veil of incorporation" which protects members of a company from liability. It is accepted that in certain circumstances the "veil" may be lifted and members may become personally liable for their acts and/or omissions.

9 INTELLECTUAL PROPERTY

WHAT IS "INTELLECTUAL PROPERTY"?

Intellectual property rights attempt to protect the creative output of individuals or **9.1** business entities. If these rights were not protected, many key products and services that we take for granted today would probably not exist: the light bulb, telecommunications and computer technology, penicillin, Dyson's cyclone vacuum cleaner and the Diesel engine, to name but a few. In today's knowledge economy, where so much emphasis is put on cutting-edge technological solutions to complicated problems, it is of great importance to have a fair and equitable intellectual property system. Without such rights that are granted to authors, inventors – or in general, "right holders" – there would be little incentive for continuous innovations, be they in a field of technology, environment, film, music or the Internet. Once these rights have been granted, their respective owners may be able to control the use of the protected subject-matter.

Intellectual property is an important concept. On the one hand, natural and legal **9.2** persons can own physical items, for example a van, a building, or a computer. Equally, they may have rights of ownership over their creative output – a new novel, a piece of art, an invention, or a particular logo, sign or name that is representative of a particular business.

As a consequence, it becomes clear that intellectual property can represent a key **9.3** personal or business asset, and it is important to know what one's rights are and how these are protected.

In more general terms, intellectual property is of huge importance to society as a **9.4** whole. If the creativity of the individual is rewarded, further innovation is encouraged. This, in turn, will stimulate the economy in the form of employment and trade. The state will benefit from greater tax revenue, and society as a whole is able to enjoy new products and enhanced cultural activities.

It is clear that intellectual property law is a broad field, covering many different **9.5** activities. The main areas concern copyright, trade marks, patents and designs which are mainly governed by specific Acts of Parliament. Two actions based on judge-made – or "common" – law are also relevant and relate to the law of confidence and an action in passing off.

Due to the limited space available, the focus of this chapter is on copyright and trade **9.6** mark law. As will be seen, in the United Kingdom copyright protection attaches automatically to protected subject-matter, while there exists a formal registration system for trade marks.

COPYRIGHT

9.7 UK copyright law is, to a great extent, contained in the Copyright, Designs and Patents Act 1988,[1] a statute that has been amended on a number of occasions, predominantly on the back of European and other international developments.[2] Copyright seeks to protect certain "works", and the 1988 Act provides the copyright owner with a number of exclusive rights which enable them to control the commercial exploitation of the work. There are also so-called moral rights available for authors.

CATEGORIES OF WORK PROTECTED – PRIMARY AND SECONDARY

9.8 The 1988 Act distinguishes between "primary" and "secondary" works in s 1. The former are categorised as literary, dramatic, musical and artistic works. Secondary works derive from these underlying works, and include sound recordings, films and broadcasts. Individuals usually are involved in creating primary works, while undertakings enter the equation in secondary works. For example, a musician may compose a melody and write lyrics for a song, but a record company may assist with producing the sound recording of it. Typographical arrangements of published editions are also protected.

Literary works

9.9 Under the 1988 Act, literary works include "any work written, spoken or sung, other than a dramatic or musical work".[3] This definition is wide enough to include, for example, song lyrics, magazines and novels, but also rather mundane subject-matter like the Yellow Pages, bus timetables, exam papers,[4] football coupons[5] and instructions on how to assemble that desk that comes in a flat pack. In *University of London Press Ltd* v *University Tutorial Press Ltd*[6] Peterson J argued that

> "the words 'literary work' cover work which is expressed in print or writing, irrespective of the question whether the quality or style is high. The word 'literary' seems to be used in a sense somewhat similar to the use of the word 'literature' in political or electioneering literature and refers to written or printed matters".[7]

Controversially, computer programs are also protected within this category.[8] A literary work will enjoy protection if it can be expressed in print. Literary *merit*, however, is not required in order to attract protection.

---

[1] "the 1988 Act" or "CDPA 1988".
[2] Membership of the European Union requires the UK to implement measures that seek to set common standards in copyright and other areas of law. In addition, international Treaties, such as the Berne Convention and the World Intellectual Property Organisation Copyright Treaties, seek to harmonise aspects of intellectual property law further.
[3] CDPA 1988, s 3(1).
[4] *University of London Press* v *University Tutorial Press* [1916] 2 Ch 601.
[5] *Ladbroke (Football) Ltd* v *William Hill (Football) Ltd* [1964] 1 WLR 273.
[6] [1916] 2 Ch 601.
[7] At 608.
[8] CDPA 1988, s 3(1)(b).

Dramatic works

A dramatic work "includes a work of dance or mime".[9] This includes stage plays, **9.10** pantomimes and works of choreography, for example, and it is crucial for a work to involve action in order to benefit from copyright protection.[10]

Musical works

The 1988 Act defines musical works as "consisting of music, exclusive of any words or **9.11** action intended to be sung, spoken or performed with the music".[11] Again, the melody in question does not have to be particularly pleasant or "melodic" in order to qualify for protection. However, like all other copyright works, it will have to be recorded in some tangible form, eg a musical notation. In *Lawson v Dundas*[12] the "four chords" theme of Channel 4's signature tune was held to be protected under this category.

Artistic works

Section 4 of the 1988 Act covers this particular category where protection is offered **9.12** irrespective of artistic merit[13] – a wise decision by the legislator, as no two individuals agree on what merits being called a work of "modern" art, for example. Included are graphic works, eg drawings, paintings, maps, charts etc, but also photographs, sculptures, collages and works of architecture. A recent Scottish case confirmed that newspaper mastheads are protected under this category.[14]

Sound recordings

This category requires a work to consist of a recording from which the sounds may be **9.13** reproduced. Naturally, it covers the recording of the whole or a part of a literary or musical work, eg a tune on its own or combined with lyrics, but it also includes "sounds where there is no underlying copyright work",[15] eg the sounds made by whales, or bird song.

Film

A film is defined as a "recording on any medium from which a moving image may by **9.14** any means be produced".[16] Movies – be they captured on celluloid or on digital media – as well as stills from movies, are covered in their own right, but it is to be remembered that there are many parts of films that attract copyright protection: the screenplay, the script and the soundtrack.

---

[9] CDPA 1988, s 3(1).
[10] See *Norowzian v Arks Ltd (No 2)* [2000] FSR 363.
[11] CDPA 1988, s 3(1)(a).
[12] *The Times*, 13 June 1985.
[13] CDPA 1988, s 4(1)(a).
[14] *Scottish and Universal Newspapers Ltd v Mack* 2004 SCLR 127; 2003 GWD 20–600.
[15] CDPA 1988, s 5A(1)(a).
[16] CDPA 1988, s 5B(1).

Broadcasts

9.15 A broadcast is defined by s 6 of the 1988 Act as "an electronic transmission of visual images, sounds or other information which is transmitted for simultaneous reception by members of the public and is capable of being lawfully received by them". This covers programmes by TV and radio stations, for example. It may also extend to cover Internet transmissions if these occur on the Web and by other means at the same time, or are concurrent transmissions of live events.[17] Hence, digital broadcasts come within the ambit of CDPA 1988.

Typographical arrangements of published editions

9.16 This category, protected under s 8 of the 1988 Act, is relevant to the layout of published editions of literary, dramatic and musical works. A publisher may invest considerable time in arranging content, eg in the newspaper and magazine industry, and the 1988 Act recognises this.

PRECONDITIONS OF LEGAL PROTECTION

9.17 While some jurisdictions use a formal registration system for copyright works,[18] there is no such arrangement in the UK. This means that copyright protection is gained automatically the moment the work is created. However, there are still some legal obstacles that need to be overcome before legal protection is achieved.

Originality

9.18 The 1988 Act requires primary works to be "original".[19] In order to fulfil this threshold, a work must simply originate from an author. As was held by the court in *University of London Press Ltd* v *Universal Tutorial Press Ltd*:

> "The word 'original' does not in this connection mean that the work must be the expression of original or inventive thought. Copyright Acts are not concerned with the originality of ideas, but with the expression of thought, and, in the case of 'literary work', with the expression of thought in print or writing. The originality which is required relates to the expression of the thought. But the Act [Copyright Act 1911] does not require that the expression must be in an original or novel form, but that the work must not be copied from another work – that it should originate from the author".[20]

Some degree of skill, labour or judgement needs to have gone into the creation of a copyright work. Copyright only protects the expression of ideas, not ideas themselves. A recent example of the idea and expression dichotomy is the legal argument relating to Dan Brown's *The Da Vinci Code*.[21]

---

[17] CDPA 1988, s 6(1A).
[18] The United States operates a Copyright Registry.
[19] CDPA 1988, s 1.
[20] *University of London Press Ltd* v *University Tutorial Press Ltd* [1916] 2 Ch 601.
[21] *Baigent* v *Random House Group Ltd* [2006] EWHC 719, Ch D (no copyright in general central themes of a literary work).

Tangibility

Copyright protects only expression of ideas in tangible form, not the ideas themselves. **9.19**
Sound recordings and films are automatically protected when recorded, but primary
works require to be recorded in whatever medium before copyright subsists in the
work: a literary work needs to exist in analogue or digital form, while a musical work is
protected when fixed by means of a notation.

De minimis

The Latin maxim *de minimis non curat lex*[22] means that copyright may not protect **9.20**
subject-matter that is trivial or insubstantial, as not enough skill and labour had been
expended on the creation of the work. For example, names,[23] newspaper headlines and
song titles have been regarded as too short to be protected by copyright law. In *Exxon
Corporation* v *Exxon Insurance Consultants International Ltd*[24] the court held that the
invented word "EXXON" could not be protected by copyright despite the skill and
labour that went into its creation. While the word may be original, its purpose was to
distinguish the products of the plaintiffs. Trade mark law would offer a better mode of
protecting words and names.

AUTHORSHIP AND OWNERSHIP

The 1988 Act states that the author of a work is to be its first owner of the copyright in **9.21**
it.[25] The following table illustrates who is to be regarded as the owner of the respective
copyright works:

Type of work	Owner of copyright	CDPA 1988
Literary, dramatic, artistic, musical	Author/creator	s 9(1)
Sound recording	Producer	s 9(2)(aa)
Film	Producer and principal director	s 9(2)(ab)
Broadcast	Person making the broadcast	s 9(2)(b)
Typography	Publisher	s 9(2)(d)
Computer-generated	Person who made the arrangements necessary for the creation of the work	s 9(3)

Joint authorship

If two or more individuals collaborate on the creation of a work then they may be **9.22**
regarded in law as joint authors.[26] The input of the respective joint authors, however,
must be significant; a mere token effort, or the supply of broad ideas, may not qualify an
individual as a joint author. In *Cala Homes* v *Alfred McAlpine Homes*[27] an employee of a
company had supplied detailed information that was used in the draft designs of

---

[22] "The law does not concern itself with trifles."
[23] *Re Elvis Presley Enterprises Inc* [1997] RPC 543; ANNE FRANK Trade Mark [1998] RPC 379 (no
copyright in names or signatures).
[24] [1981] 3 All ER 241.
[25] CDPA 1988, s 11(1).
[26] CDPA 1988, s 11(2).
[27] [1995] FSR 818.

buildings. Laddie J held that that individual was to be regarded as a joint author and stated that:

> "to have regard merely to who pushed the pen is too narrow a view of authorship. What is protected by copyright in a drawing or a literary work is more than just the skill and effort involved in creating, selecting or gathering together the detailed concepts, data or emotions which those words or lines have fixed in some tangible form which is protected. It is wrong to think that any person who carries out the mechanical act of fixation is an author. There may well be skill and expertise in drawing clearly and well but that does not mean that it is only that skill and expertise which is relevant. Where two or more people collaborate in the creation of a work and each contributes a significant part of the skill and labour protected by the copyright then they are joint authors".[28]

In the recent case of *Brown v Mcasso Music Production Ltd*[29] Judge Fysh QC held that the plaintiff was the joint author in a song. Brown's contribution was original and involved sufficient skill and labour entitling him to damages.

The creative employee

9.23   If employees create copyright works in the course of their employment, ownership of the copyright will vest in their respective employers.[30] Employees are already rewarded by a salary and employed to be creative. However, if it can be proved that the work had been created outside the scope of the employment, the employee may well be able to claim ownership. For example, in *Byrne v Statist Co*[31] an employee was held to be the owner of a translation from Portuguese which he made for his employer in his own time because translations were not part of his normal employment duties.[32] Sometimes a court must establish whether the individual in question is an employee, ie under a contract of service or employment, or rather an independent contractor, ie under a contract for services. A good example is *Beloff v Pressdram Ltd*.[33] The court took into account, among other things, that the *Observer* newspaper provided the journalist with office space, stationery and secretarial support, and PAYE and pension contributions were deducted from her salary, all of which suggested employee rather than freelance writer status.

DURATION OF COPYRIGHT PROTECTION

9.24   The 1988 Act covers a variety of different works to which different terms of protection have been afforded. The following table offers a simplified summary to the most prevalent copyright works.[34]

---

[28] [1995] FSR 818 at 835. See also *Robin Ray v Classic FM plc*, *The Times*, 8 April 1998 (cataloguing of musical tracks); *Brighton v Jones* [2005] FSR 16 (alleged joint authorship in a dramatic work).
[29] [2005] FSR 40.
[30] CDPA 1988, s 11(2).
[31] [1914] 1 KB 622.
[32] See also *Stevenson, Jordan & Harrison Ltd v McDonnell* [1952] 69 RPC 10 (copyright in lectures on accounting prepared by an accountant held not to vest in the employer).
[33] [1973] 1 All ER 241.
[34] For more detailed coverage, see, for example, D Bainbridge, *Intellectual Property* (5th edn, 2002).

Type of work	Duration	CDPA 1988
Literary, dramatic, artistic, musical	Life of the author plus 70 years	s 12(2)
Computer-generated	50 years from the end of the year it was made	s 12(7)
Sound recordings	50 years from the making or its release	s 13A
Films	70 years from the end of the year in which the last to die of principal director; author of film screenplay or dialogue; composer of film music	s 13B
Broadcasts	50 years from the end of the year it was made	s 14
Typographical arrangement of published editions	25 years from the year of the first publication	s 15
Moral rights	As long as the copyright in the work for integrity and paternity right; 20 years for the right to object to false attribution of authorship	s 86

INFRINGEMENT OF COPYRIGHT

The 1988 Act covers both primary and secondary infringement. Primary infringement **9.25** relates to an individual carrying out restricted acts in relation to the whole or a substantial part of the work without authorisation by its owner who may be able to seek civil remedies. If copyright is infringed knowingly on a grand scale, eg for the purposes of copyright piracy, then secondary infringement occurs, most of which carries criminal penalties.

The owner of copyright in a work has the exclusive rights to do any of the restricted **9.26** acts stated in s 16(1) in respect of the relevant copyright work, namely:

- to copy the work;[35]
- to issue copies of the work to the public;[36]
- to rent or lend the work to the public;[37]
- to perform, show or play the work in public;[38]
- to communicate the work to the public;[39]
- to make an adaptation of the work, or to do any of the above acts in relation to an adaptation of the work.[40]

Instances of secondary infringement are elaborated upon under ss 22–26 of the 1988 Act. **9.27** Individuals who import, possess or deal, sell, exhibit or distribute an infringing copy or provide the means for making infringing copies without authorisation by the copyright owner fall foul of these provisions. Such actions constitute criminal offences which are stipulated under s 107 and carry penalties of a fine or imprisonment between 6 months and 10 years or both. It remains to be seen whether these somewhat draconian measures are effective deterrents to copyright pirates.

---

[35] CDPA 1988, s 17.
[36] CDPA 1988, s 18.
[37] CDPA 1988, s 18A.
[38] CDPA 1988, s 19.
[39] CDPA 1988, s 20.
[40] CDPA 1988, s 21.

Primary infringement and substantiality

9.28   A controversial notion, because of its unpredictability, is copying of a substantial part of a work. If a work is copied in its entirety without permission, eg in cases of illegal downloading of copyrighted MP3 files, then it may be quite straightforward to prove primary infringement. If only a part of the work is taken, it needs to be "substantial" in order to constitute infringement. Since the 1988 Act does not offer a definition of this term, the courts had to develop tests in order to assess substantiality. While this largely depends on the specific facts of relevant cases, a few principles may be distilled from earlier decisions.

9.29   There must be a link between the original work and the allegedly infringing version.[41] When the amount of what has been taken is considered, the court will assess both the quality and the quantity of the subject-matter that was allegedly taken without permission. In *Hawkes & Son (London) Ltd v Paramount Film Service Ltd*[42] the most recognisable part of the march "Colonel Bogie", amounting to 20 seconds of a four-minute tune, were used in a news programme. This was held to be a substantial part. Problems may also occur in cases where a prior work has been used as inspiration. In *Ravenscroft v Herbert*[43] the plaintiff had written a scientific work on the Spear of Destiny. He complained about the alleged unauthorised use of parts of his work by Herbert in a work of fiction. The court found for Ravenscroft, as Herbert had taken details of characters and incidents of the underlying work. While overall only 4 per cent of the non-fictional work had been taken, this amounted to 15 per cent of Herbert's novel.[44]

Permitted acts

9.30   The 1988 Act permits the use of copyrighted work under certain circumstances without constituting infringement.[45] Examples are fair dealing for the purposes of non-commercial research and private study,[46] criticism and review,[47] reporting current events[48] and incidental inclusion. Others cover, for example, educational institutions,[49] libraries and archives,[50] and the time-shifting provisions for the recording of TV and radio programmes.[51] Another controversial defence is that the copyright infringement was in the public interest.[52] This defence will rarely succeed, as publication may often be

---

[41] *Francis Day & Hunter v Bron* [1963] Ch 587 (subconscious copying of a song).
[42] [1934] Ch 593.
[43] [1980] RPC 193.
[44] See also *Baigent v Random House Group Ltd* [2006] EWHC 719, Ch D (the "*Da Vinci Code* case").
[45] CDPA 1988, ss 28–76, the "permitted acts".
[46] CDPA 1988, s 29.
[47] CDPA 1988, s 30(1). See eg *Hubbard v Vosper* [1972] 1 All ER 1023, CA; (extracts from memos and internal documents), *Time Warner Entertainments Company LP v Channel Four Television Corporation plc* [1994] EMLR 1, CA (extracts from *A Clockwork Orange* in a documentary); *Pro Sieben Media AG v Carlton UK TV Ltd* [1999] FSR 610 (extracts of a previously broadcast interview).
[48] CDPA 1988, s 30(2). See eg *BBC v British Satellite Broadcasting Ltd* [1992] Ch 141 (highlights of football matches); *Newspaper Licensing Agency Ltd v Marks & Spencer plc* [2001] 3 All ER 977 (newspaper cuttings).
[49] CDPA 1988, ss 32–36A.
[50] CDPA 1988, ss 37–44.
[51] CDPA 1988, s 70.
[52] CDPA 1988, s 171(3).

motivated by commercial exploitation rather than an overriding public interest to the detriment of copyright protection.[53]

Civil remedies

Once primary infringement is established, pursuers may seek a number of remedies as appropriate to their respective cases. A copyright owner may claim damages which are assessed according to the facts of the case, including the flagrancy of the infringement and to what extent the defender benefited from the illegal activity.[54] Other remedies include interdicts, and account of profits, seizure of infringing copies and delivery up of infringing copies.[55]   **9.31**

MORAL RIGHTS

Authors of literary, dramatic, artistic and musical works, as well as directors of films, enjoy certain moral rights that are not as economically important as the restricted acts reserved to copyright owners. Authors may waive these rights.   **9.32**

Under s 77 of the 1988 Act authors have the right to be identified as such, once the right has been asserted. Authors and directors may also object to derogatory treatment of their work when it has been distorted, mutilated or otherwise prejudicially treated.[56] In addition, any individual has the right to object to false attribution of a work.[57] If photographs were commissioned, the commissioner enjoys a right of privacy with regard to those photographs under s 85. Finally, the Artist's Resale Right Regulations 2006[58] provide for a right to royalties in the event of artist's works of art being re-sold following the original first sale, thereby introducing the *droit de suite*, a well-known moral right in many European jurisdictions, to the UK arena.[59]   **9.33**

TRADE MARKS

In a world of commerce where goods and services are pivotal, we are surrounded by trade marks: the Nike "swoosh", the McDonald's "golden arches", the distinctive Coca-Cola bottle, the Bass red triangle, Levi's garments, to name but a few. Businesses, from the small company around the corner to the large multi-national Leviathan, invest a lot of time and money in the research and development of their brands in order to   **9.34**

---

[53] See *Ashdown v Telegraph Group Ltd* [2001] 4 All ER 666 (copyright in private memoirs of a politician trumped the freedom of expression of a newspaper).
[54] CDPA 1988, ss 96 and 97.
[55] CDPA 1988, ss 96, 99 and 100.
[56] CDPA 1988, ss 80–83; see eg *Morrison Leahy Music v Lightbond* [1993] EMLR 144 (the singer George Michael was granted an injunction against the inclusion of parts of one of his songs in a *Bad Boy Megamix*).
[57] CDPA 1988, ss 84–86; see eg *Clark v Associated Newspapers Ltd* [1998] 1 All ER 959 (injunction granted to Alan Clark MP against the publication of a spoof diary that gave the wrongful impression of the MP being the author).
[58] SI 2006/346.
[59] For comment, see eg D Gourlay, "The art of cashing in" 2006 51(2) JLSS 44.

distinguish their products from those offered by competitors and stop others from taking unfair advantage of their hard-earned reputation. The best brand image will attract the highest number of customers. Trade mark law, consequently, is of crucial importance to offer legal protection in this fast-moving area.

9.35   In the United Kingdom, the Trade Marks Act 1994[60] is the main statutory provision for UK-wide marks. In order to gain protection, an application has to be filed with the Patent Office which maintains a Trade Mark Registry.[61] The European Union also plays a pivotal role in this field: Council Regulation 40/94 established the so-called Community Trade Mark which, once granted by the Office for Harmonisation in the Internal Market in Alicante,[62] will provide legal protection throughout the EU Member States.[63]

APPLICATION

9.36   Since there is a formal Trade Mark Registry, applicants have to file formal applications which consist of

- a request for registration of a trade mark;
- the name and address of the applicant;
- a statement of the goods or services in relation to which it is sought to register the trade mark;
- a representation of the trade mark;
- a declaration by the applicant that the trade mark is used or being used; and
- payment of the appropriate fees, depending on how many classes the application covers.[64]

9.37   Once examined and accepted, the new trade mark is published in the *Trade Marks Journal*.[65] If anyone wants to dispute the legality of the trade mark and oppose it, this may be done within 3 months of its publication. If unopposed or unsuccessfully opposed, the trade mark will finally be registered.[66]

LEGAL DEFINITION

Sign

9.38   The notion of what qualifies as a "sign" for the purposes of TMA 1994 is predictably wide and inclusive. While s 1 does provide some examples, a "sign" goes well beyond the traditional ones such as a word or a logo. In theory, anything that conveys information may be potentially registrable.[67] It is possible to register slogans, which

---

[60] "the 1994 Act" or "TMA 1994".
[61] See http://www.patent.gov.uk. This website holds a wealth of information on all matters of intellectual property and should rank highly in every student's research plans!
[62] "OHIM".
[63] [1994] OJ L11/1.
[64] TMA 1994, s 32.
[65] TMA 1994, s 38.
[66] TMA 1994, s 40.
[67] *Philips Electronics NV* v *Remington Consumer Products Ltd* [2003] RPC 2.

is of great importance to businesses in terms of their advertising strategies. It may also be possible to register colours, sounds or even smells, the obstacles here being graphic representation and distinctive character.

Graphic representation

In order to be successful, a potential trade mark must be able to be represented **9.39** graphically – individuals must be able to assess what the mark *is*. Again, this may be straightforward in terms of words or logos, or even shapes,[68] where a drawing or a photograph may be sufficient. Sounds, eg in advertising jingles, may be graphically represented by their musical notation. Colours may be registered if a specific shade of a colour is identified and it is supported by a reference to an internationally recognised colour identification code.[69] The registration of smells has been subjected to lively debate and will be considered below.

Capable of distinguishing

The third obstacle for a trade mark is that it must be capable of distinguishing goods or **9.40** services of one business from those of another. On the face of it this is a comparatively low threshold, but it will be used to rule out applications for signs that cannot function as a trade mark. In *H Quennel Ltd's Application*[70] the court refused an application for the term "PUSSIKIN" in relation to cat food, arguing that it was describing the product rather than distinguishing it from products of other manufacturers. In another important case, *British Sugar plc v James Robertson & Sons*,[71] the registration of the trade mark "TREAT" for dessert sauces and syrups was revoked on the basis that it was devoid of distinctive character and it constituted a "sign which had become customary in the current language" contrary to s 3(1)(d). More recently, the European Court of Justice confirmed that the distinctive character of a trade mark may be acquired through its use as part of an already registered mark. In *Société des Produits Nestlé SA v Mars UK Ltd*,[72] the English Court of Appeal asked the ECJ whether it was possible to register the term "HAVE A BREAK", part of the well-known and trade-marked slogan "HAVE A BREAK . . . HAVE A KITKAT", in its own right. This situation will be revisited as part of the next section.

ABSOLUTE GROUNDS OF REFUSAL

If an application falls foul of any of the absolute grounds of refusal, which are based on **9.41** the mark itself, contained in s 3 of the 1994 Act, registration will not be granted.

---

[68] Eg the distinctive shape of the Coca-Cola bottle is registered as a trade mark – although this was not possible under the previous legislation: *Re Coca-Cola Co's Applications* [1986] 2 All ER 274.
[69] See the judgment by the European Court of Justice in *Libertel Groep BV v Benelux Merkenbureau* (C–104/01) [2004] FSR 4 (application to register the colour "orange" as a trade mark for telecommunications products and services).
[70] [1954] RPC 36.
[71] [1996] RPC 281.
[72] [2006] All ER (EC) 348.

Signs which do not satisfy the requirements of s 1(1)

9.42   If the mark fails the tests of graphical representation or capability of distinguishing goods and services it may not be registrable.[73] As stated earlier, graphical representation is normally not that high a hurdle. However, it has proved to be almost insurmountable in respect of applications to register scents as trade marks. Merely describing the smell applied for is not enough. In *John Lewis of Hungerford Ltd's Trade Mark Application*[74] the application to register the "smell, aroma or essence of cinnamon" for furniture and fittings in Class 20 failed. However, OHIM granted a trade mark for "the smell of fresh cut grass" for tennis balls, arguing that that particular smell was distinct, unambiguous and universally recognised.[75] The ECJ arguably made it more difficult to register olfactory marks in its decision in *Sieckmann v Deutsches Patent- und Markenamt.*[76] In this case the German applicant attempted to register the chemical methyl cinnamate, duly writing down the chemical formula in the application. This proved not to be enough to represent the smell graphically because the formula was indicative of the chemical substance rather than the odour; also, a sample of the odour would not satisy the requirement for graphic representation. More recently, the European Court of First Instance (CFI) refused an application for the "smell of ripe strawberries" for soaps, face cream, stationery, leather goods and clothing by Laboratoires France Parfum.[77] The picture of a strawberry was not enough to fulfil the requirement, as there are many different kinds of strawberries having different smells. The CFI noted that there is no international classification of smells – comparable to international colour codes or musical notation that is generally accepted and which would make it possible to identify a scent precisely and objectively.

Trade marks which are devoid of any distinctive character

9.43   Unless made distinctive through its use, a trade mark may not be registered if it is not distinctive, eg merely describes the product or service in question.[78] In *Smith Kline & French Laboratories v Sterling-Winthrop Group Ltd*[79] the House of Lords held that colour combinations on drug capsules had become distinctive through use and were therefore registrable. Contrast this case with *Unilever plc's Trade Mark*[80] where an application of red and white stripes for toothpaste was refused. Here, the colours were fulfilling a particular purpose – the red stripes being the mouthwash component – and, hence, were purely functional, rather than distinctive.

Trade marks which are exclusively descriptive

9.44   Section 3(1)(c) of the 1994 Act states that "trade marks which consist exclusively of signs or indications which may serve, in trade, to designate the kind, quality, quantity, intended purpose, value, geographical origin, the time of production of goods or of

---

[73] TMA 1994, s 3(1)(a).
[74] [2001] ETMR 36.
[75] *Vennootschap Onder Firma Senta Aromatic Marketing's Application* [1999] ETMR 429.
[76] (C–273/00) [2003] RPC 38.
[77] *Eden SARL v OHIM* (T305/04) [2006] ETMR 14.
[78] See *H Quennel Ltd's Application* [1954] RPC 36.
[79] [1975] 2 All ER 578.
[80] [1984] RPC 155.

rendering of services, or other characteristics of goods or services" may not be registered, again subject to the proviso that they have not become distinctive through use. Examples may include everyday terms like "BEST" relating to quality, "BUY THREE FOR THE PRICE OF TWO". However, in *Procter & Gamble v OHIM*[81] the ECJ held that trade mark protection should be granted to "BABY-DRY" for nappies. While each word on its own may be descriptive, their combination made the product in question distinctive in the eyes of the court.

Unregistrable shapes

The 1994 Act permits the registration of shapes, unlike its 1938 predecessor. Section 3(2) provides for some exceptions to the rule. If the shape of the product in question is dictated by its inherent function, registration may be refused. Footballs or keys may fall into this category. Also, where the shape is necessary to achieve a particular technical result, or adds substantial value to the product, this may preclude registration.[82]   **9.45**

Offensive or deceptive marks

Under s 3(3)(a) a trade mark shall not be registered if it is contrary to public policy or to accepted principles of morality, or under s 3(3)(b) of such a nature as to deceive the public, eg in respect of the nature, quality or geographical origin of the goods or service. Recently, French Connection UK succeeded in registering the mark "FCUK" for its products after some opposition on the ground that this is an anagram of a swear word. In *Dick Lexic Ltd's Community Trade Mark Application*,[83] OHIM granted the registration of "DICK & FANNY" for stationery and photographic equipment. In formal English usage these terms did have a neutral meaning, and the different connotations based on slang words could not preclude registration.   **9.46**

Protected emblems and bad faith applications[84]

Certain emblems are not registrable, eg connotations to Royalty, national flags and Olympic emblems. In addition, bad faith applications may be refused if the party in question does not have *bona fide* intention to use the mark.[85]   **9.47**

RELATIVE GROUNDS OF REFUSAL

Marks that are the same as or similar to earlier marks may be refused registration under s 5 of the 1994 Act. An earlier mark is defined in s 6(1) as being   **9.48**

- a registered trade mark, international trade mark or Community trade mark which has a date of application for registration earlier than that of the trade mark in question;

---

[81] [2002] RPC 17.
[82] See *Philips Electronics NV v Remington Consumer Products Ltd* [1998] RPC 2.
[83] [2005] ETMR 99.
[84] TMA 1994, s 3(5) and (6).
[85] See *Imperial Group Ltd v Philip Morris & Co Ltd* [1982] FSR 72.

- a Community trade mark which has a valid claim to seniority from an earlier registered trade mark or international trade mark; or
- a trade mark which, at the date of application for registration of the trade mark in question, was entitled to protection under the Paris Convention as a well-known trade mark.

9.49 A mark cannot be registered if it is likely to cause confusion in the minds of the general public. The ECJ provided some guidance on the concept of likelihood of confusion in the minds of the public in *Sabel BV v Puma AG*.[86] It was held that likelihood of confusion had to be appreciated globally. The visual, aural or conceptual similarity of the marks must be based on the overall impression given by the marks, bearing in mind in particular their distinctive and dominant components. In addition, it was established that the more distinctive the earlier mark was, the greater the likelihood of confusion would be. In *Oasis Stores Ltd's Trade Mark Application*[87] Oasis's application to register the mark "EVEREADY" for contraceptives was opposed by the proprietors of the mark "EVER READY" for batteries, citing likelihood of confusion, but this was not entertained by the court. Merely being reminded of another, similar trade mark is not enough to lead to confusion in the minds of the public.

9.50   If a mark conflicts with earlier rights, eg other intellectual property rights including passing off, that mark may not be registered, according to s 5(4).

INFRINGEMENT

9.51 Section 9 provides a number of rights to the owner and exclusive licensee of a registered trade mark, and legal action can be taken against those who use a trade mark without permission. Under s 10 the scenarios which constitute infringement are listed:

- usage of the mark in relation to the same goods or services for which the mark was registered;
- usage in relation to similar goods or services and there is likelihood of confusion;
- usage of a similar mark in relation to the same goods or services.[88]

DEFENCES

9.52 Section 11 provides for the defences for infringement of a trade mark. Under the notion of "honest concurrent use" it is a defence to use the mark in question if it is also registered. However, there may well be an action to seek a declaration of invalidity, ie that the mark of the alleged infringer should not have been registered in the first instance. Under s 11(2) it is also a defence to use one's name or address or the geographical origin if this is "in accordance with honest practices in industrial or

---

[86] (C–251/95) [1998] RPC 199.
[87] [1998] RPC 631.
[88] The cases cited earlier are relevant here, in particular *British Sugar plc v James Robertson & Sons* [1996] RPC 281. In addition, you may consult, for example, *Baywatch Production Co Inc v Home Video Channel* [1997] FSR 22; *Re Elvis Presley Enterprises Inc* [1997] RPC 543; and *Wagamama Ltd v City Centre Restaurants plc* [1995] FSR 713.

commercial matters". In addition, a mark may not be infringed by usage in the course of trade in a particular locality of an earlier right which applies only in that locality.[89] Section 12 states that trade mark rights are exhausted when the owner has agreed to putting the products bearing the mark on the market within the European Economic Area (EEA). In other words, once the goods have been lawfully introduced to the market in the UK, the trade mark owner may not prohibit their reselling on the market of any other EEA Member State unless there are legitimate reasons for doing so.[90] Finally, an alleged infringer may apply for an interdict if he faces groundless threats of an action for trade mark infringement under s 21 of the Act.

CIVIL REMEDIES

The civil remedies available for trade mark infringement are similar to those available **9.53** under copyright law. The 1994 Act provides for damages, an account of profits or interdicts under s 14. An application to erase the offending sign, delivery up of infringing articles, and the destruction or forfeiture of infringing products may also be available.[91]

CRIMINAL OFFENCES

The 1994 Act does provide for criminal offences in terms of unauthorised use of a trade **9.54** mark, falsification of the register or falsely representing the trade mark as registered.[92] Enforcement is by the local Weights and Measures authorities, who may also use the Trade Descriptions Act 1968 or the Consumer Protection Act 1987 for the purposes of tackling trade mark piracy and counterfeit products. In addition, Customs and Excise play a pivotal role in the detection and seizure of counterfeit material. A number of business associations and other organisations are also active in this area.[93]

ESSENTIAL FACTS

- Intellectual property rights attempt to protect the creative output of **9.55** individuals or business entities.
- Intellectual property is therefore an important concept for those individuals and business entities and for society as a whole, in the consequent encouragement of innovation and stimulation of trade.

---

[89] TMA 1994, s 11(3).
[90] TMA 1994, s 12(2)
[91] TMA 1994, ss 15–19.
[92] TMA 1994, s 92–95.
[93] See, for example, the Federation Against Copyright Theft (FACT). Its website contains up-to-date information on the latest successes in this quixotic battle: http://www.fact-uk.org.uk.

COPYRIGHT

- The Copyright, Designs and Patents Act 1988 distinguishes between "primary" and "secondary" works. The former are further categorised as literary, dramatic, musical and artistic works. Secondary works include sound recordings, films and broadcasts.
- Copyright protection is gained automatically the moment the work is created.
- In order to receive protection under the 1988 Act, a work must be original; in tangible form; and not trivial or insubstantial in nature.
- The author is the first owner of copyright in a work.
- Copyright protection subsists for different terms specified in the 1988 Act, depending on the type of work.
- Primary infringement of copyright relates to an individual carrying out restricted acts in relation to the work, without authorisation by the copyright owner. Secondary infringement can consist of importing, possessing, dealing in, selling, exhibiting or distributing an infringing copy or providing the means for making such copies, without authorisation by the copyright owner.
- The 1988 Act permits the use of copyrighted work under certain circumstances without constituting infringement.
- Authors of certain works enjoy moral rights that are not as economically important as the restricted acts reserved to copyright owners. Authors may waive these rights.
- Remedies for infringement of copyright include damages, interdicts, account of profits, and seizure and delivery up of infringing copies.

TRADE MARKS

- The Trade Marks Act 1994 is the main statutory provision covering UK-wide trade marks.
- In order to gain protection for a mark, an application must be filed with the Trade Mark Registry maintained by the Patent Office.
- A potential trade mark must qualify as a "sign"; must be able to be represented graphically; and must be capable of distinguishing goods or services of one business from those of another.
- An application for registration which falls foul of the absolute grounds of refusal contained in the 1994 Act will not be granted.
- Marks that are the same as or similar to earlier marks may be refused registration under the 1994 Act.
- The owner or exclusive licensee of a registered trade mark may take legal action against those using that mark, or a similar mark, without permission.
- Defences to a complaint of infringement include "honest concurrent use".
- Remedies for infringement of trade marks are provided by the 1994 Act (damages, interdicts, account of profits, orders to erase the offending sign, delivery up, destruction or forfeiture of infringing articles). Other enforcement measures are provided by the Trade Descriptions Act 1968 and the Consumer Protection Act 1987.

ESSENTIAL CASES

Ladbroke (Football) Ltd v *William Hill (Football) Ltd* (1964): This case addressed the question of whether football coupons could attract copyright protection as original literary works. It was argued that it had to be established first whether a particular work as a whole was entitled to copyright protection before any assessment of an alleged breach by taking a substantial part of that work without permission could be made. It was held that the respondent's coupon was a compilation and so an original literary work entitled to copyright protection.

9.56

Scottish and Universal Newspapers Ltd v *Mack* (2004): The pursuers complained that Mack had breached an interdict and infringed their copyright in the masthead of a newspaper. This masthead, it was argued, attracted copyright protection as an artistic work. Mack used the masthead in a spoof or parodying manner. The court agreed with the publishers and held that there was deliberate copying of a substantial part of the visual aspects of the masthead. This Scottish case illustrates that parodies do not enjoy special status under UK copyright law.

Brighton v *Jones* (2005): This case concerns the issue of joint authorship. Brighton raised an action against Jones in respect of a play. Jones had been commissioned to write the original script, with Brighton being the director. In 1999, the script was revamped by Jones. The existing two versions constituted different dramatic works and each enjoyed copyright protection in their own right despite being based on the same script. Brighton claimed, *inter alia*, that she had contributed to the work in rehearsals, and this made her a joint author and owner of the copyright in the work. It was held that joint authorship of a dramatic work required a significant contribution towards the creation of the work. While Brighton's contributions were important during the rehearsals, they were not significant enough to make her a joint author.

Stevenson, Jordan & Harrison Ltd v *McDonnell* (1952): A person was employed as an accountant. He gave some lectures in accounting and later moulded these into a book. His employer claimed ownership of copyright. While his employer had provided some secretarial assistance, it was held that this was not sufficient to qualify for ownership of the copyright in the lectures, nor the book. The accountant was employed to advise clients, not to provide lectures. Consequently, he was the first owner of those parts of the book which were not based on a report for his employer he had written during the course of his employment.

Hubbard v *Vosper* (1972): Vosper was a former member of the Church of Scientology, and he proceeded to write a book that was very critical of the cult. In doing so, he used parts of books and internal memos written by Ron Hubbard, the cult leader. Hubbard argued, *inter alia*, that this infringed his copyright in the material. Vosper relied on the fair dealing provisions for the purposes of criticism and review. The court held that the fair dealing defence is not confined to criticising or reviewing someone's literary work, but may be available for criticising or reviewing the doctrine or philosophy underlying a particular work. So, while the material was protected by copyright, and Vosper had made substantial use of it, he had also commented on these extracts to a great extent which allowed him to rely on the fair dealing provisions.

Philips Electronics NV v *Remington Consumer Products Ltd* (2003): Philips alleged, *inter alia*, that, in marketing its own three-headed rotary shaver, Remington had infringed its registered trade mark. Philips argued that once the whole or part of a particular item was recognised by the public as being produced by one manufacturer, a picture of it or its shape could be registered as a trade mark and that registration could then be used to prevent others from copying that product at any time in the future. Certain shapes may not be registered as trade marks, and the Court of Justice held in a preliminary ruling that protection is unavailable where it would grant a monopoly on technical solutions or functional characteristics of a product. As a consequence, the ECJ confirmed what had already been decided by the English High Court and the Court of Appeal, and the mark registered by Philips was declared invalid.

British Sugar plc v *James Robertson & Sons* (1996): British Sugar had registered "TREAT" as a trade mark under the specification "Dessert sauces and syrups". It was used for particular syrups for desserts. Robertson proceeded to put a spread known as "Robertson's Toffee Treat" on the market. British Sugar was not impressed and alleged trade mark infringement, arguing that Robertson's product was likely to cause confusion on the part of the public. Robertson disputed the allegations. The court held against British Sugar. There was no likelihood of confusion in the eyes of the court, as the products had different purposes and were presented differently. In addition, Robertson's product was not marketed as a dessert sauce and therefore fell outside the specification used by British Sugar. The two products also lacked similarity because they were not in direct competition, they would be stacked on different shelves, and were of a differing physical nature. To make matters worse, the court also held that "TREAT" was devoid of any distinctive character based on the insufficient evidence provided by British Sugar and, therefore, should not be registrable.

GLOSSARY

Appellate – an appellate court or body is one which decides appeals, such as the Appellate Committee of the House of Lords.

Articles of association – the internal "constitutional" document of a limited company, regulating its management.

Bill/Act – a Bill is a proposal for legislation in either the UK or the Scottish Parliament. Once the Bill has passed through all the required stages and received the Royal Assent, it becomes an Act of Parliament or an Act of the Scottish Parliament.

Civil law – all law (public or private) which is not criminal law.

Consensus – agreement.

Contract of services – a contract between an employer and employee.

Contract for services – a contract between an employer and an independent contractor or self-employed person.

Contributory negligence – a careless action or omission of the pursuer which contributes, alongside the defender's negligence, to the pursuer's loss or injury.

Copyright – the exclusive right to exploit a copyright work by the right holder. It is an incorporeal right in, for example, original literary, dramatic, musical or artistic works, as well as sound recordings, films and published texts.

Criminal law – body of law regulating behaviour prohibited by the state for which sanctions exist in the form of imprisonment or some other penalty.

Custom – an unwritten rule which may be treated as a source of law through general long-held acceptance by a community.

Damnum fatale – sometimes known as an "Act of God"; loss caused by an extraordinary event which cannot be foreseen, such as a ferocious storm or other natural event. Any loss resulting from such an event is generally not recoverable in delict.

Defender – the person against whom a civil action has been raised in Scots law.

Delict – a civil wrong arising through the intentional or negligent breach of a legal duty, which in turn may give rise to a liability to compensate for loss and injury.

Damnum injuria datum – loss caused by a legal wrong which forms the basis of liability in delict.

Dissolution – the termination of Parliament made by means of a Royal Proclamation. When the term of either the UK Parliament or the Scottish Parliament comes to an end, the Queen is asked by the Prime Minister or the Presiding Officer of the Scottish Parliament respectively to dissolve the Parliament to enable a general election to be held.

EC/EU – EC is the European Community while EU is the European Union. All countries which are in the EC are also in the EU as they are the same body. The term "EC" is used in connection with the law relating to the Common Market etc and the term "EU" is used in relation to the political union.

Error – a misunderstanding or a misrepresentation of fact which occurs during pre-contractual negotiations or in the contract itself.

Federal government – a system of government which consists of two co-ordinate tiers of government: a central or federal tier and a state or provincial tier, each with its own legislature, executive and judiciary. Examples include the United States of America and the Federal Republic of Germany.

Frustration – an event which supervenes to terminate the obligations under the contract.

Implied – a term, especially in a contract, which is deemed to exist in the particular circumstances, notwithstanding an absence of express provision.

Incorporation – the forming of a distinct legal entity comprising at least one member and one director together with a company secretary.

Infringement – illegal acts taken without the right holder's permission (eg by downloading copyrighted files from the Internet without permission of the owner of those files). Infringements of intellectual piogenty rights may lead to the right holder taking legal action and pursuing certain remedies.

Insolvency – the state of being unable to pay debts as they fall due.

Institutional writings – encyclopaedic legal texts treated as authoritative sources of law dealing with Scots civil and criminal law. Examples include Stair, Erskine and Hume.

Intellectual property rights – rights offering legal protection for subject-matter that is created by a person's intellect, skill, labour and investment of time or money. IPRs encompass copyright, patents, trade marks, design, trade secrets and the goodwill of a business.

Judicial precedent – source of law consisting of court decisions regarded as authoritative in deciding later cases.

Legislation – laws enacted by Parliament. Encompasses Acts of the UK Parliament, the Scottish Parliament and Acts of the European Community institutions.

Legislative competence – the legislative competence of the Scottish Parliament means the areas in which the Parliament can make a valid law.

Limited liability – the principle whereby the liabilities of a member of a company are limited to the capital they invest.

Liquidation – the process of winding up a limited company which can be either voluntary, if agreed upon by shareholders, or judicial, if ordered by a court.

Memorandum of association – the external "constitutional" document of a limited company, signed by persons seeking its incorporation. Contains, for example, the name, objects and powers of the company.

Minister – Ministers are MPs (and sometimes Members of the House of Lords) who hold a promoted post in the UK Government. The most senior Ministers are Ministers of the Crown and hold the chief political offices in the Government. Most, but not all, are in charge of a Department of State and have the title of "Secretary of State". The Chancellor of the Exchequer and the Lord Chancellor are also Ministers of the Crown. The Scottish Parliament has Ministers and Junior Ministers who are MSPs who hold similar promoted posts.

Monarch – "monarch" and "sovereign" are both used as terms for the king or queen who is the head of the UK state.

Moral rights – the non-economic rights that remain with the author of a copyright work. An author has the right to be identified as such, and to object to derogatory treatment of the work. In addition, any person has the right not to have a work falsely attributed to him.

Negligence – failure to carry out a duty required by law to exercise reasonable care to avoid loss or harm to persons or property.

Novus actus interveniens – a new intervening act which may break the chain of causation between cause and effect.

Obiter dictum – things said "by the way" in a judgment; an opinion expounded by a judge on a legal point which is not essential to the decision.

Permitted acts – this offers a defence against an allegation of copyright infringement for some narrowly defined purposes, eg non-business research and private study, for purposes of criticism and review, and the reporting of current events.

Personal bar – a party is prevented from enforcing his rights if he has placed himself in the position of not being entitled to do so in law.

Personal rights – rights which accrue to a party under contract and which he can enforce against the other party to the contract.

Pure economic loss – financial loss sustained as a result of an action or omission which has not caused any physical injury or damage.

Pursuer – person raising a civil action in Scots law.

Private law – branch of law regulating the relationships between individuals.

Public law – branch of law regulating the relationships between the state and individuals, and between agencies of government.

Ratio decidendi – literally "the reason of the decision". A term used to describe the principle of law which justifies the decision of a court; the ground upon which a case is decided. A *ratio* may be used as a precedent in a later case.

Real rights – these rights differ from personal rights in that they can be enforced against the world (eg land owners have real rights over the ownership of their land and those real rights are registered in public registers).

Rescission – the right of an innocent party to terminate the contract in response to a material breach by the other party.

Reduction – to have a contract set aside, usually through court action.

Repeal – an Act of Parliament (or section of an Act) is said to be repealed when subsequently Parliament passes another Act which cancels or revokes the earlier Act or provisions. Normally it is explicitly stated in the later Act that the earlier law is being repealed. If this is not done and the provisions of the later Act are inconsistent with the earlier one, the earlier Act (or section) is said to be repealed by implication.

Repudiation – the refusal by one party to perform a contract.

Resile – a legal method of withdrawing from a contract.

Restitutio in integrum – to put the parties back to their original position before the contract was concluded

Royal Prerogative – the residue of discretionary common law power which is legally left in the hands of the Crown. It dates back to the time when the monarch held power and could do whatever he or she wished. Today, however, "the Crown" normally means Government Ministers rather than the Queen, although the Queen still exercises some prerogative powers, such as choosing the Prime Minister and dissolving Parliament.

Sovereign – has a number of meanings. First it is used of the king or queen (see "Monarch", above). Secondly, it means "supreme" and it is used to describe the UK Parliament whose Acts cannot be successfully challenged in any UK court.

Stare decisis – literally "to stand by decisions". A term used to describe the concept of judicial precedent.

Subordinate legislation – laws made under the authority of an Act of Parliament. Also known as delegated legislation. Includes Orders in Council, statutory instruments, byelaws etc.

Trade mark – a sign (eg a logo, name, colour etc) that is used to identify the product or service of one business from those of another. Once registered, the owner of the trade mark can control its use and take legal action against those who infringe it. Unregistered trade marks may be protected under the common law of passing off.

Vicarious liability – liability of a person for the delictual act or omission of another, especially an employee.

Void – null; of no legal effect.

Volenti non fit injuria – a defence to an action in delict for damages for personal injury or death. Literally "to those who are willing no harm can be done", ie a person who voluntarily accepts the risk of an injury cannot claim damages should the injury actually be sustained.

Voidable – a contract which is voidable is open to challenge on certain legal grounds and has effect up until the point that it is reduced.

INDEX